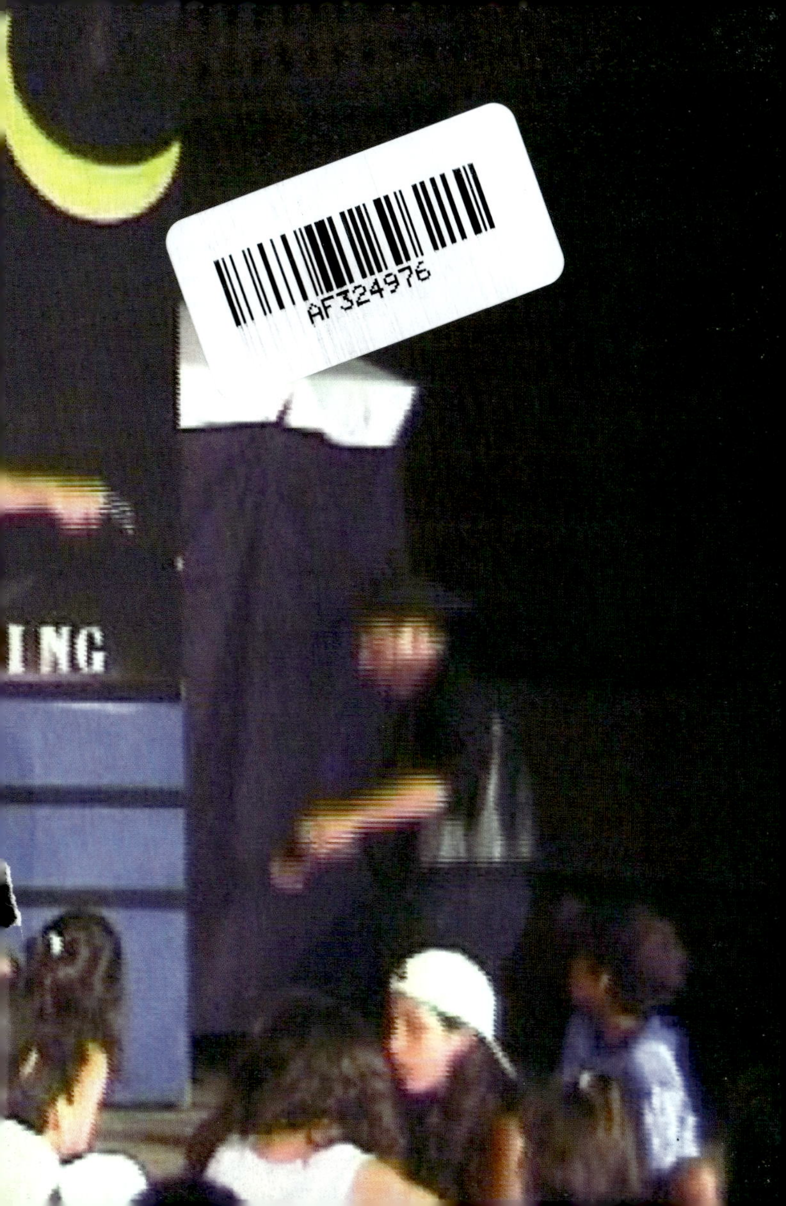

AF324976
ING

stefan banz

a shot away some flowers

what it's like. everlast

edited by christoph doswald

stefan banz

a shot away some flowers

video works 1997 – 1999

edition patrick frey

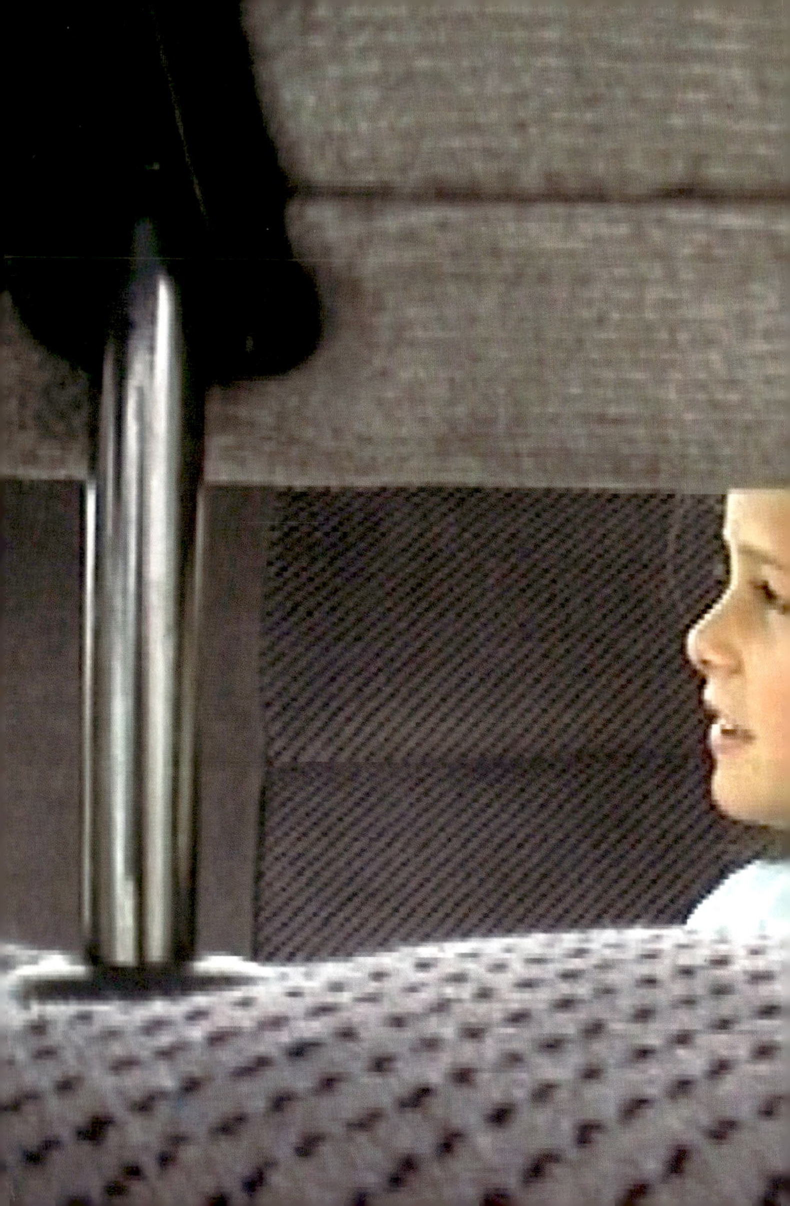

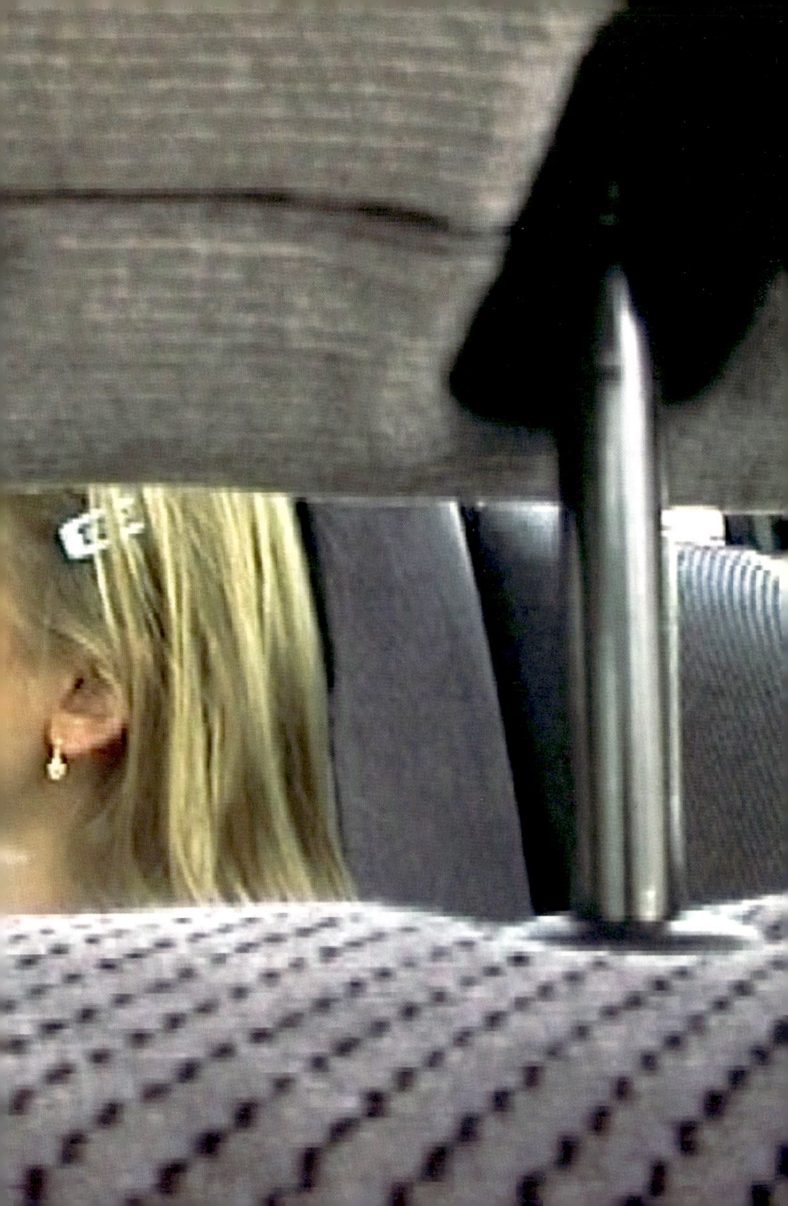

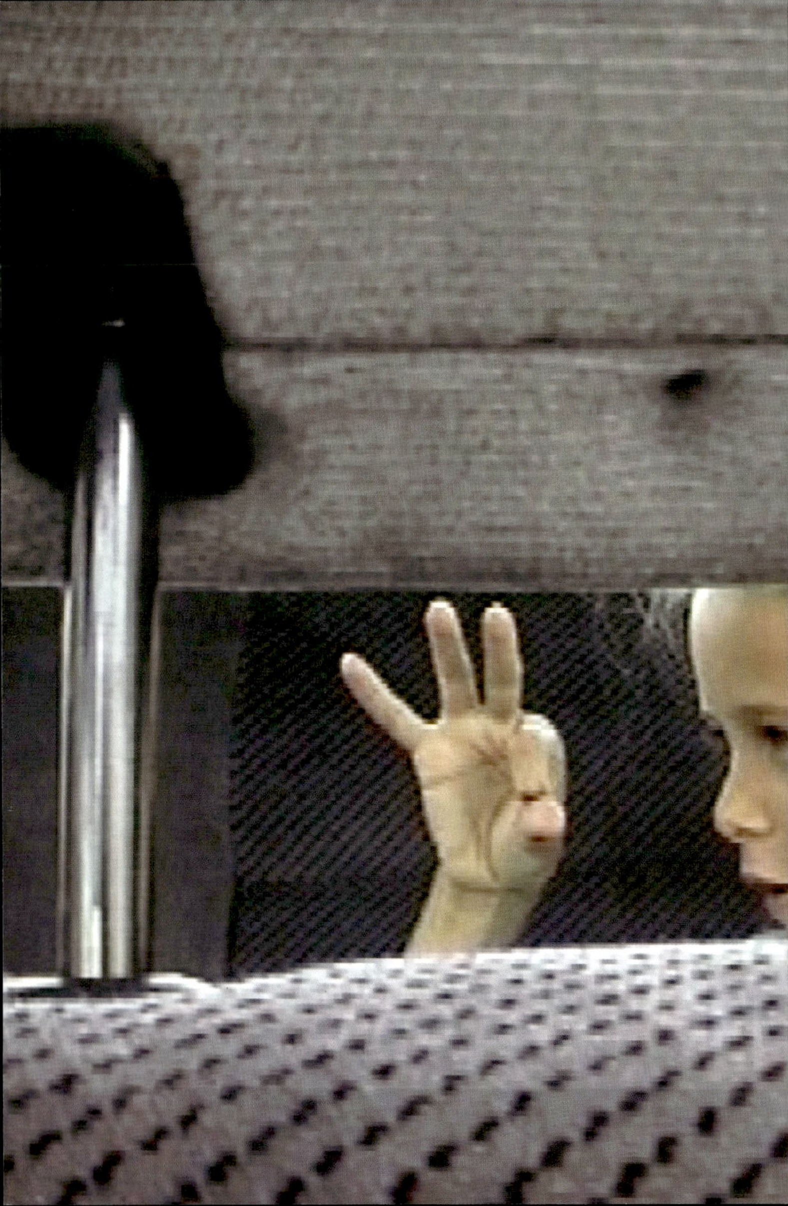

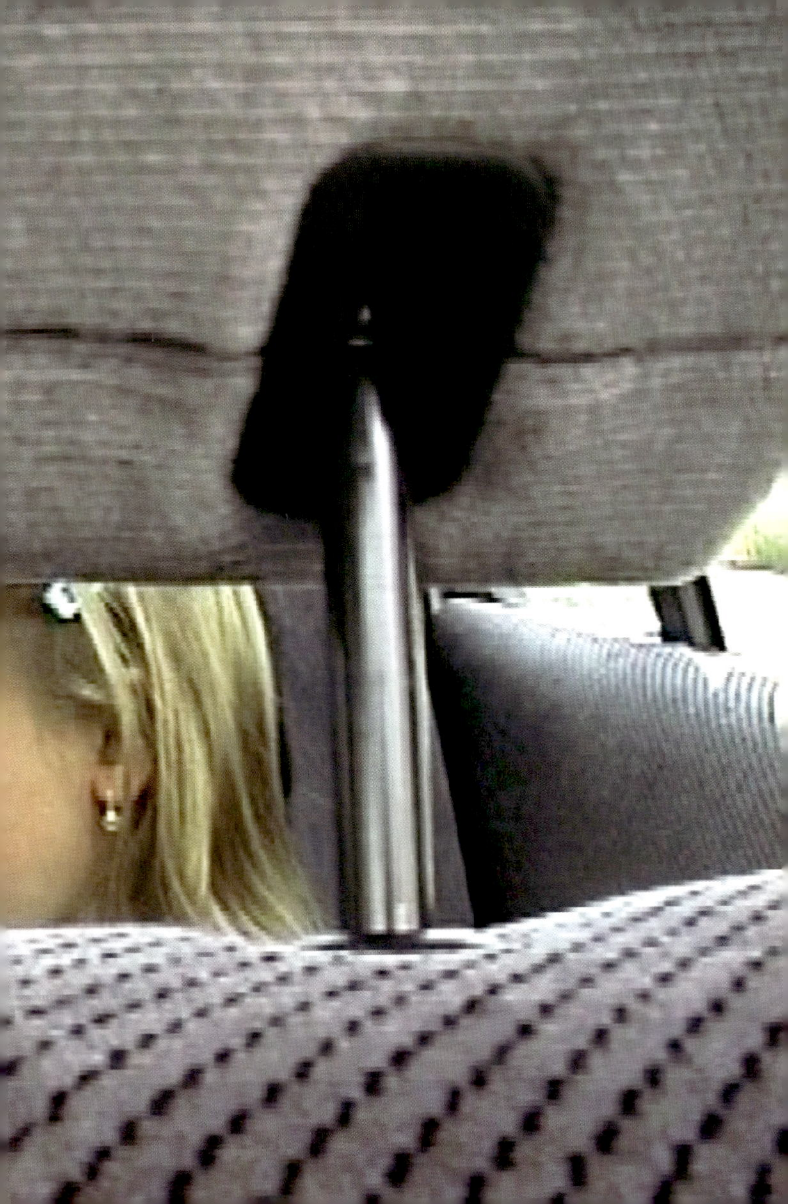

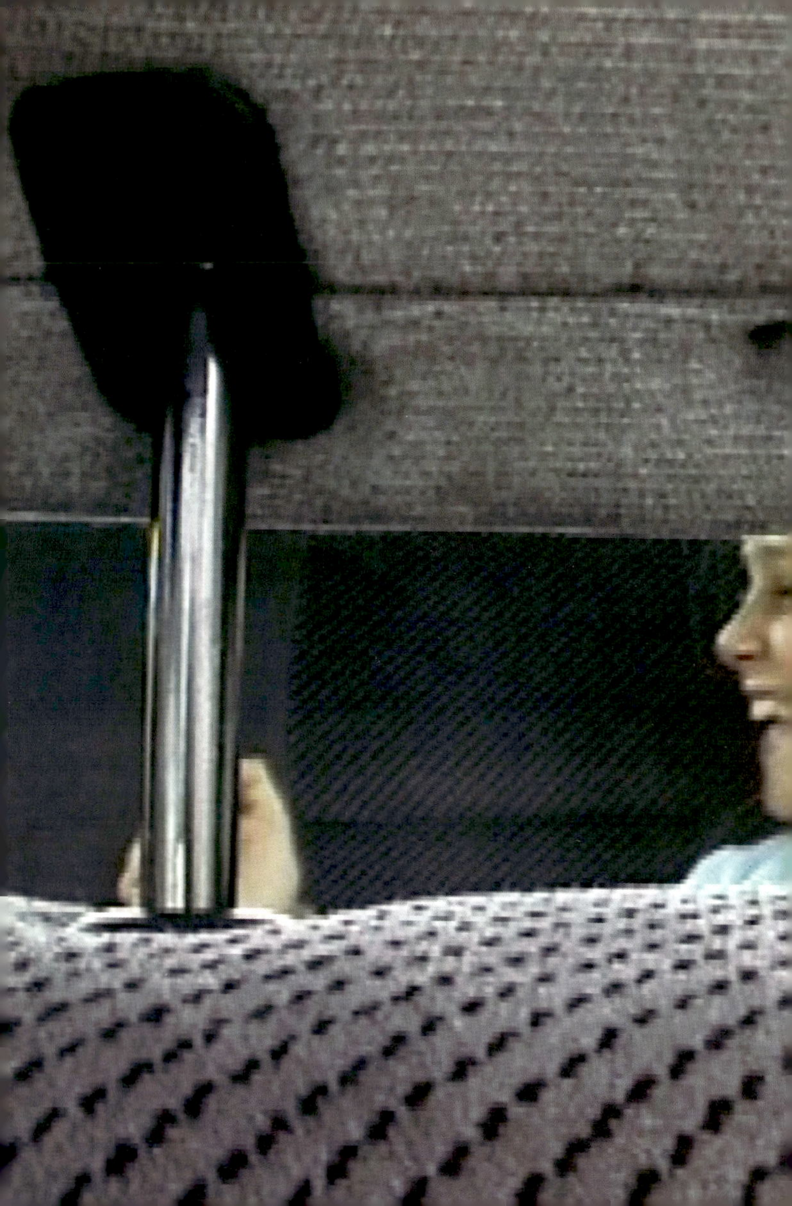

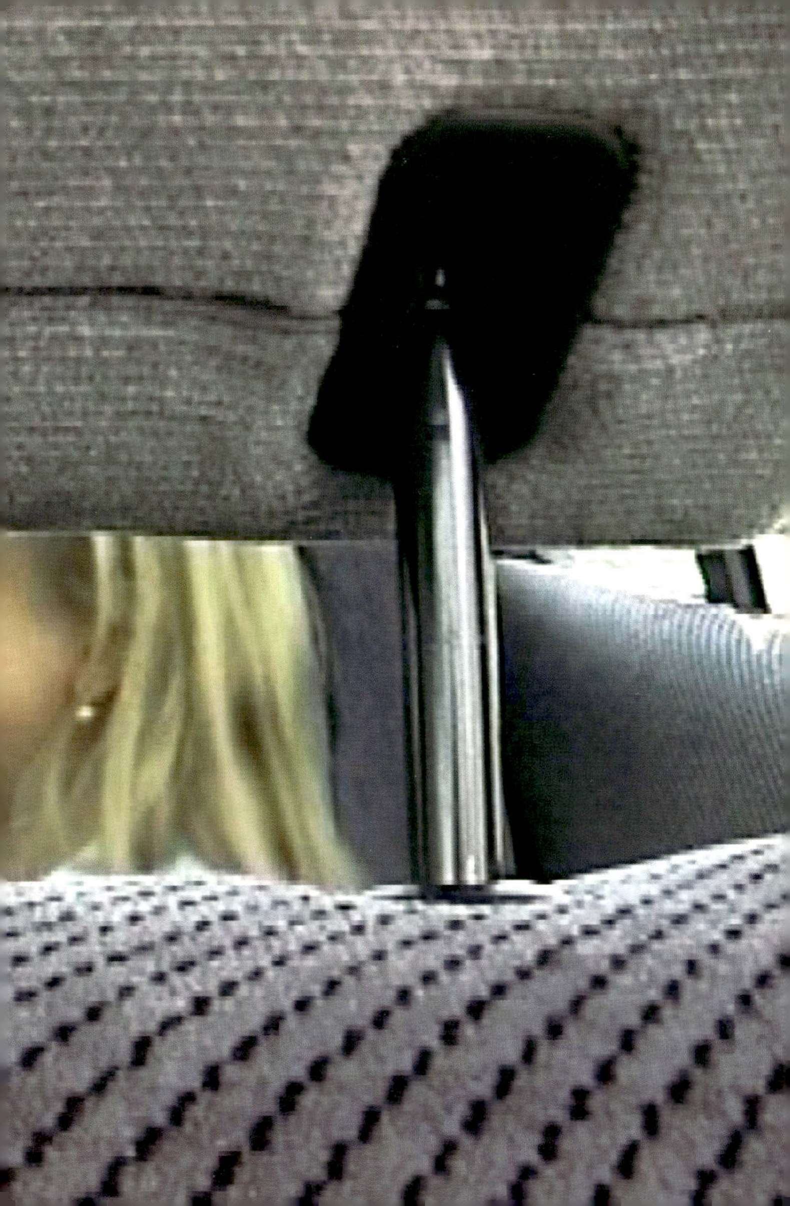

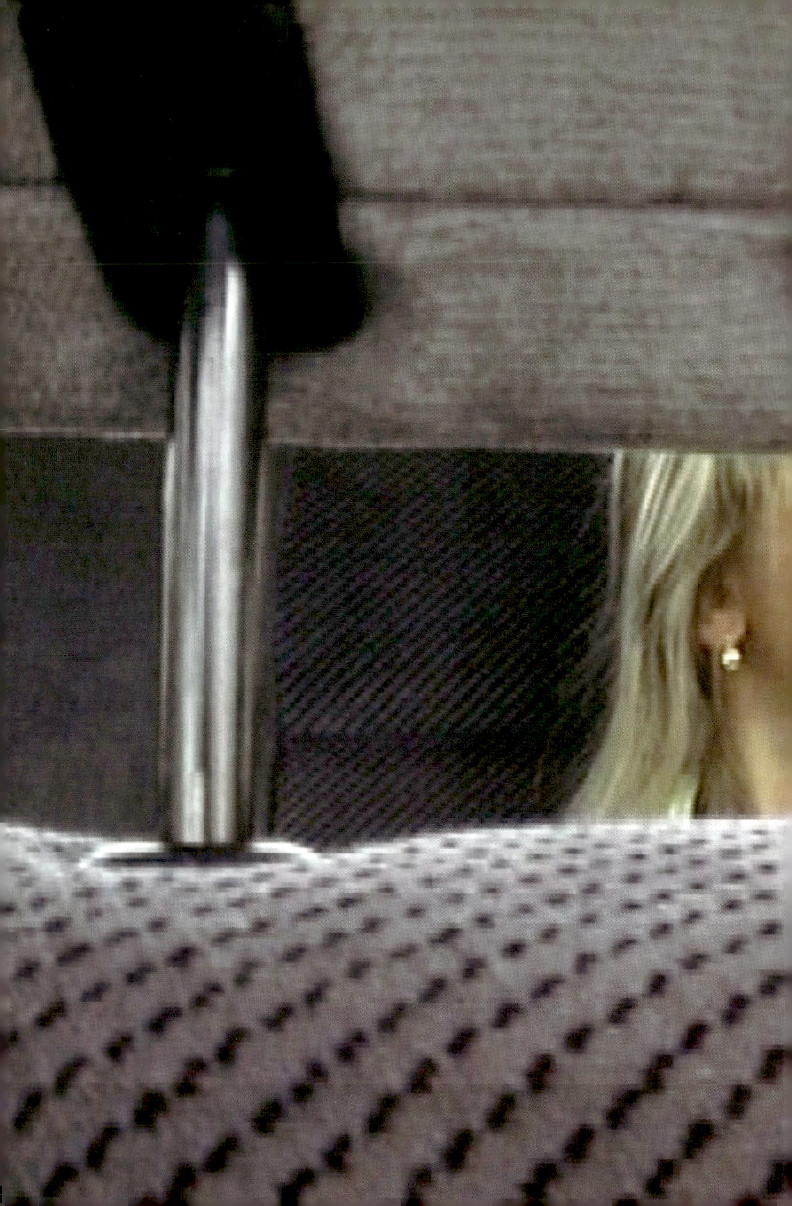

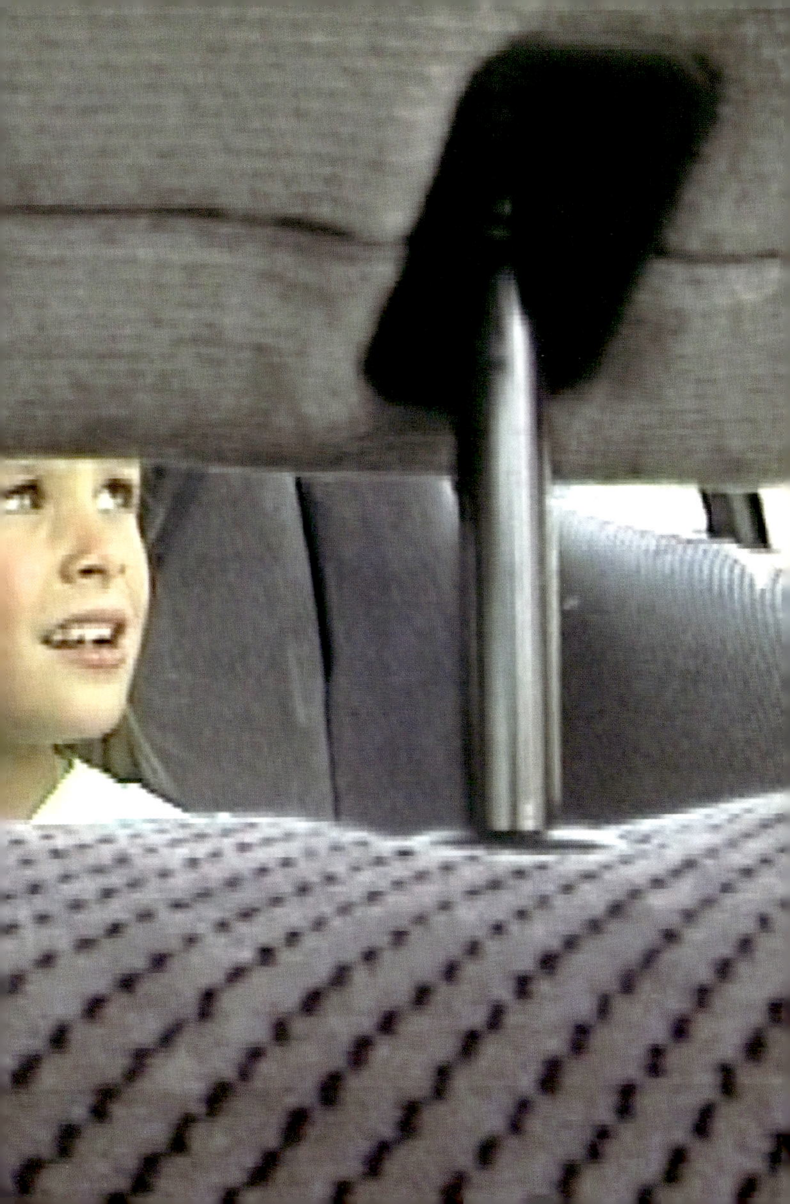

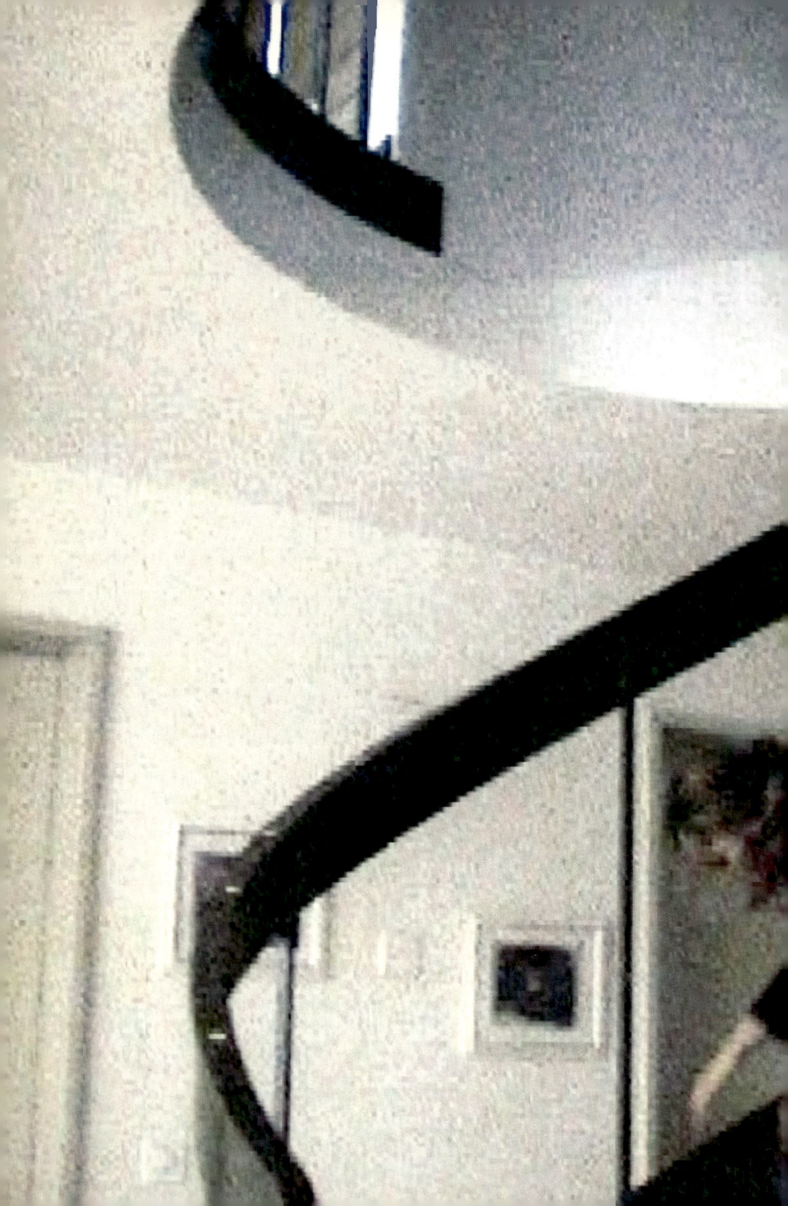

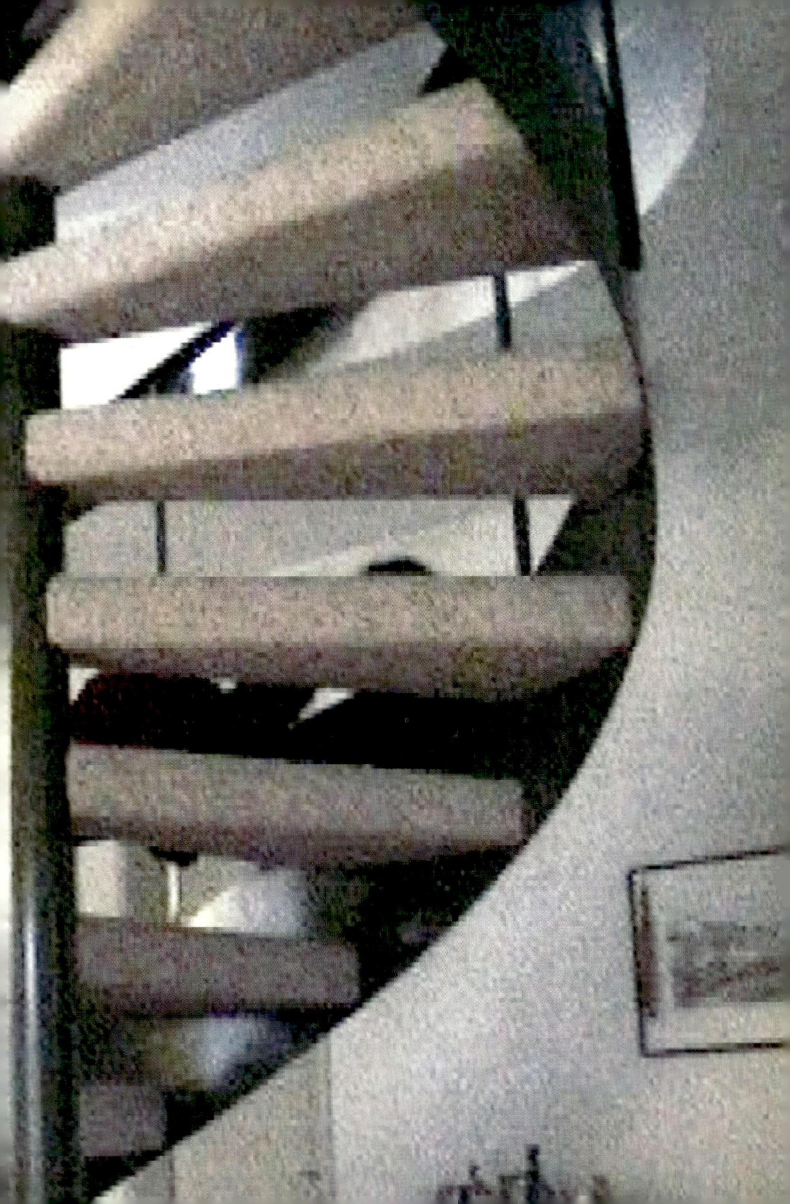

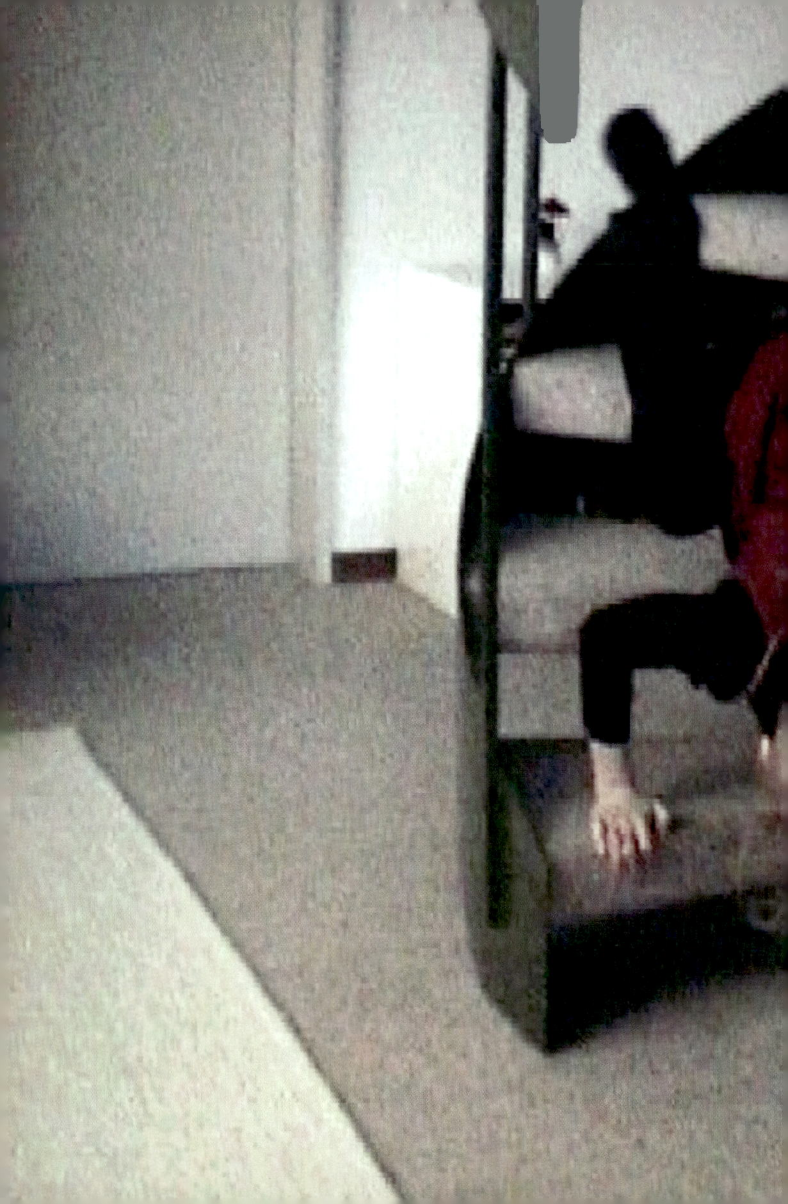

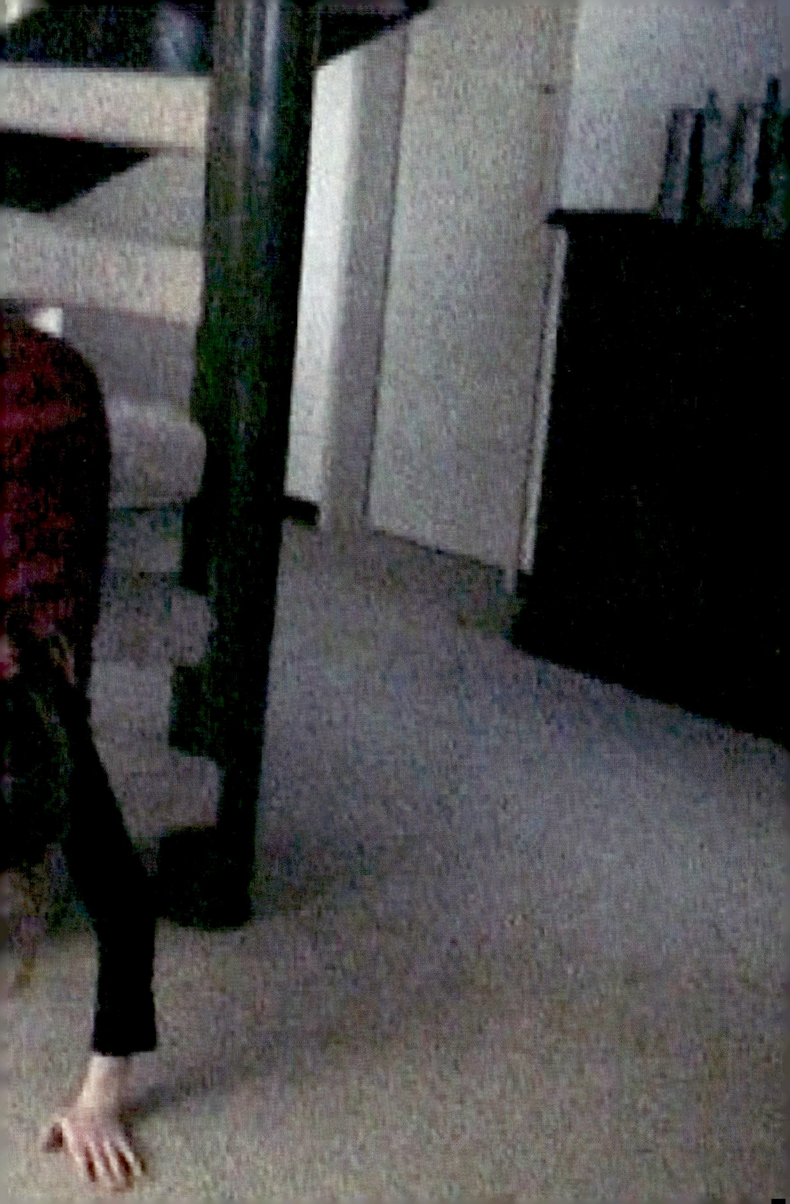

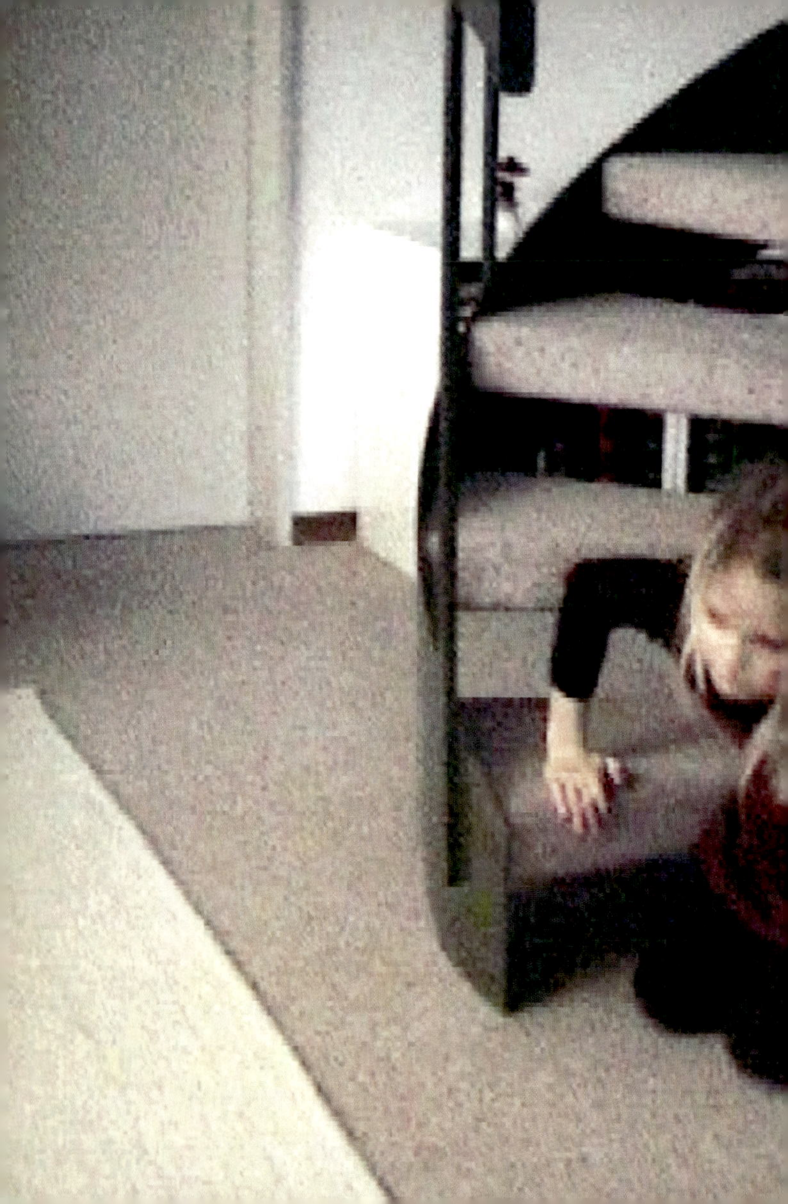

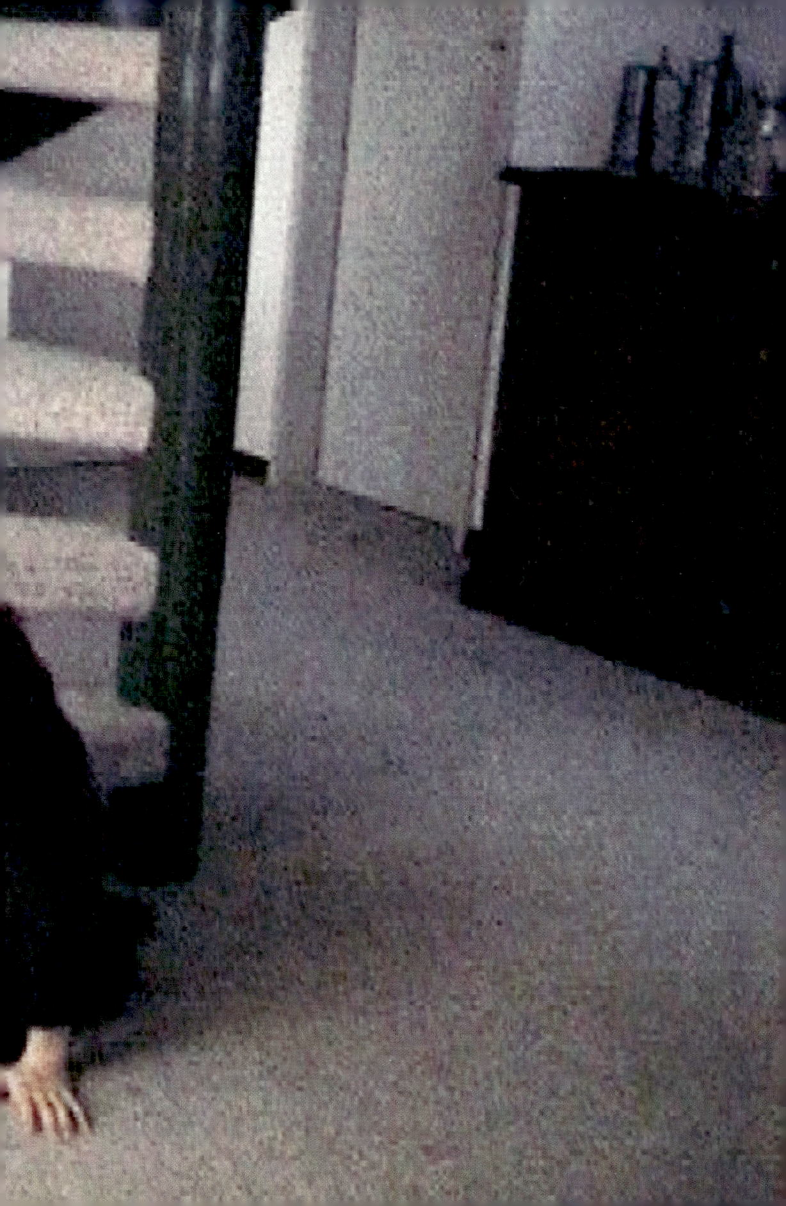

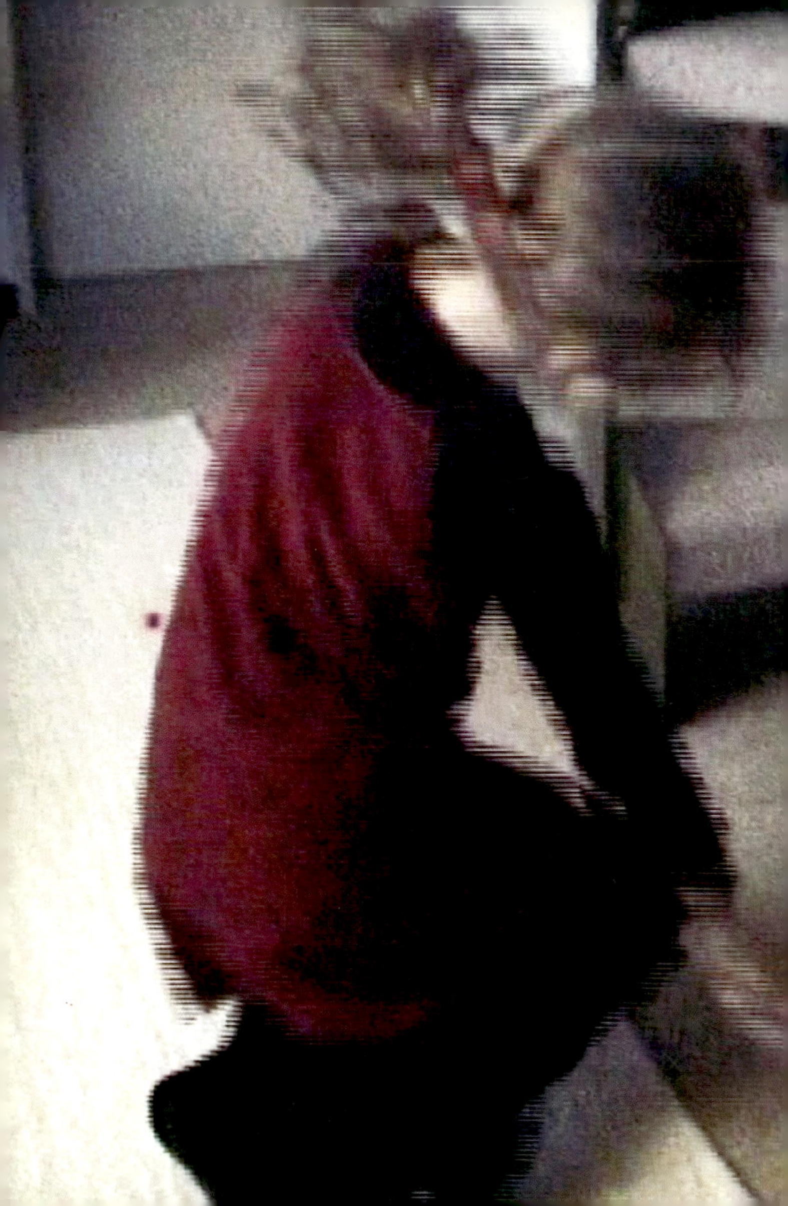

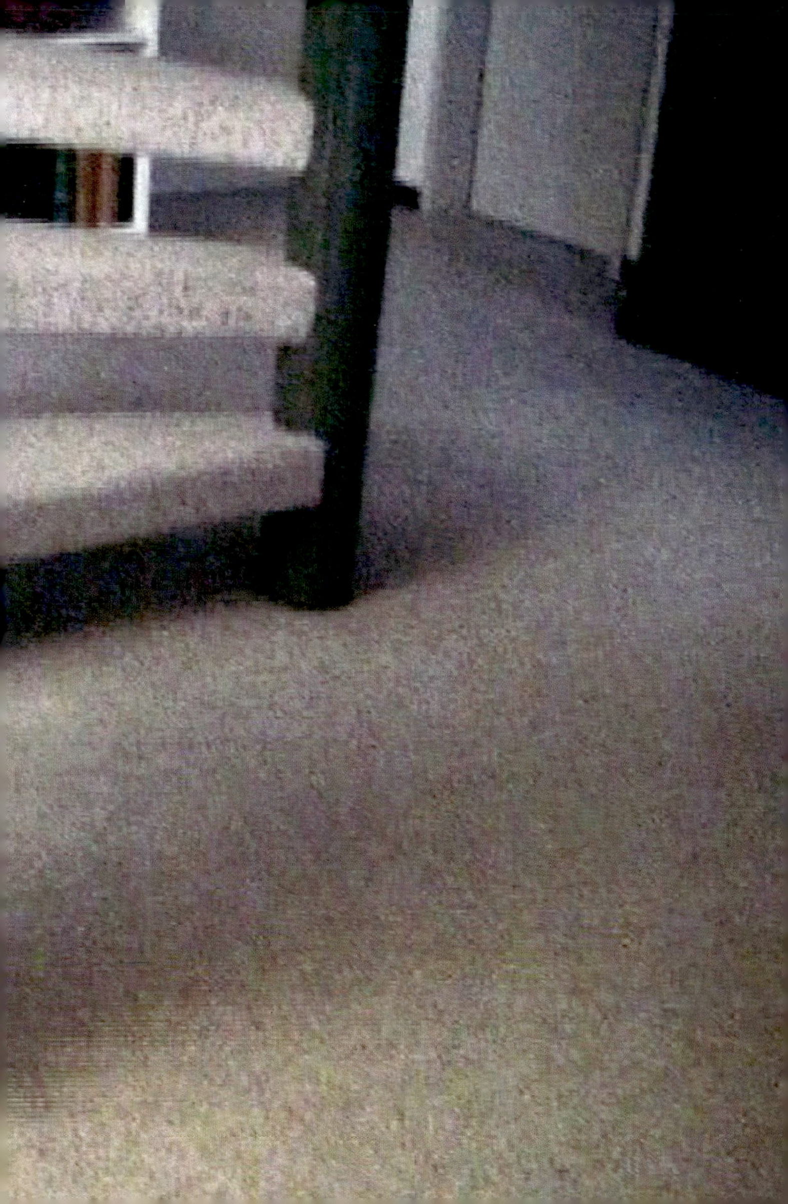

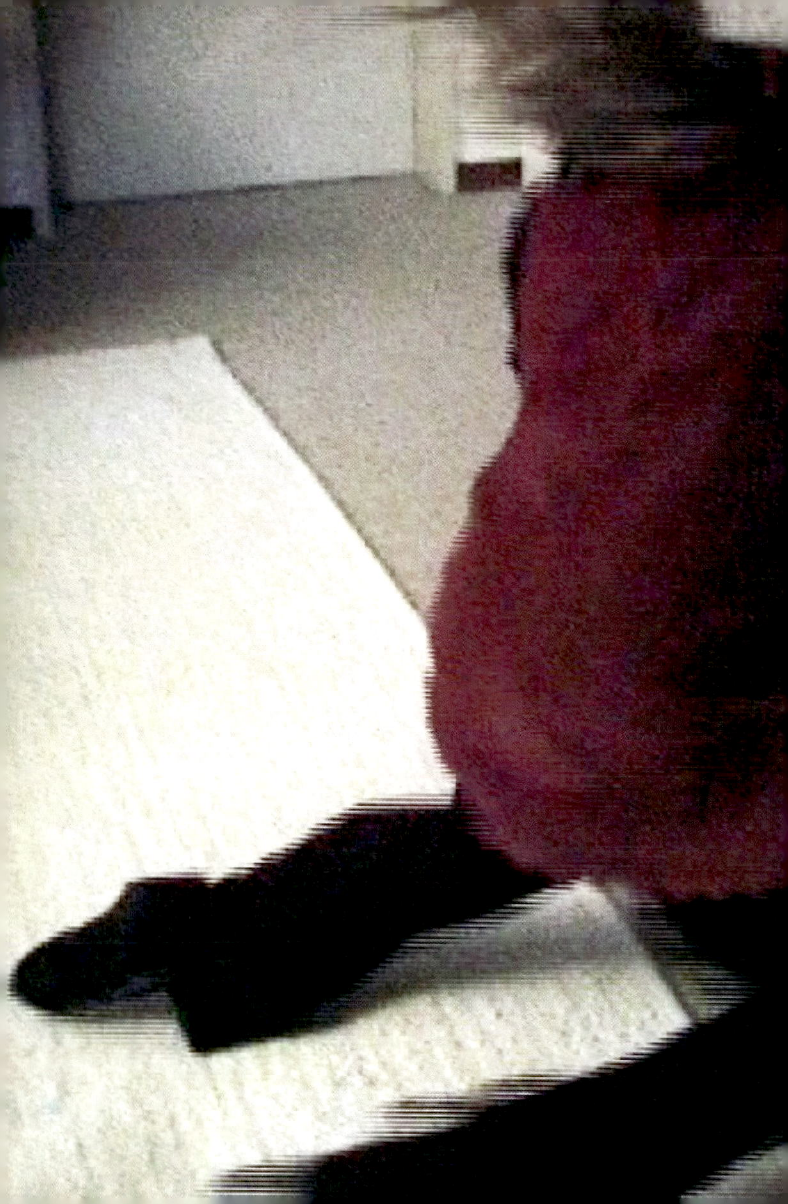

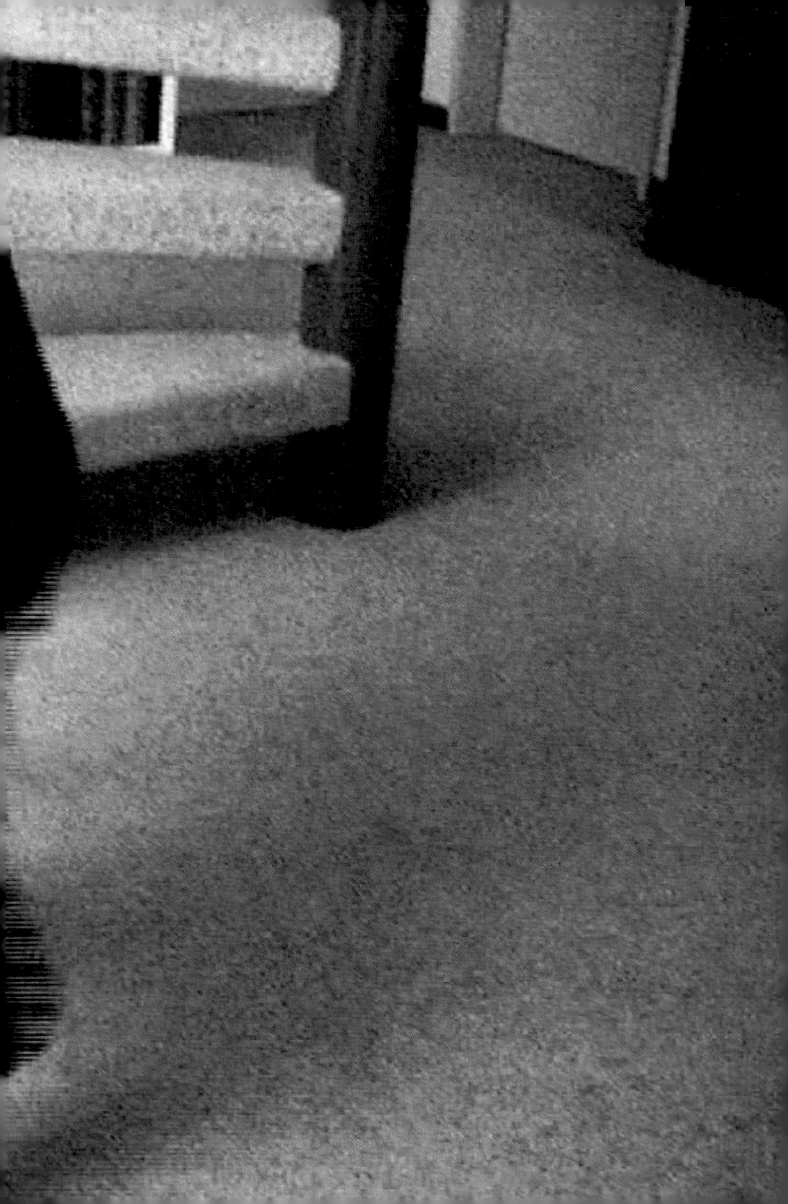

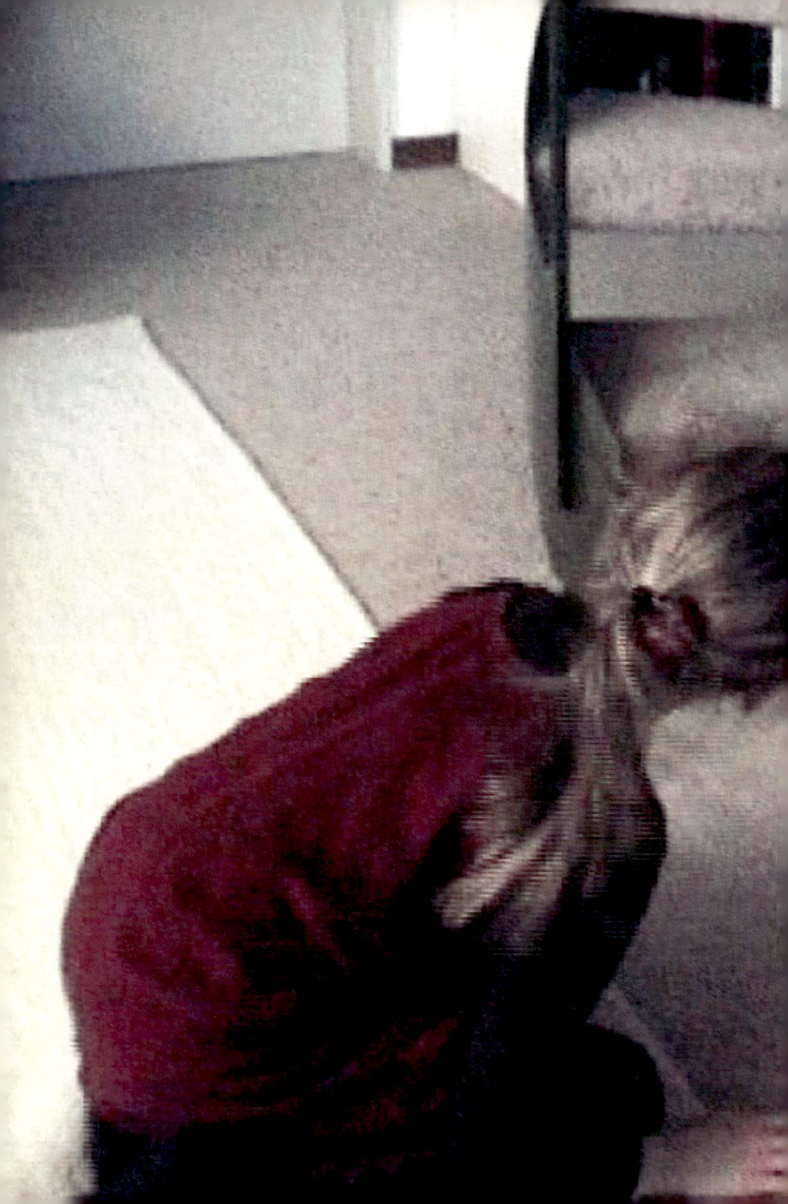

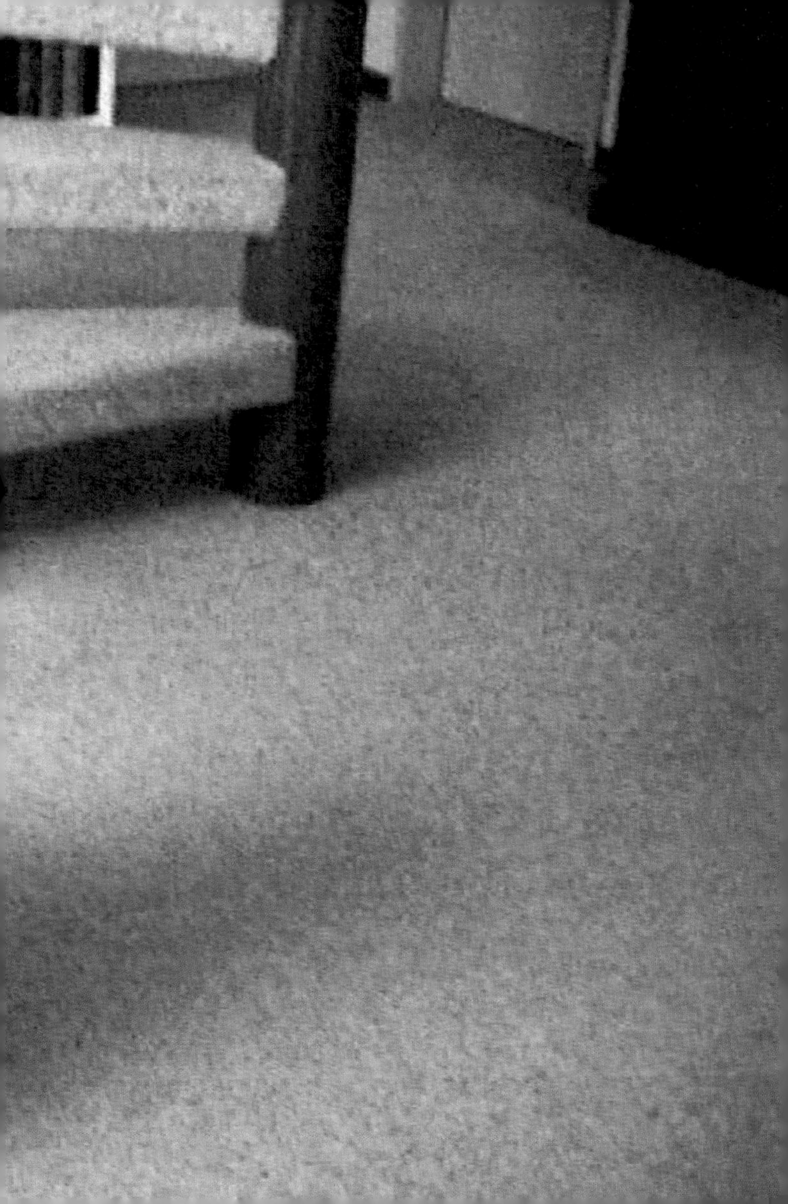

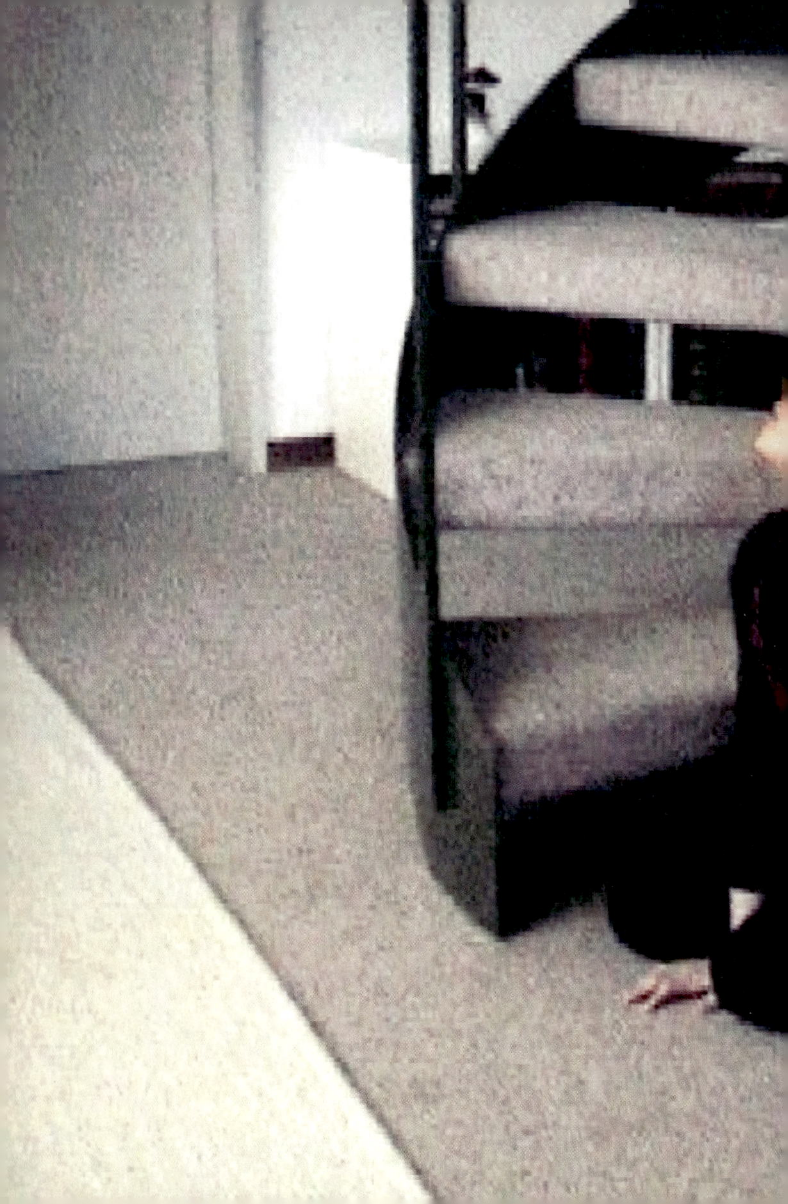

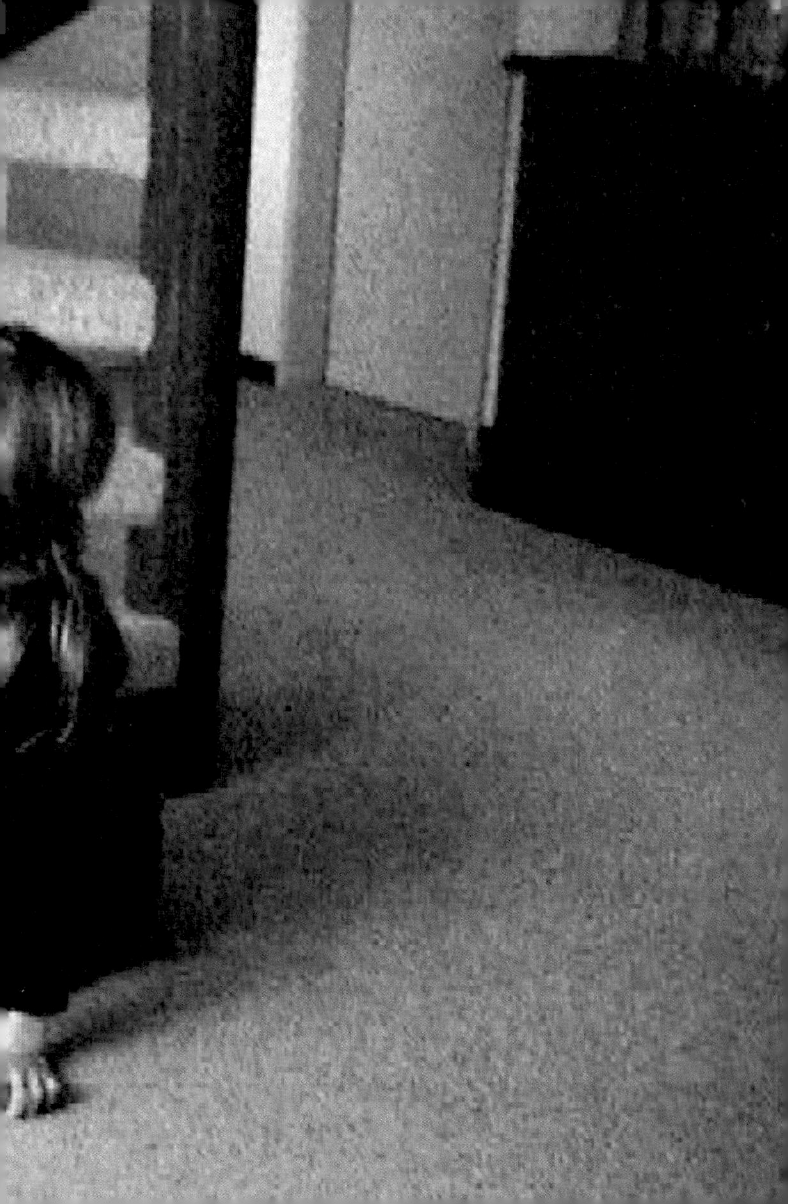

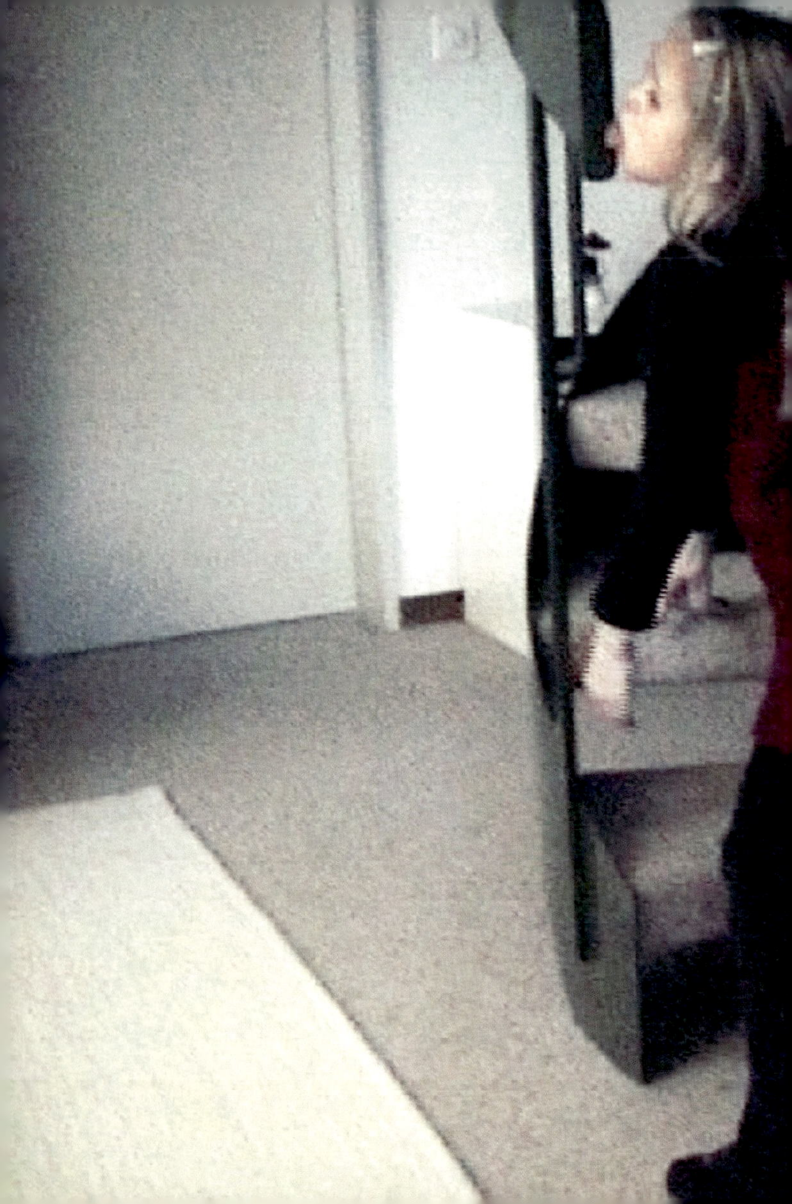

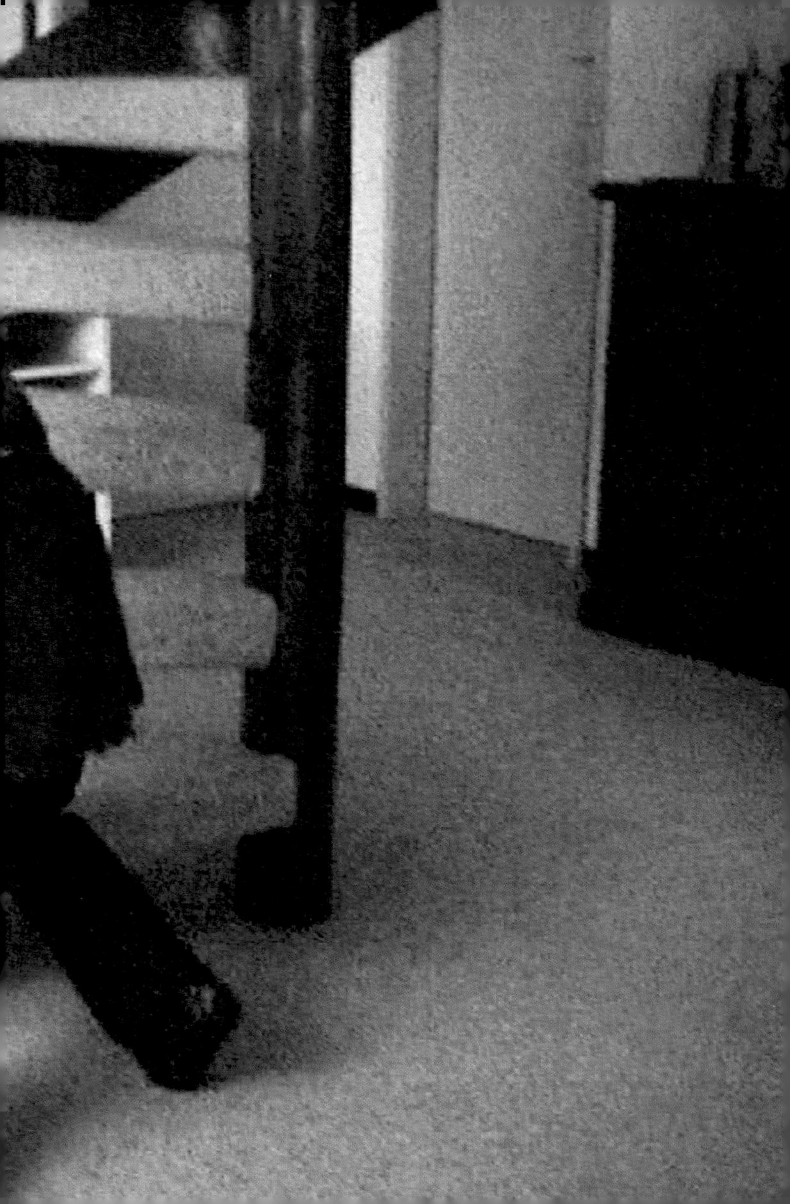

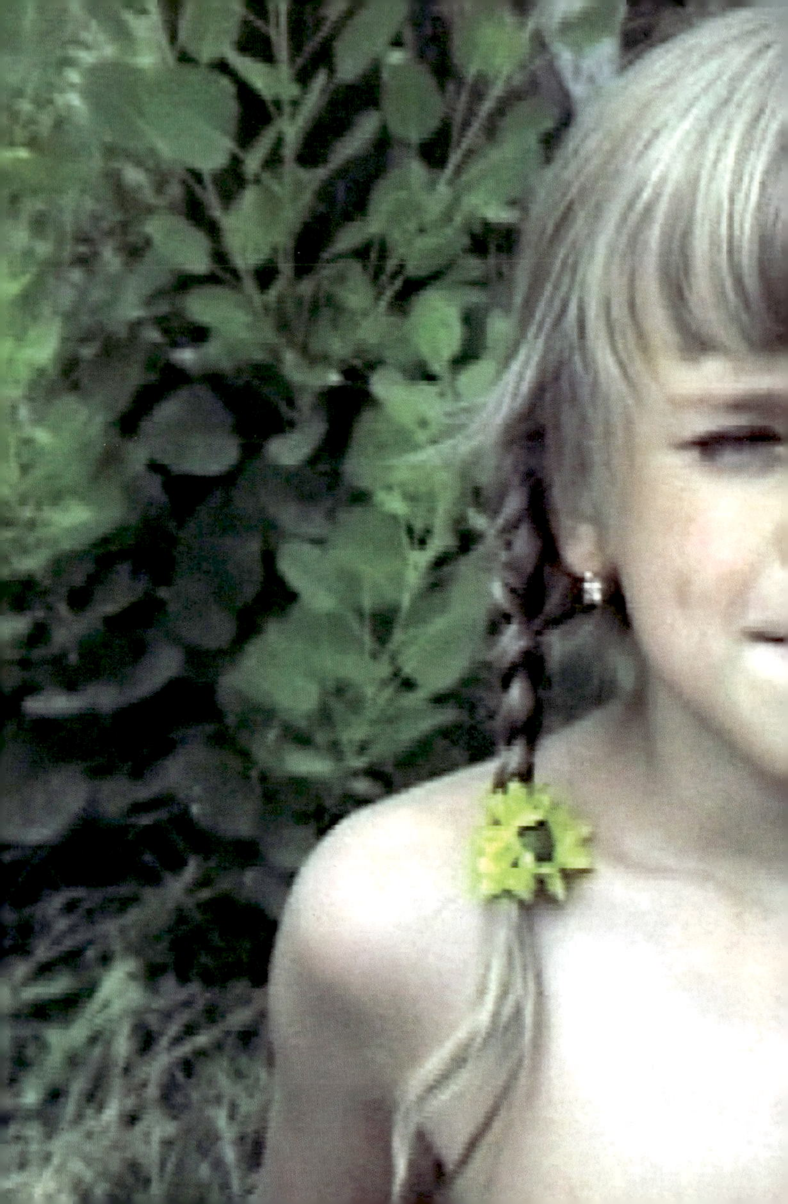

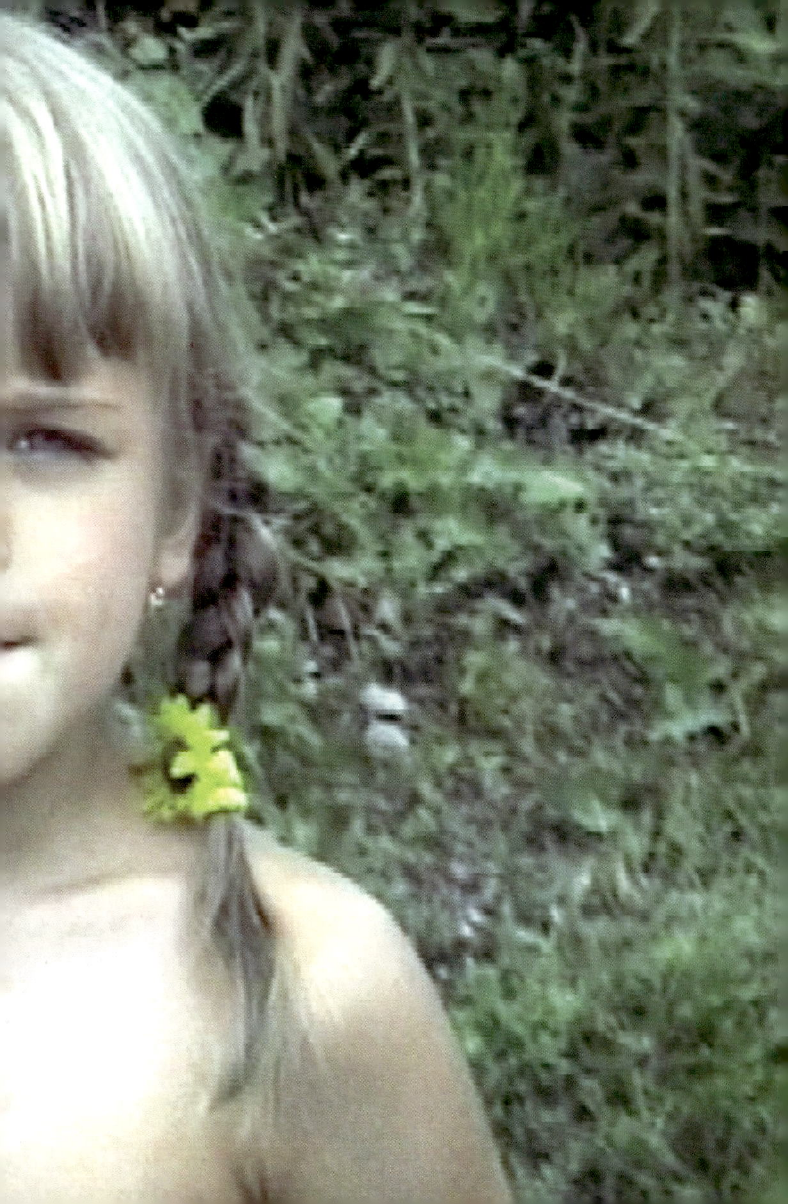

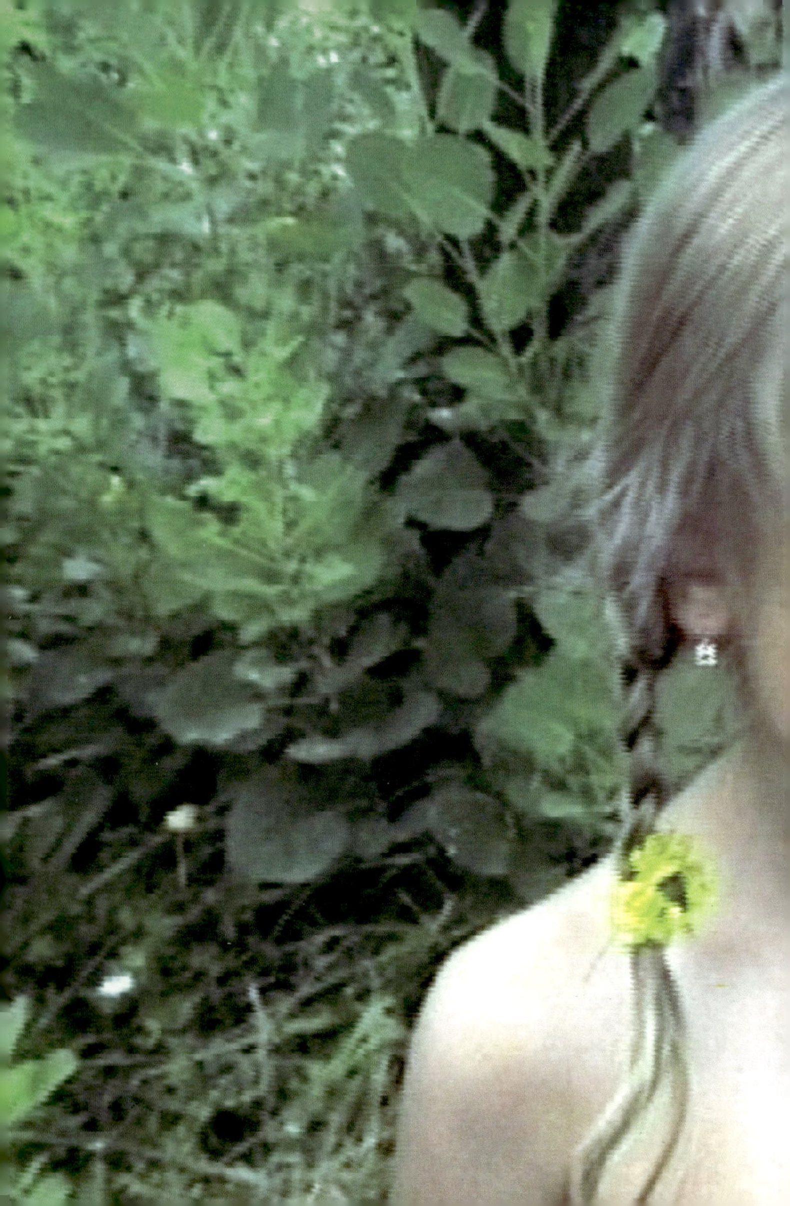

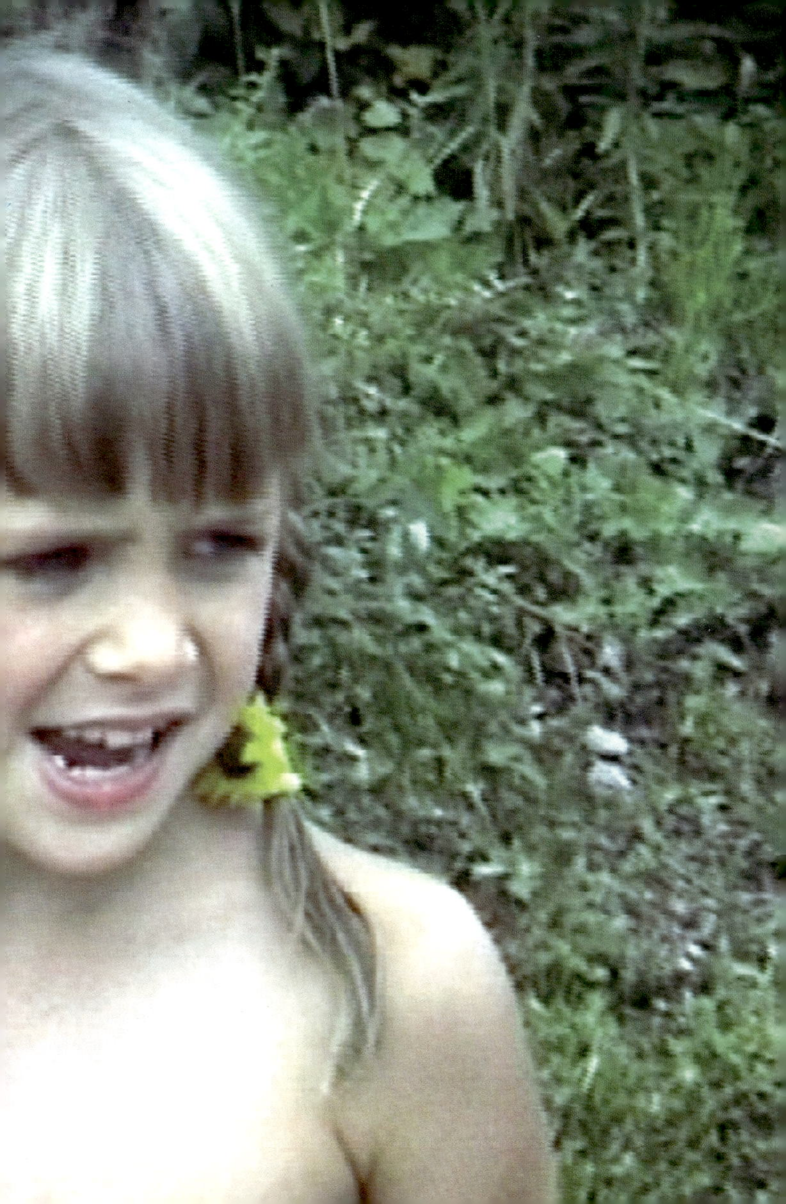

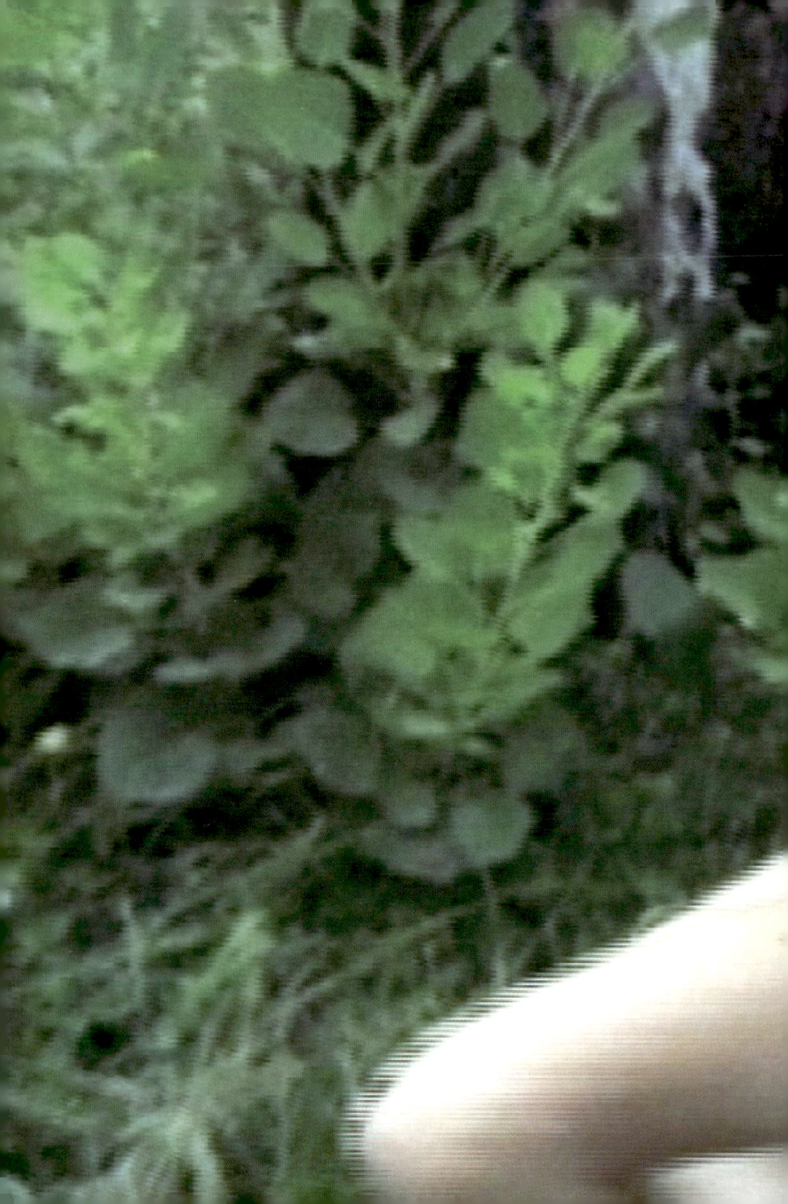

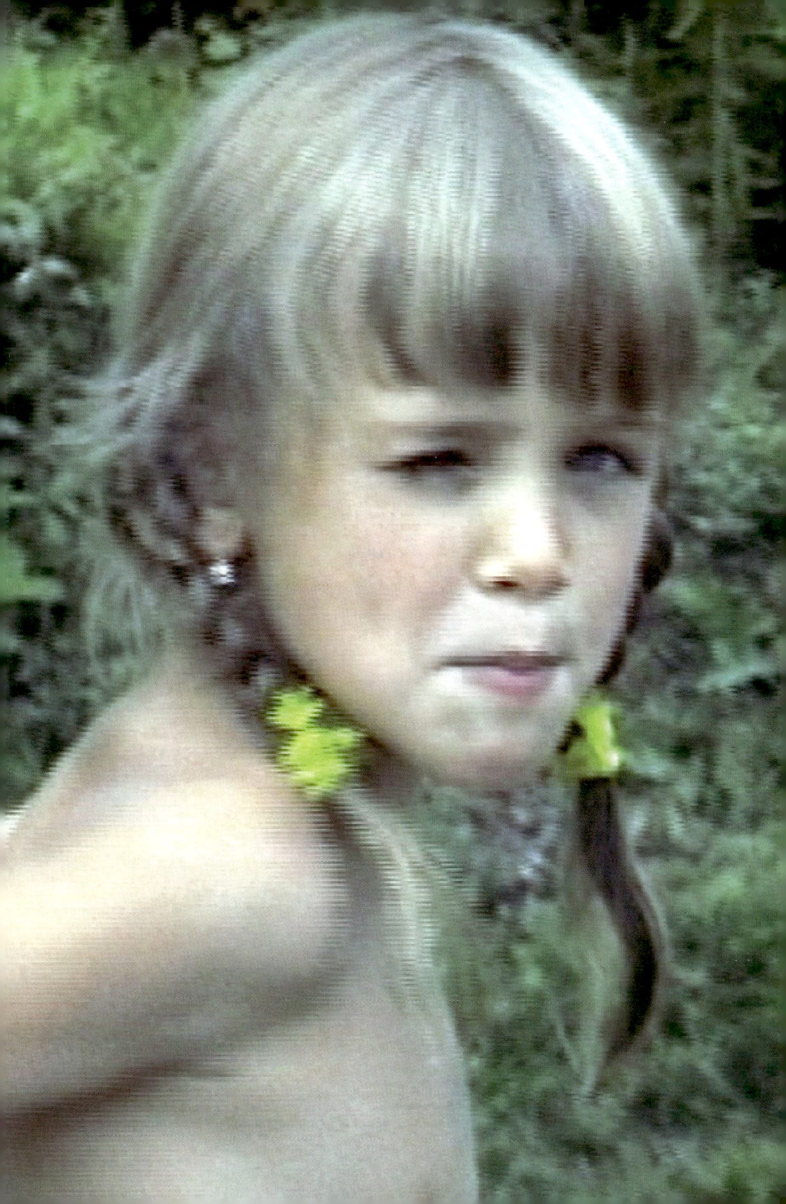

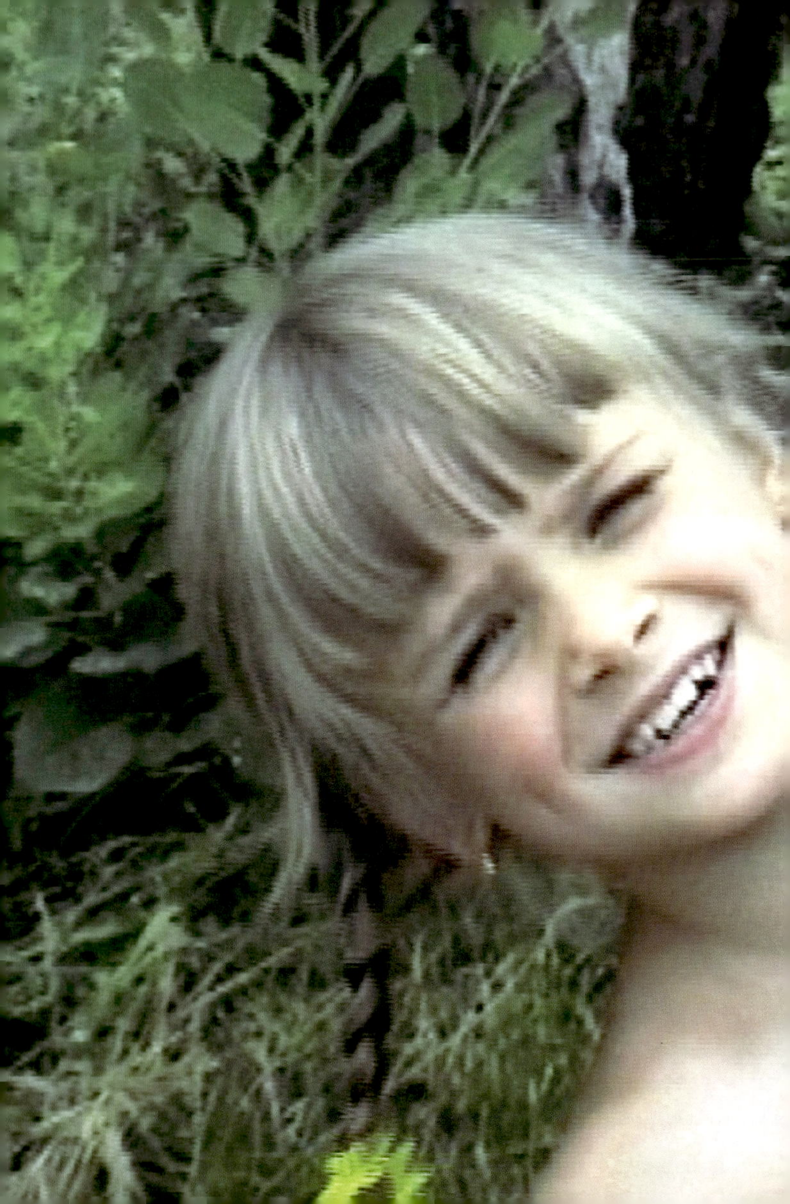

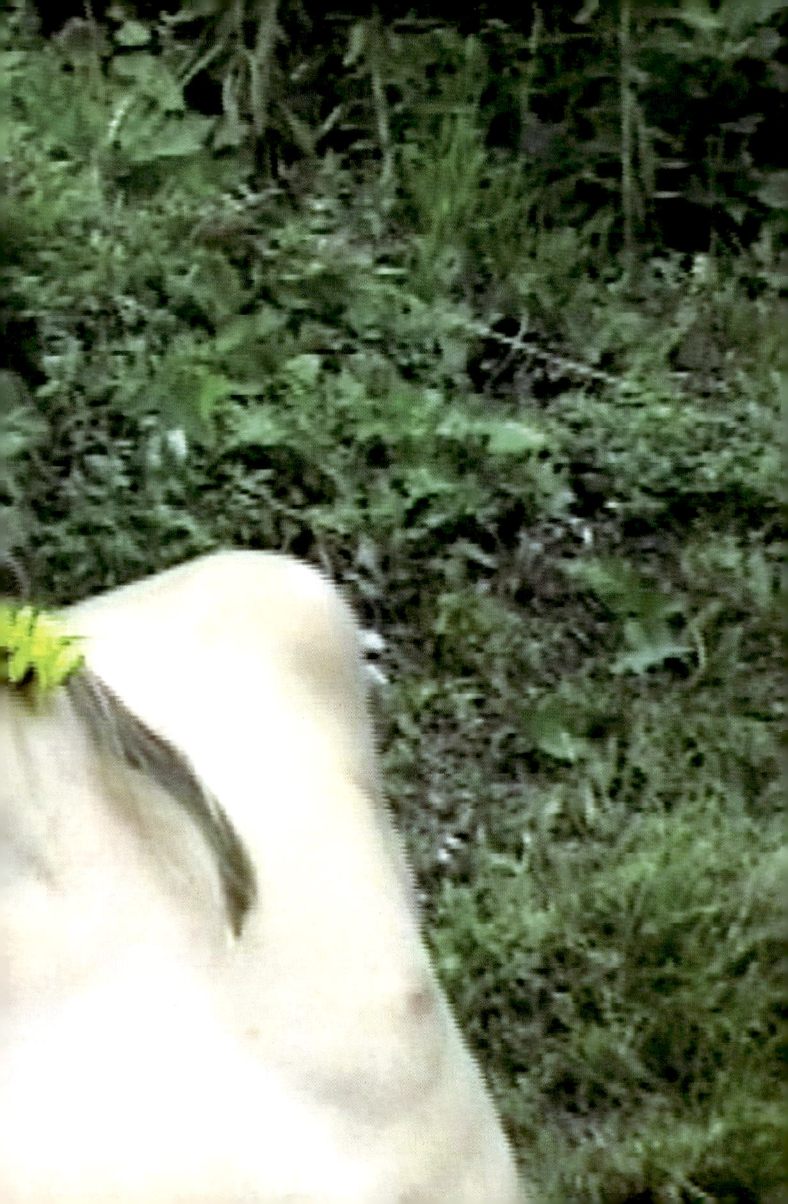

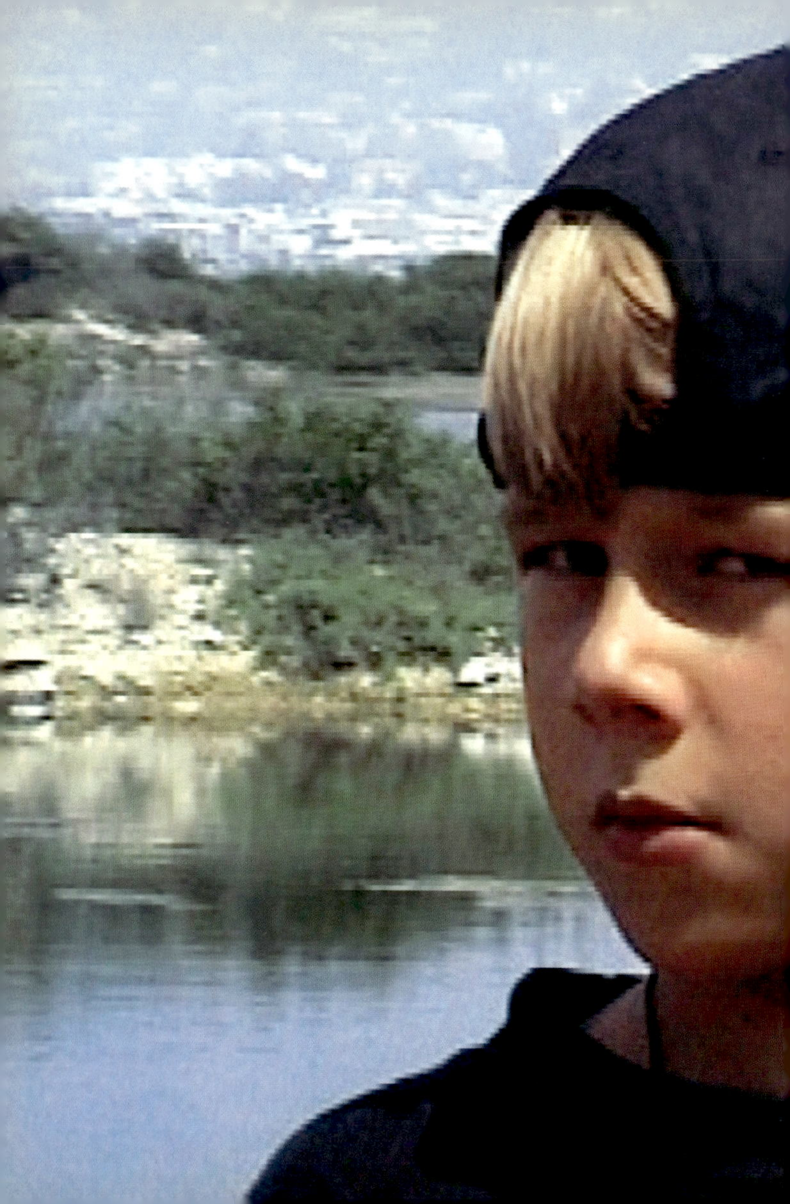

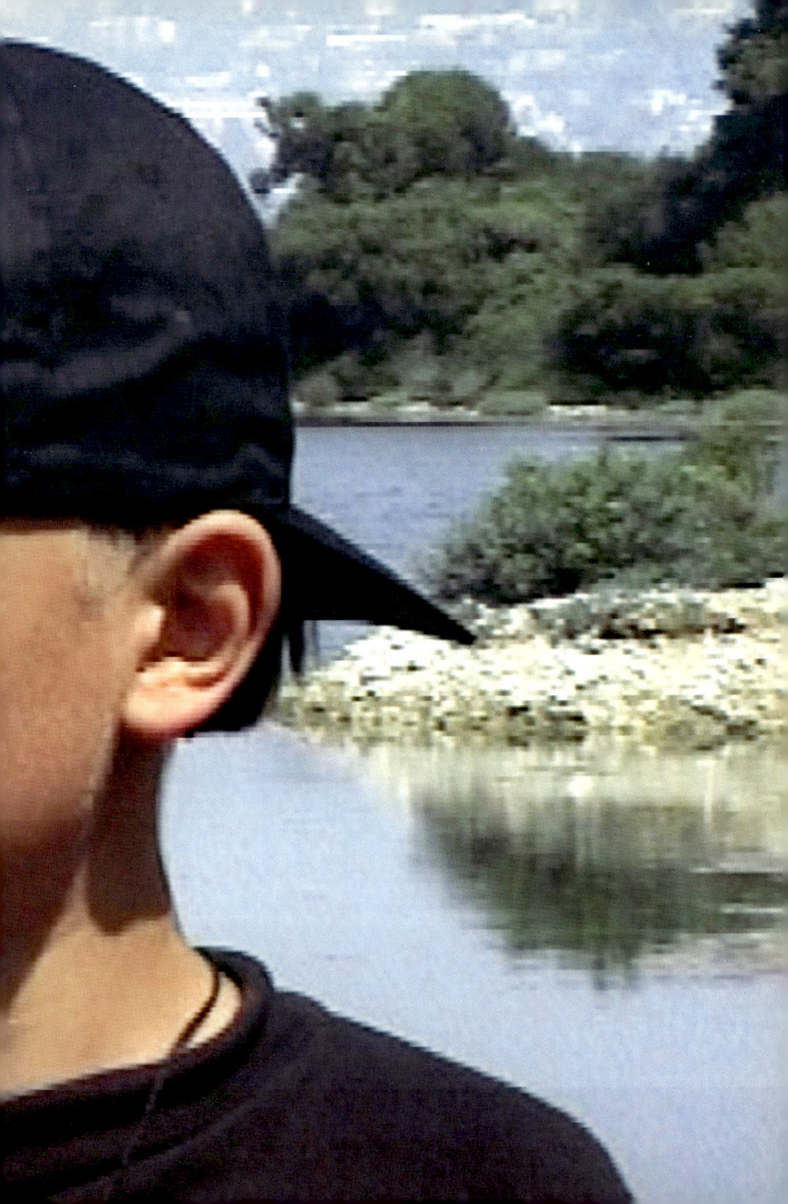

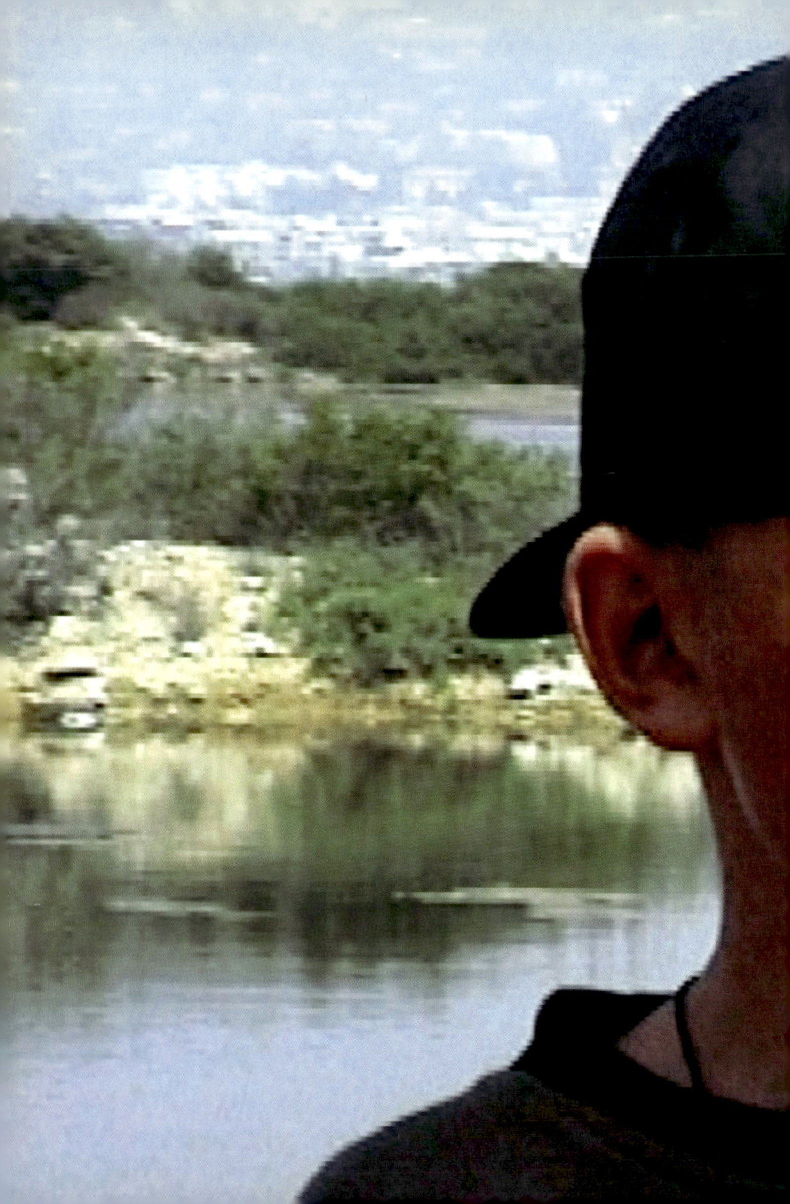

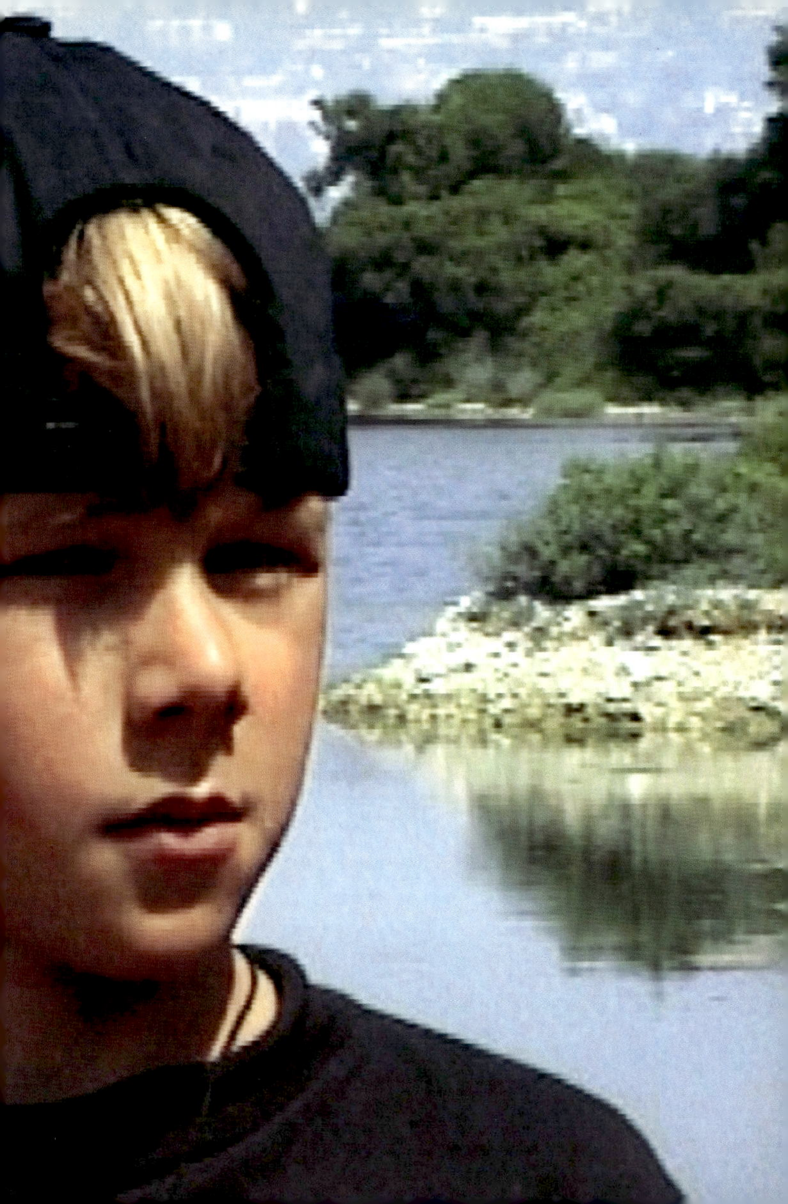

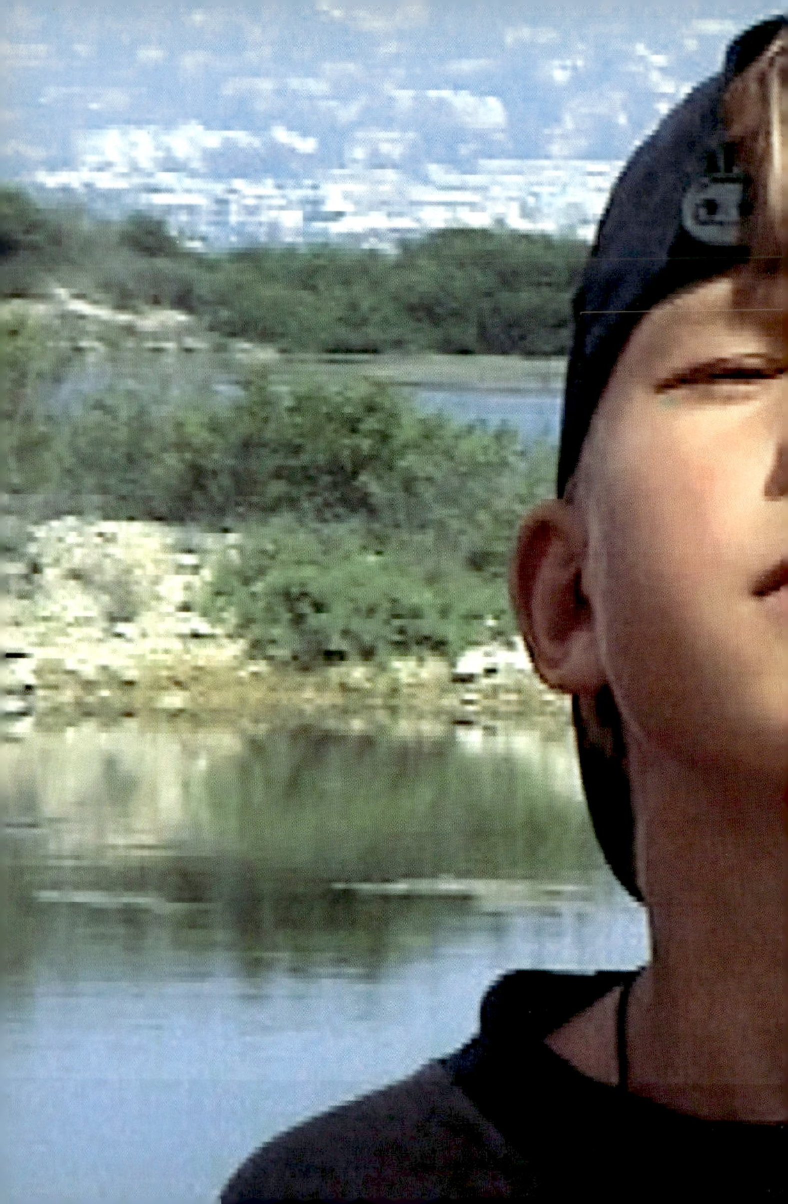

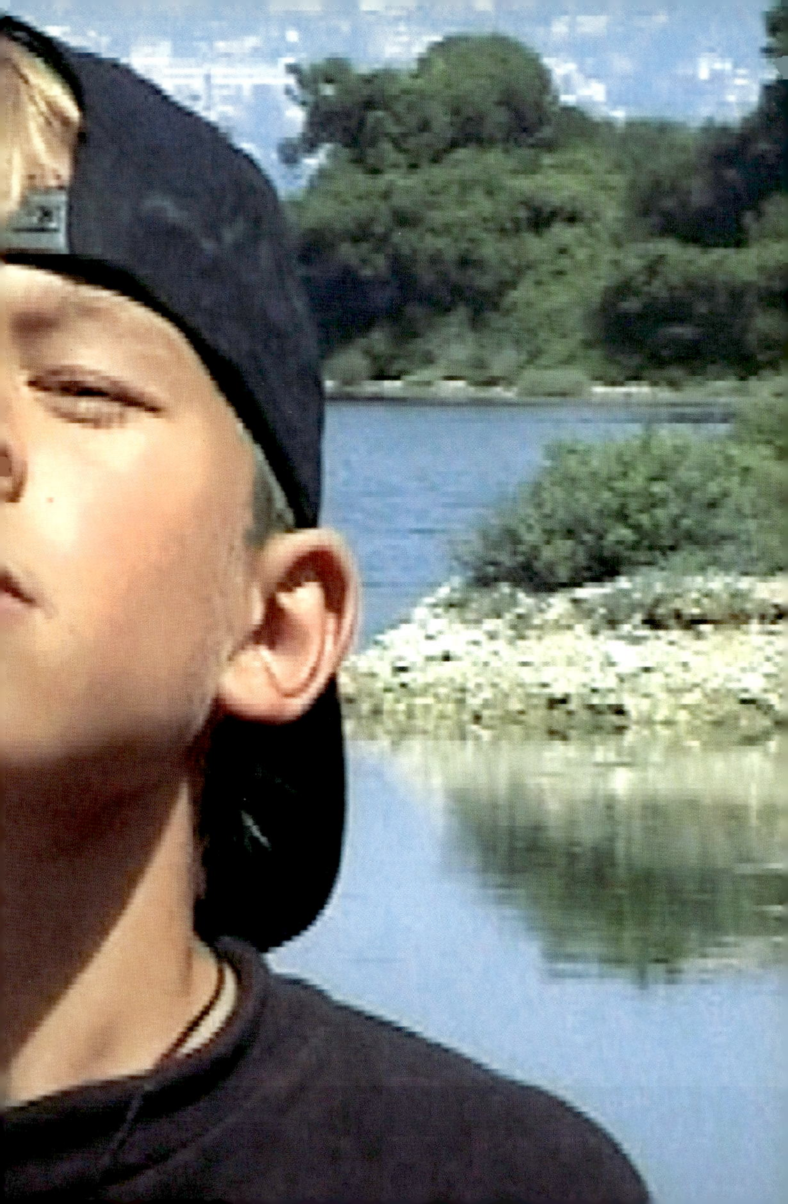

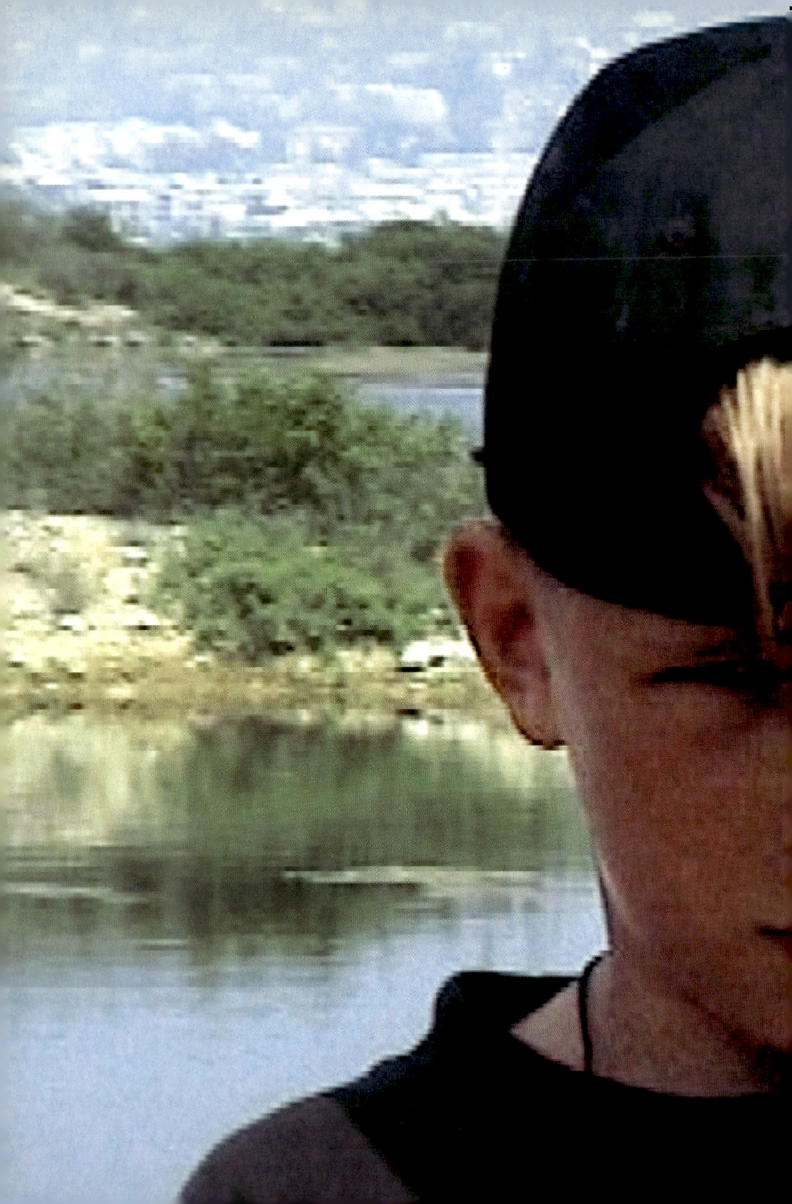

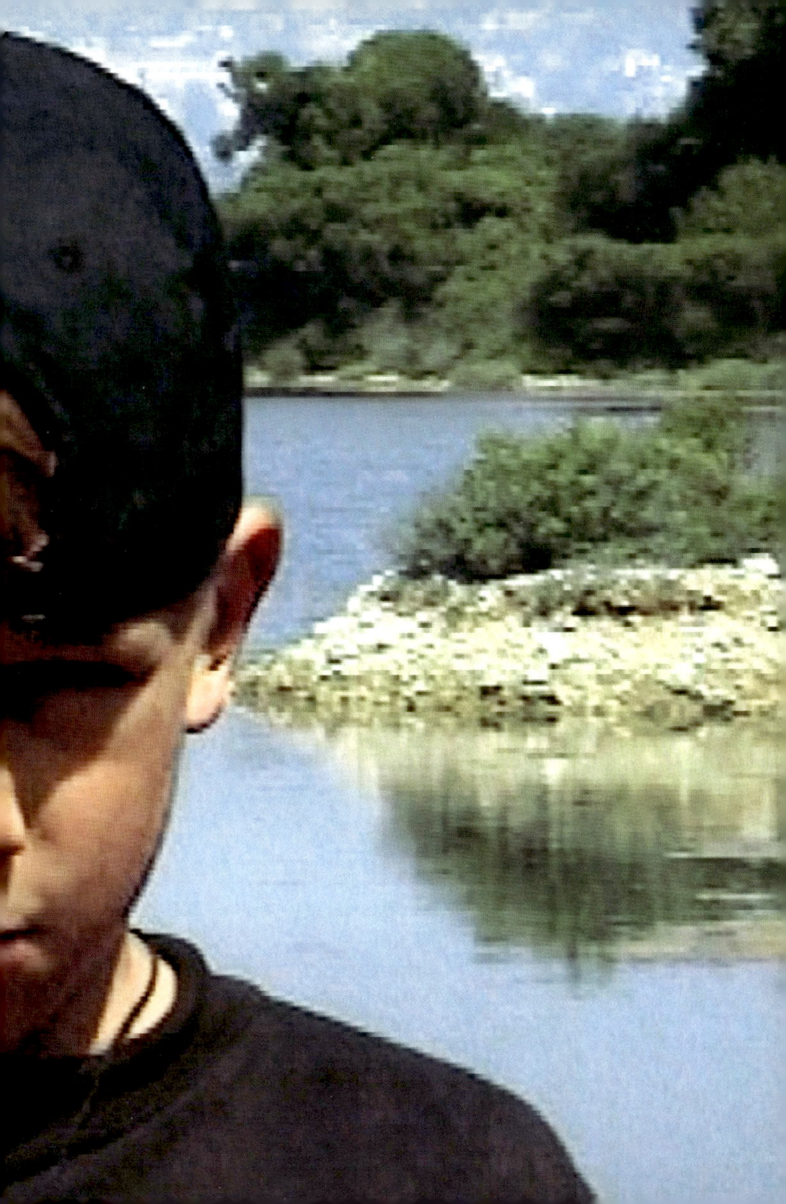

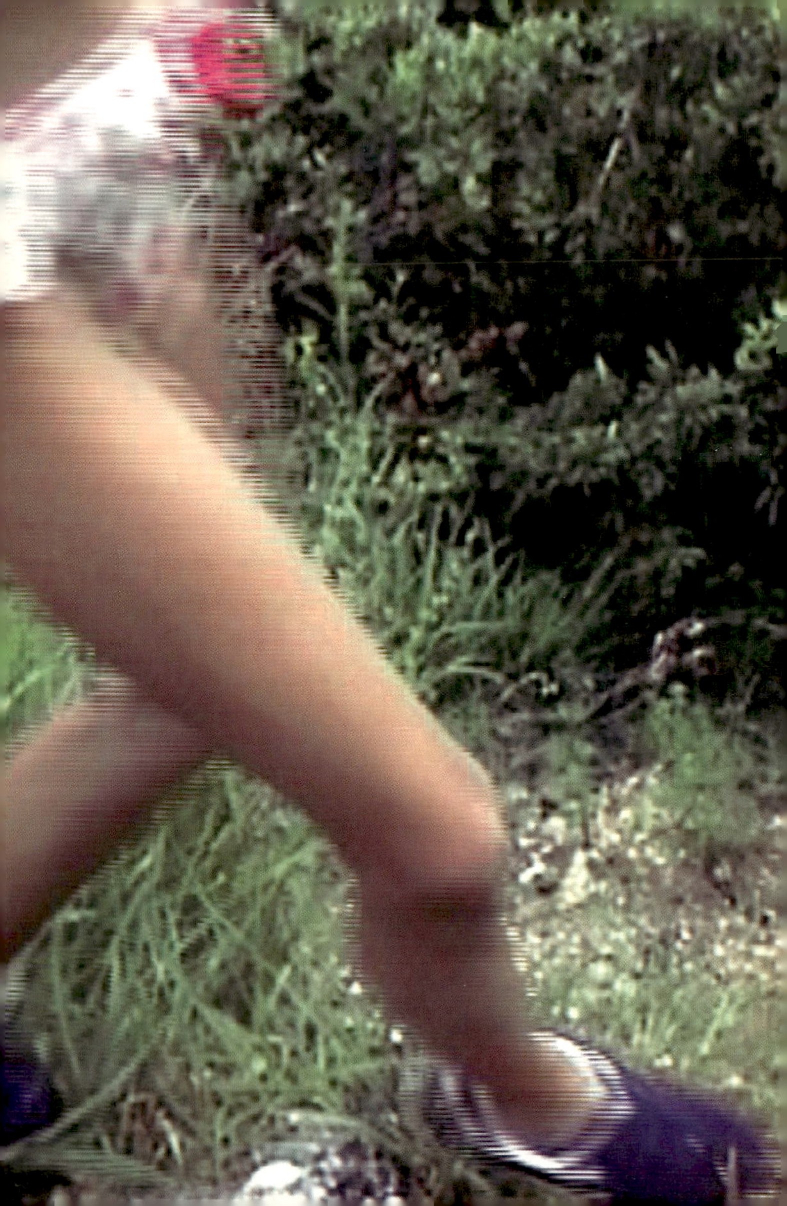

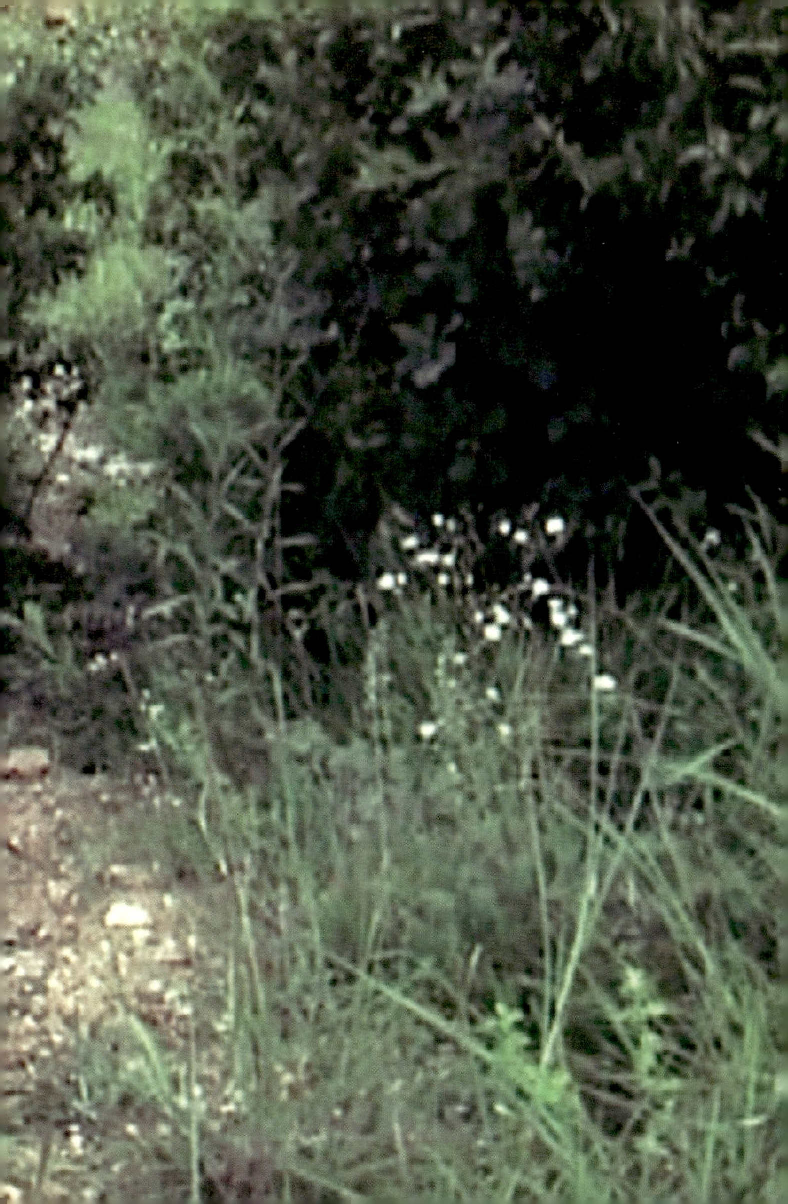

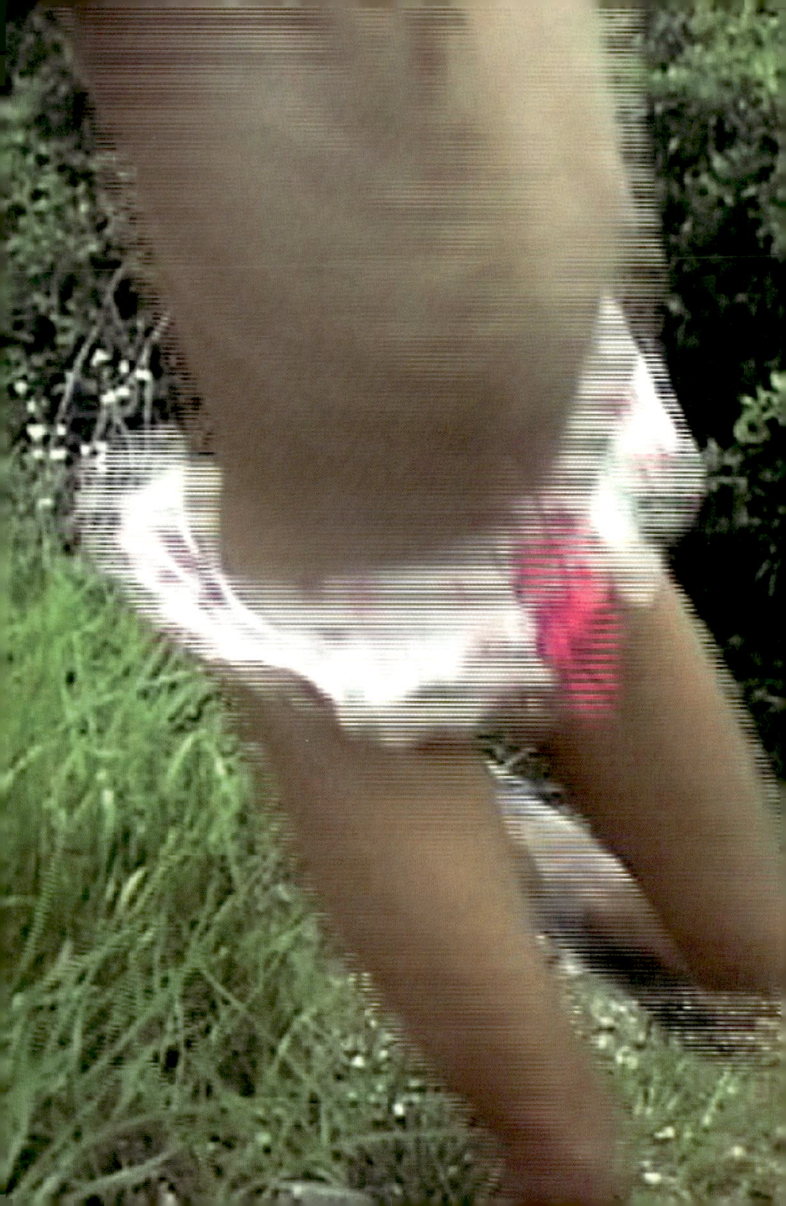

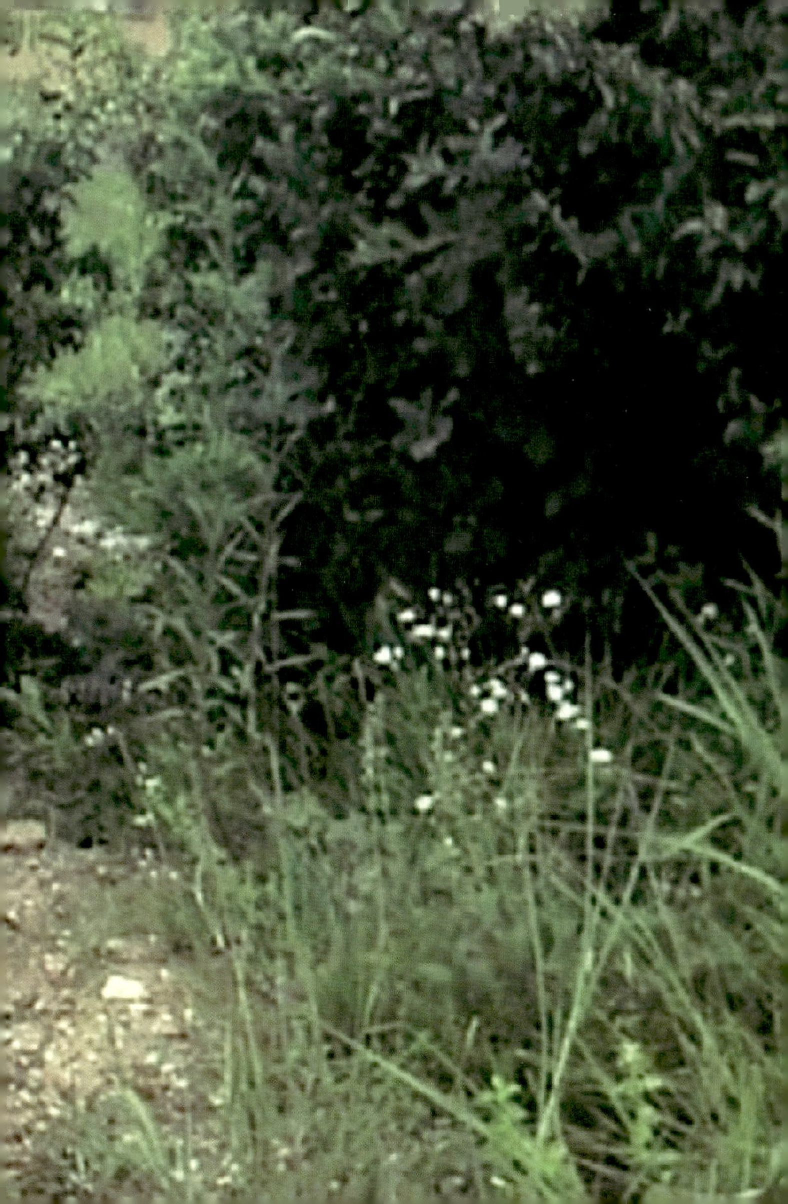

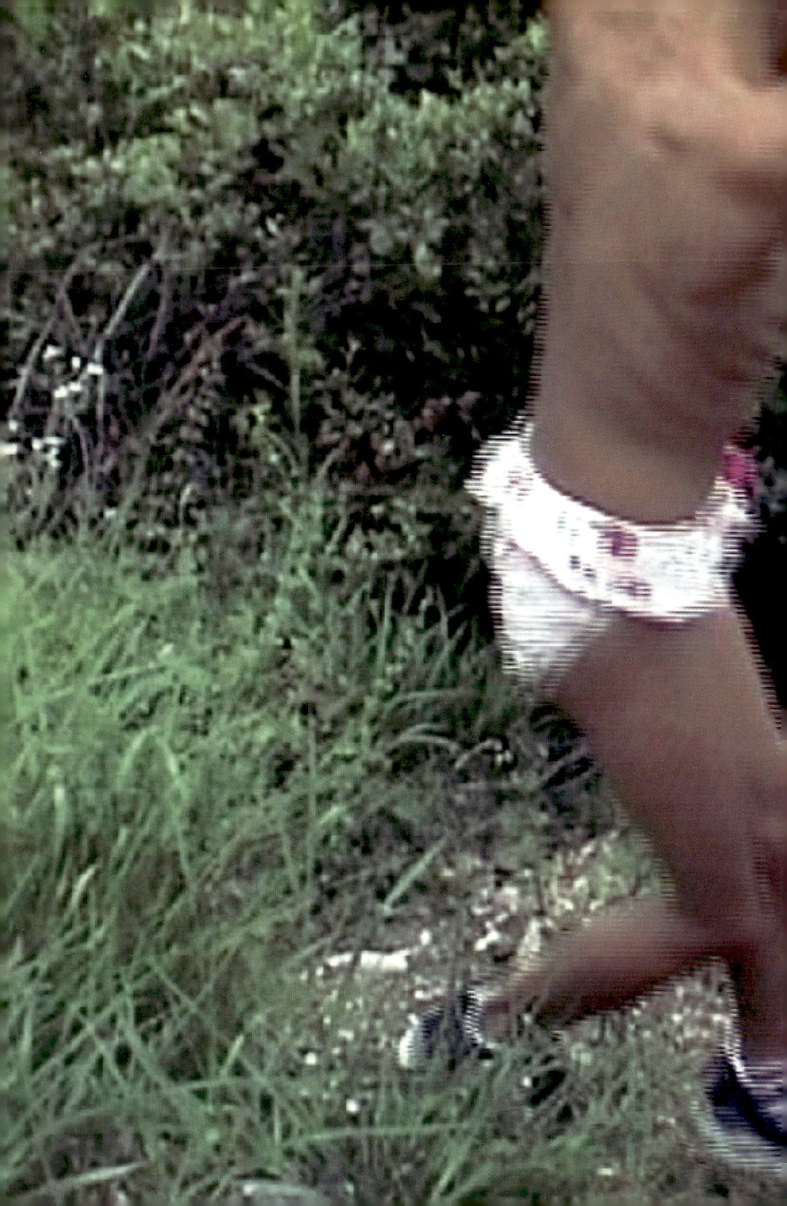

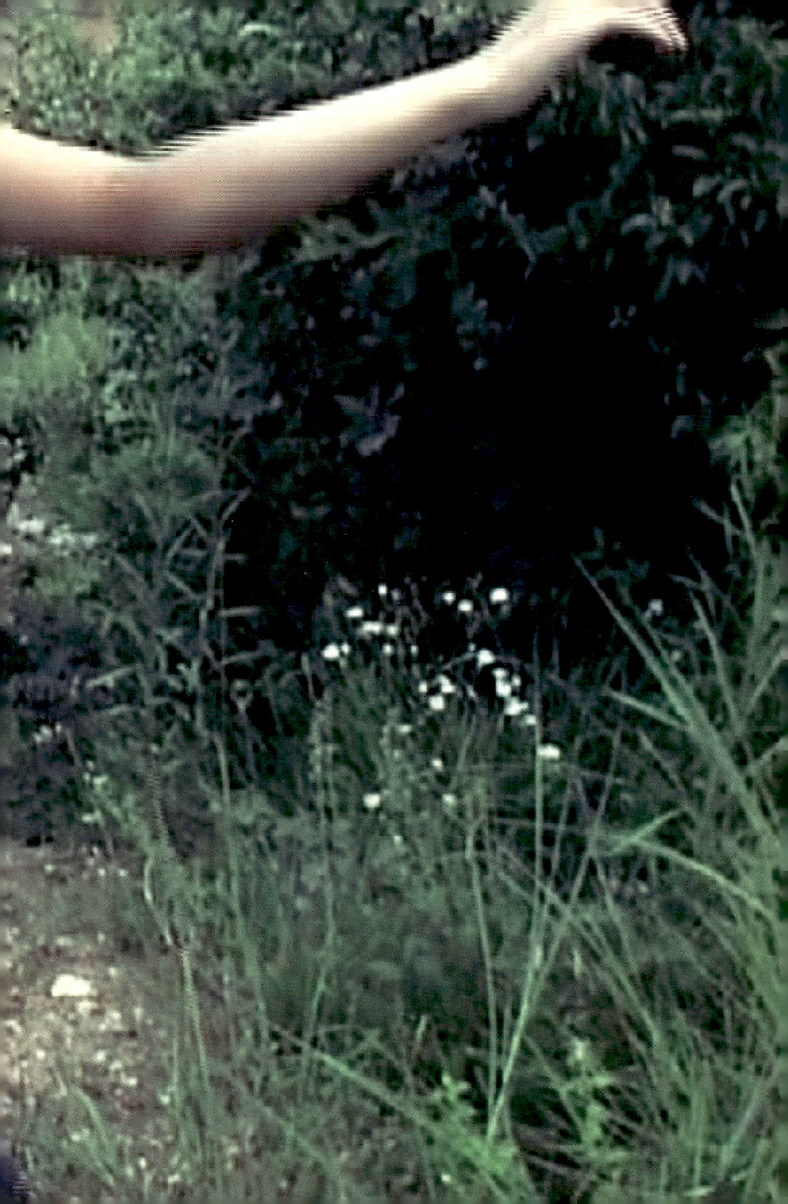

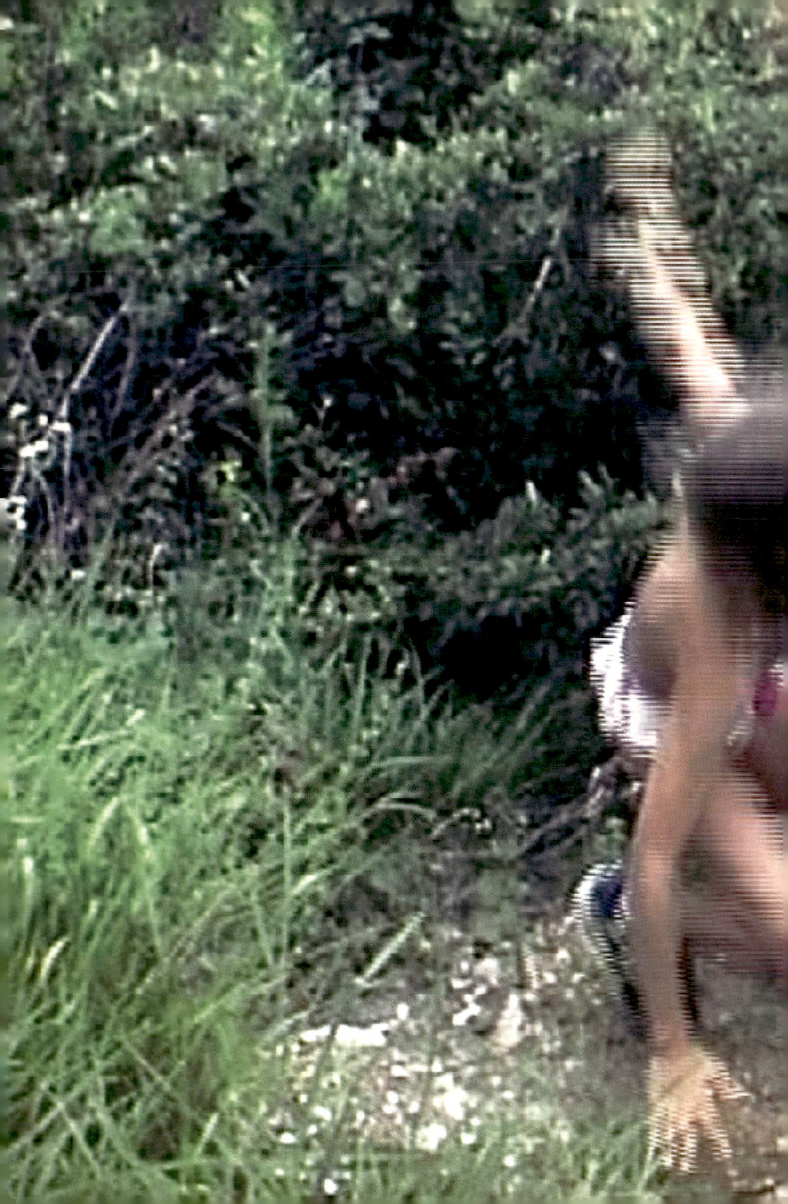

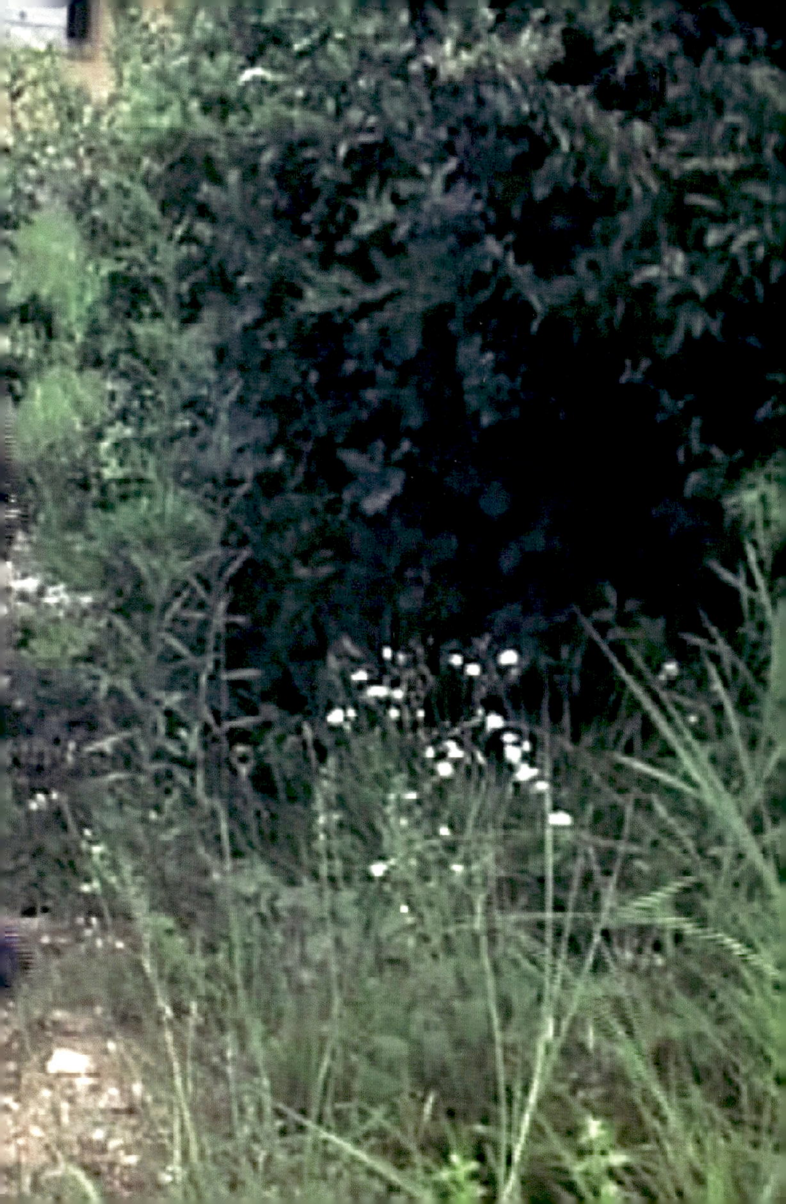

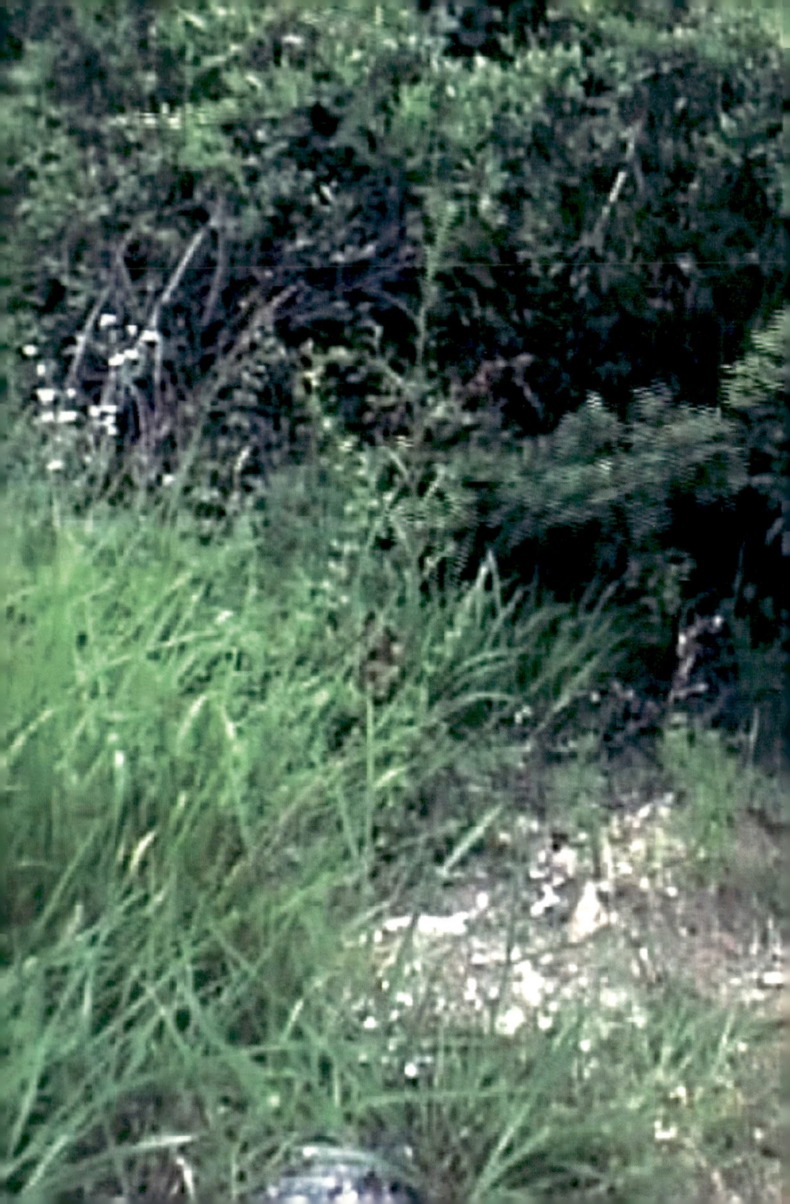

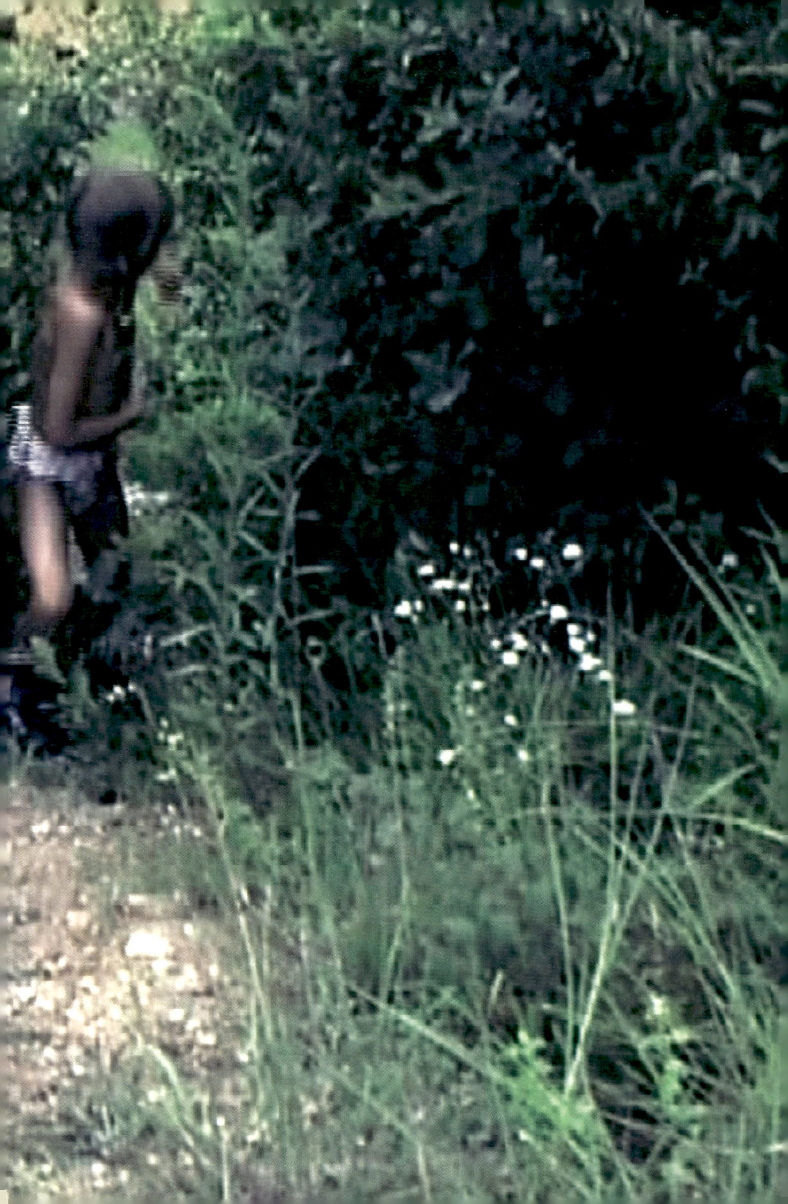

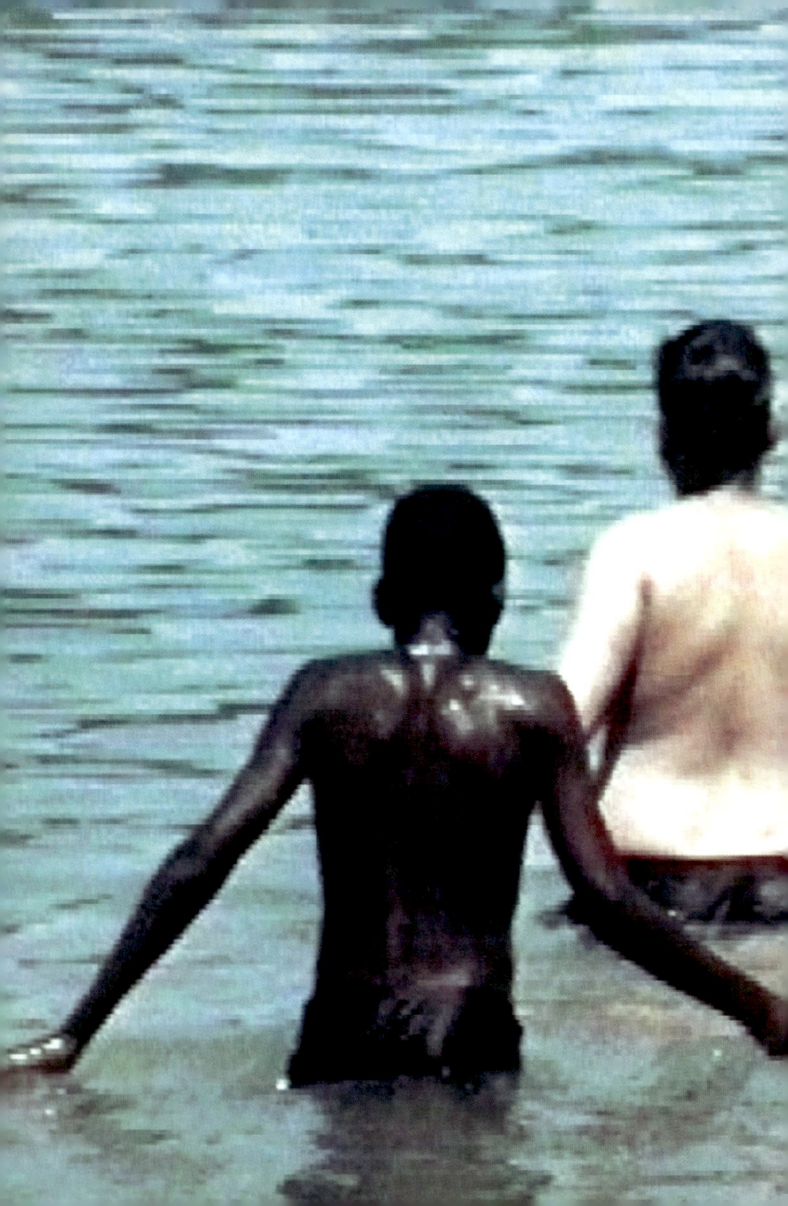

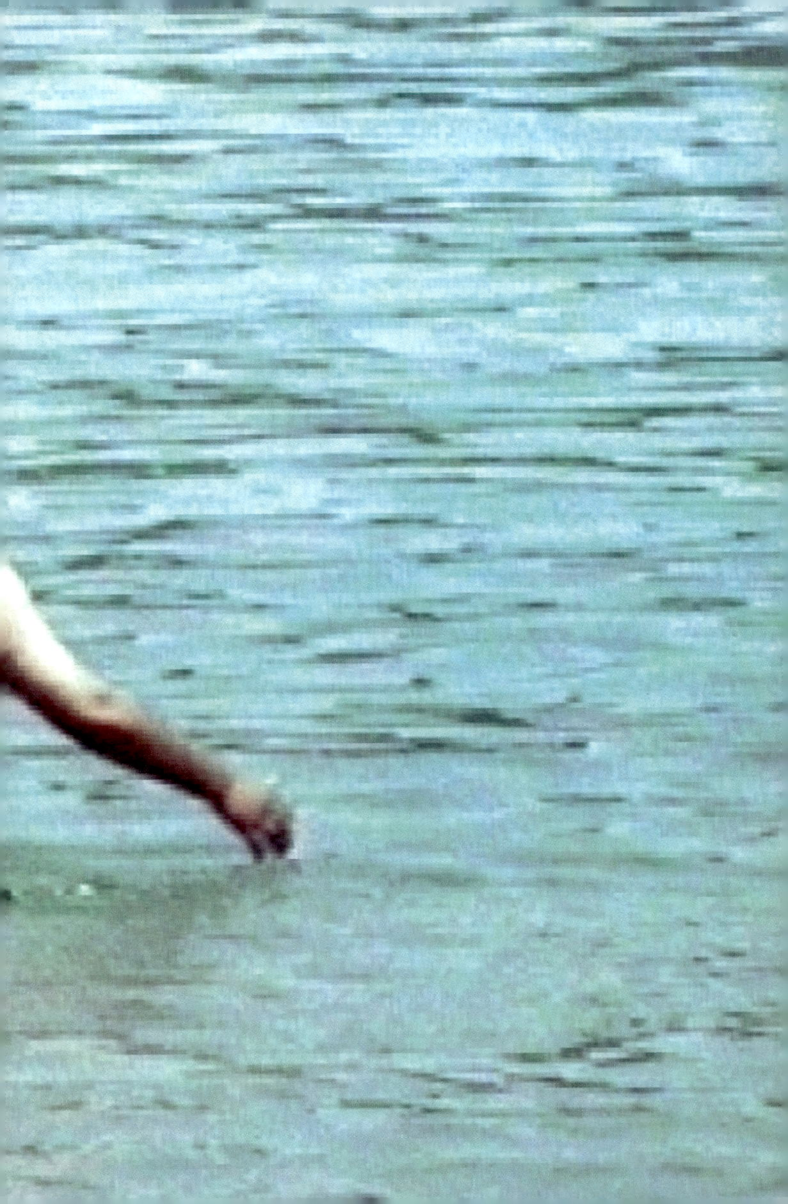

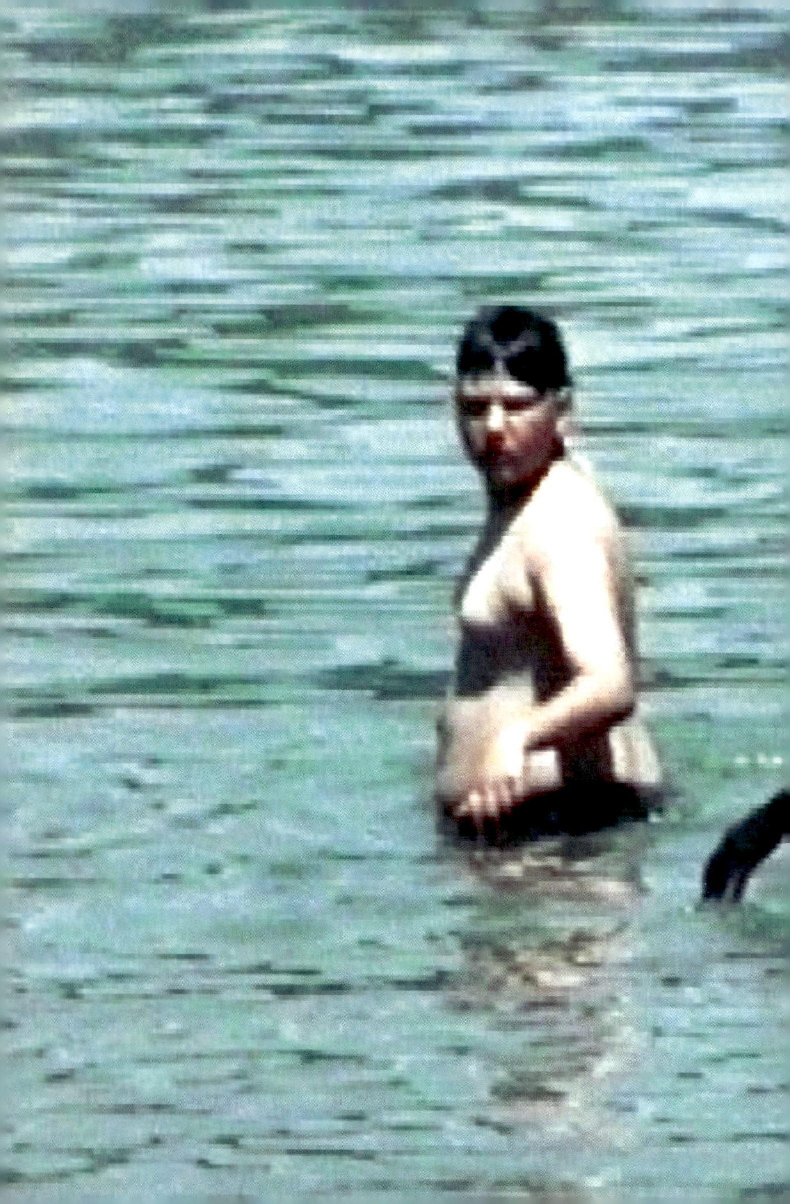

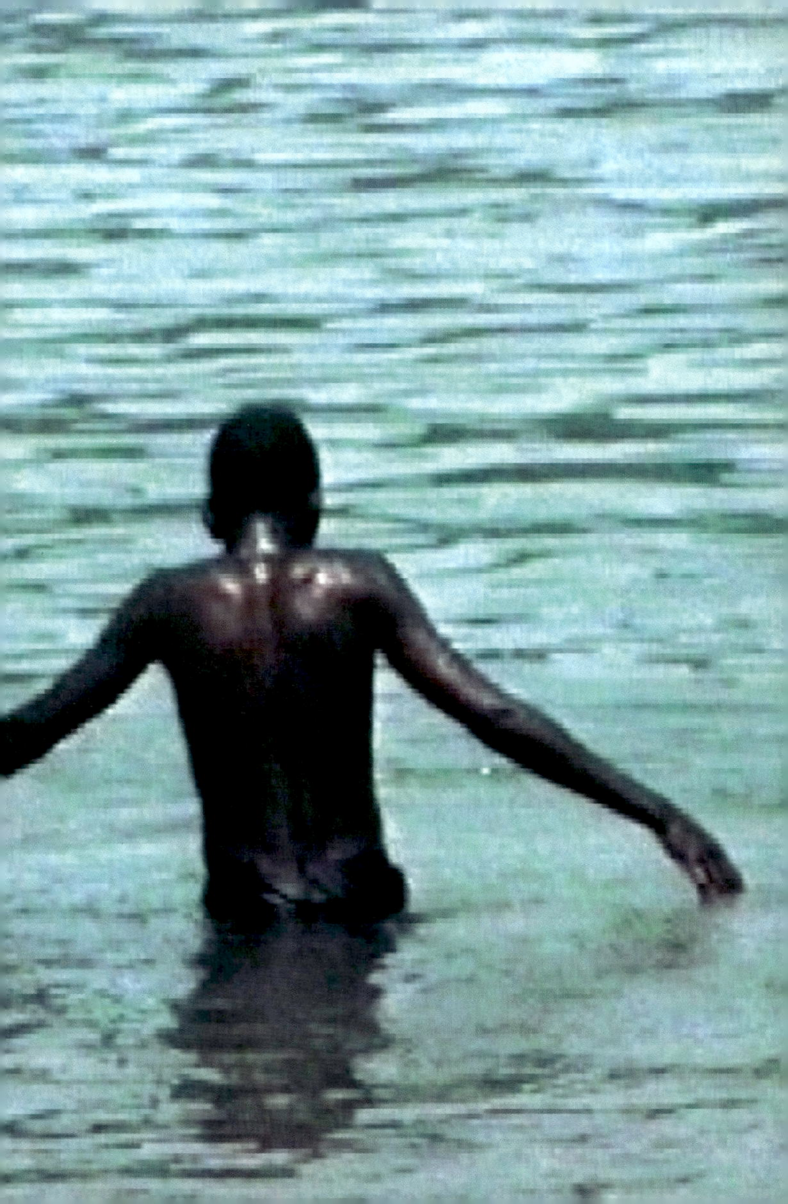

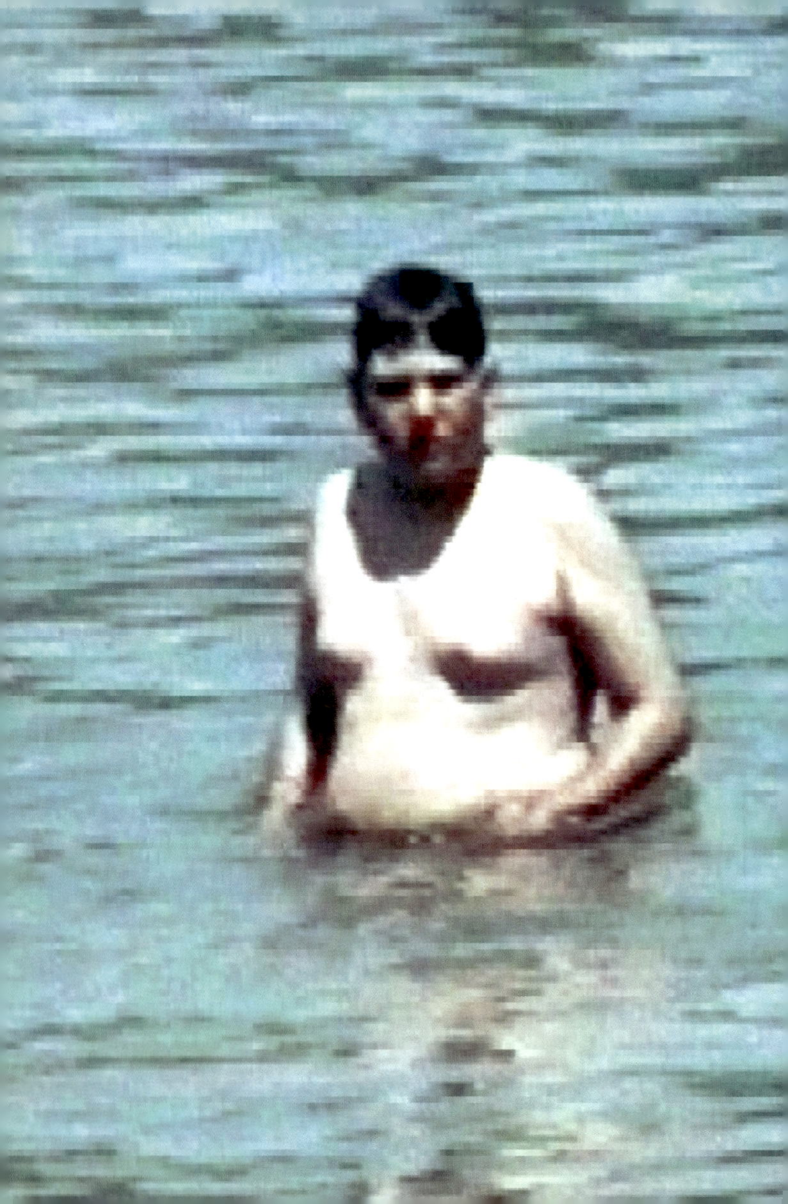

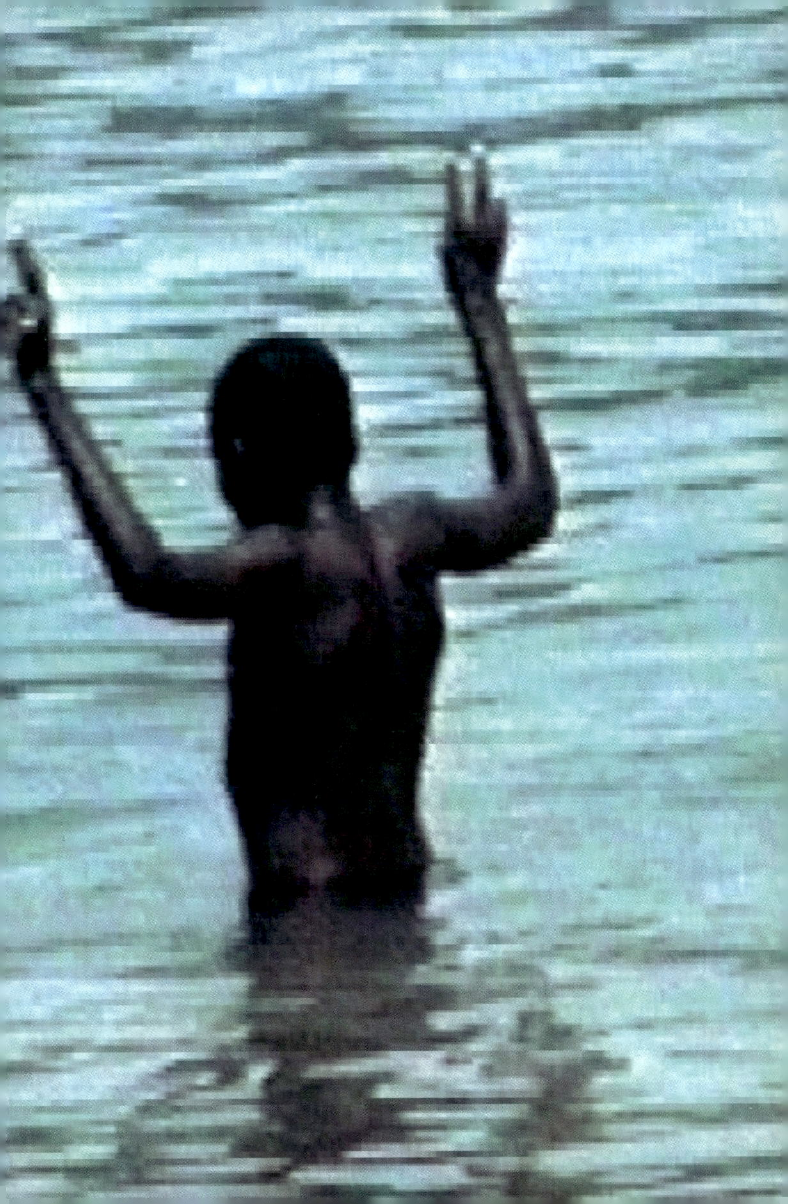

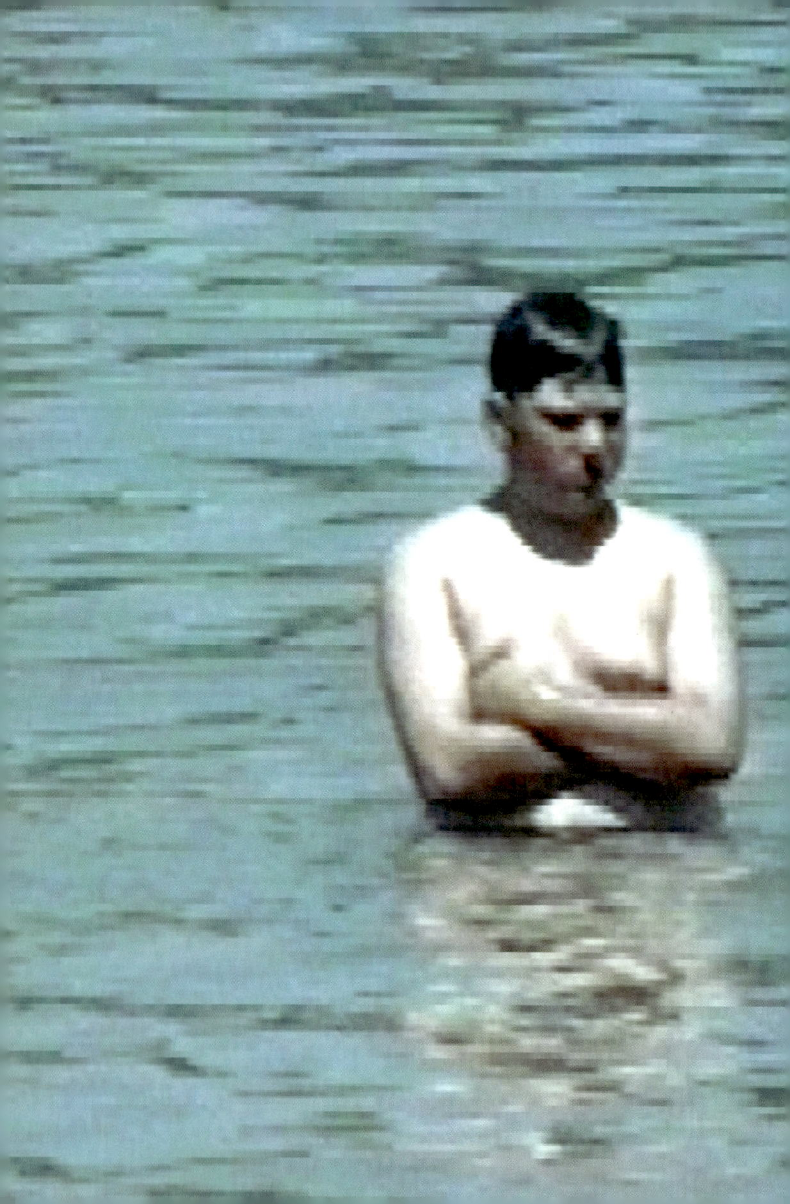

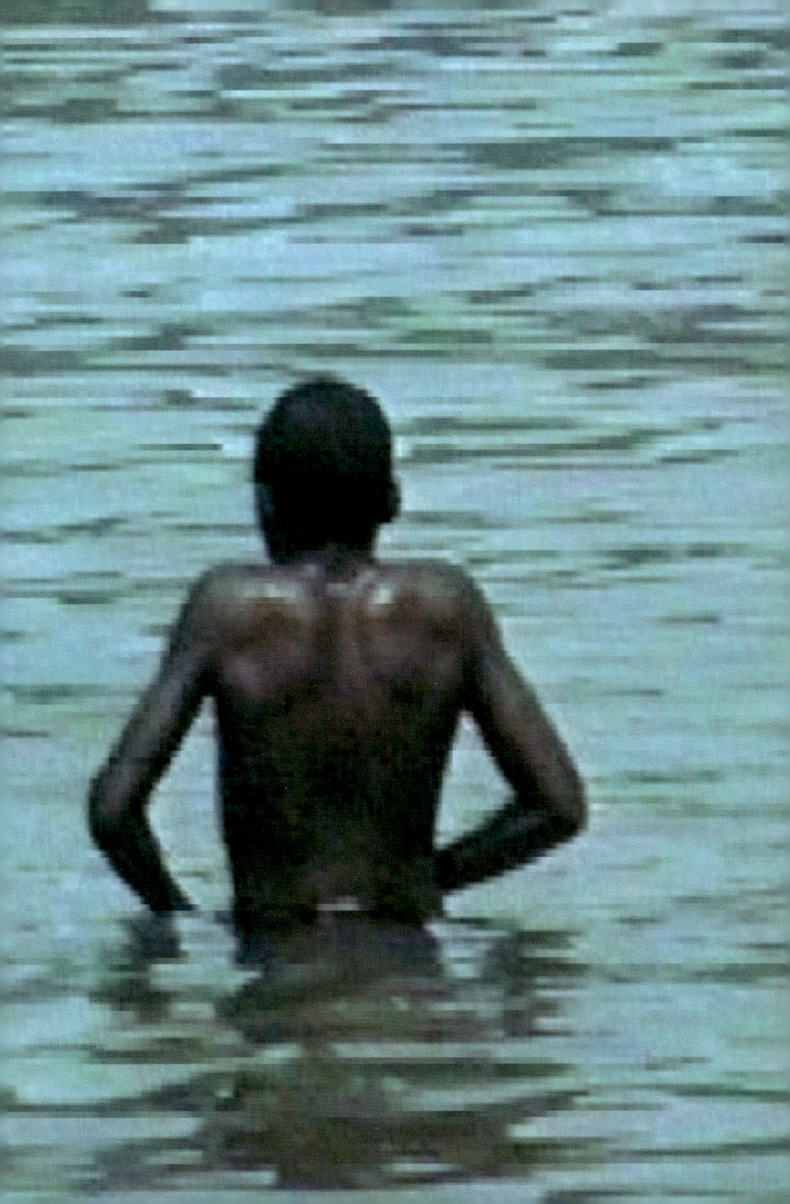

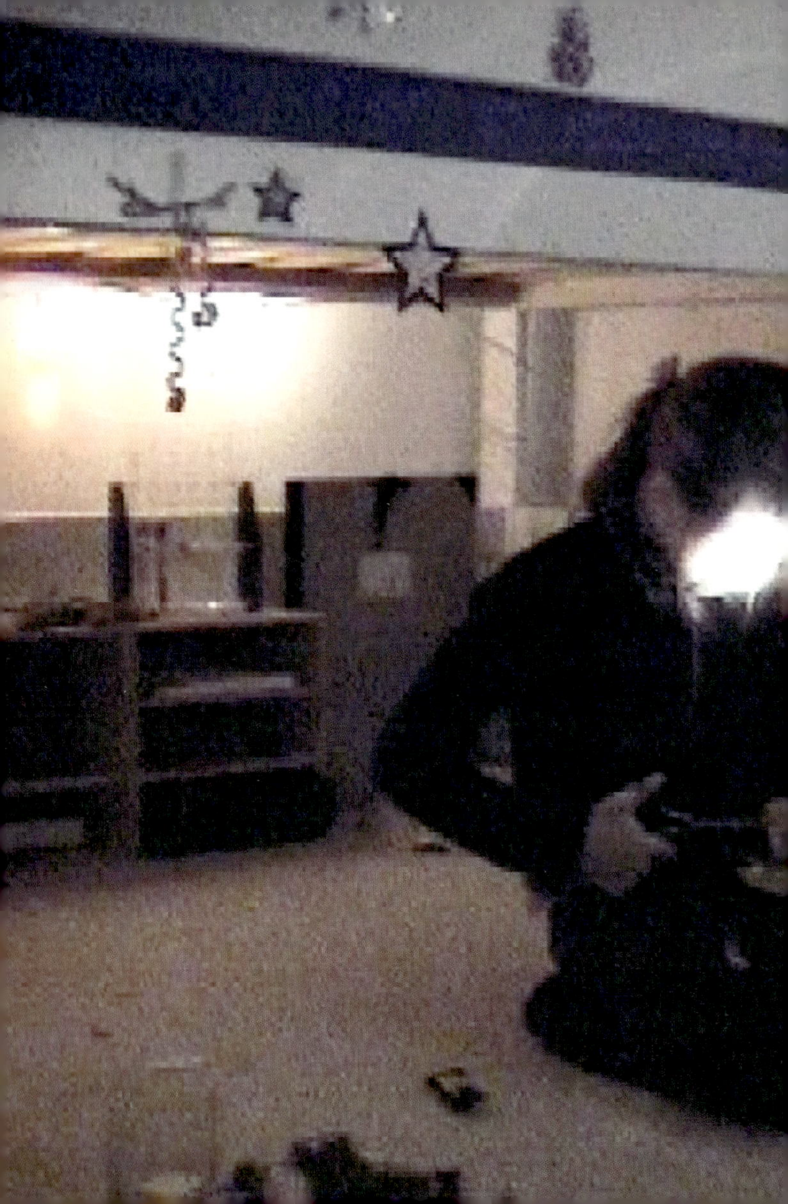

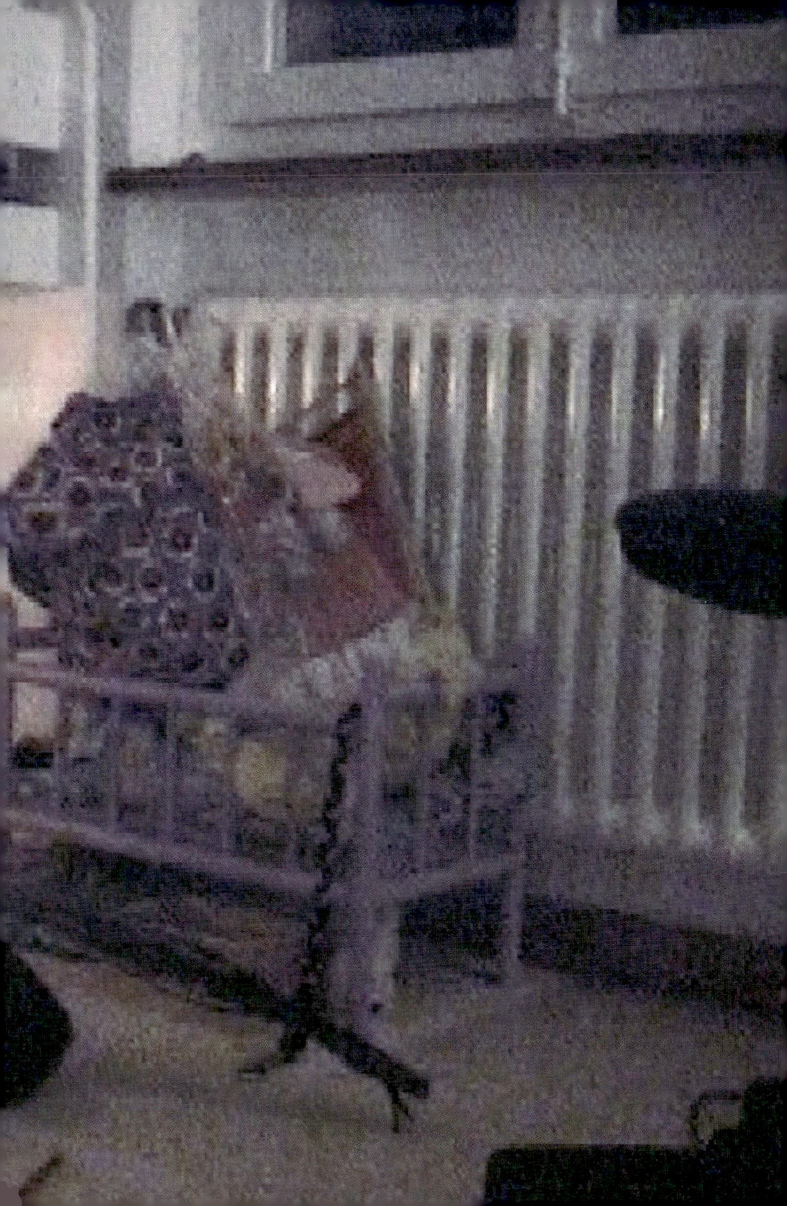

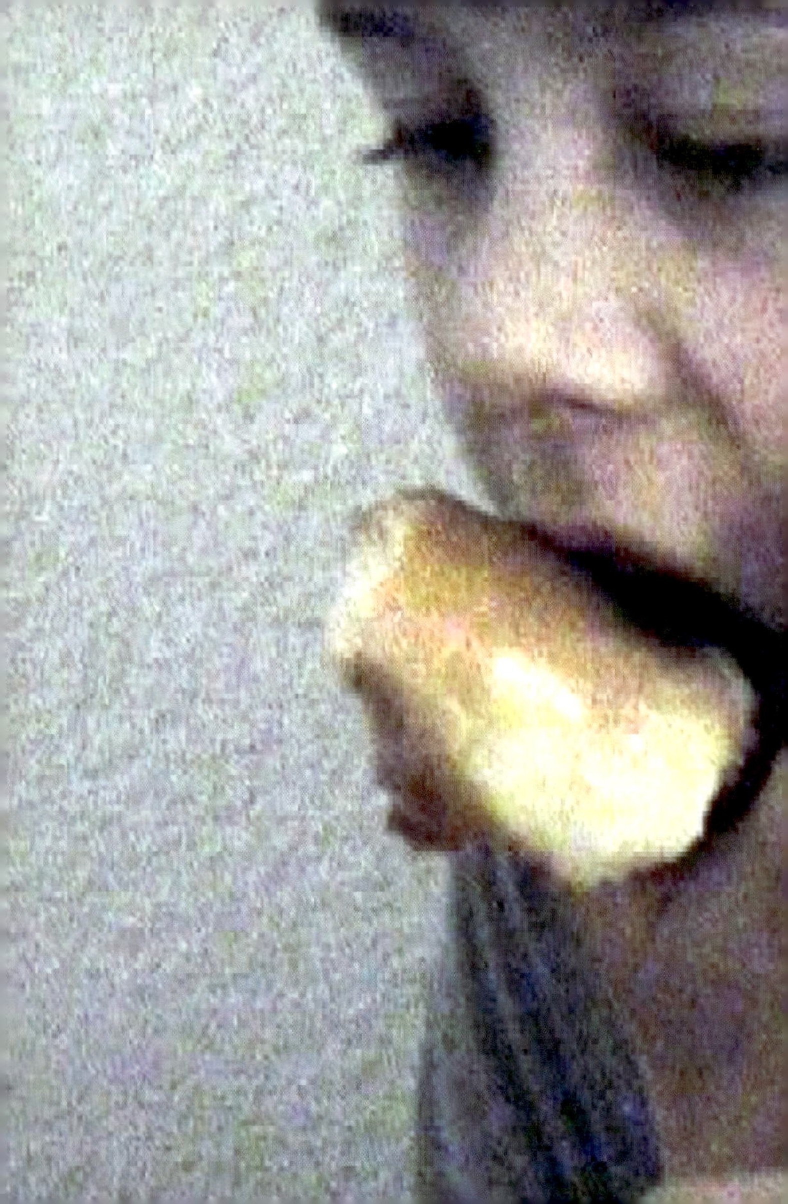

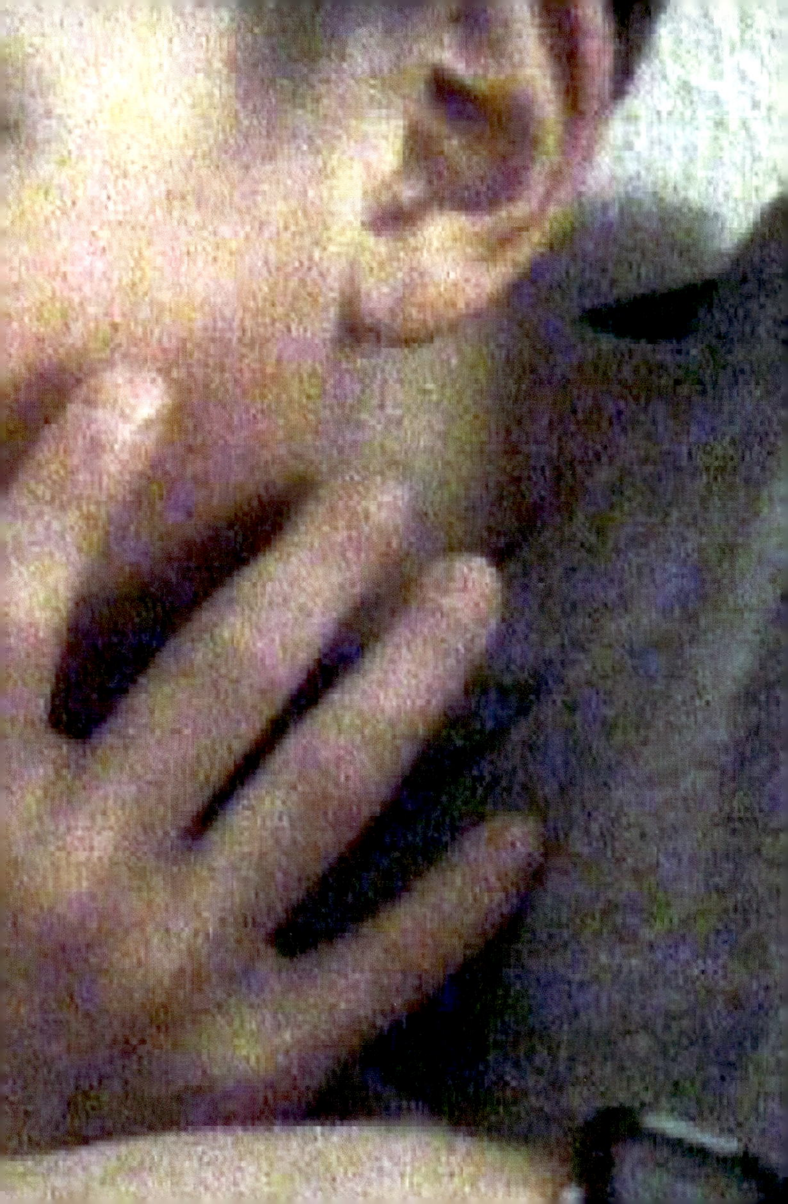

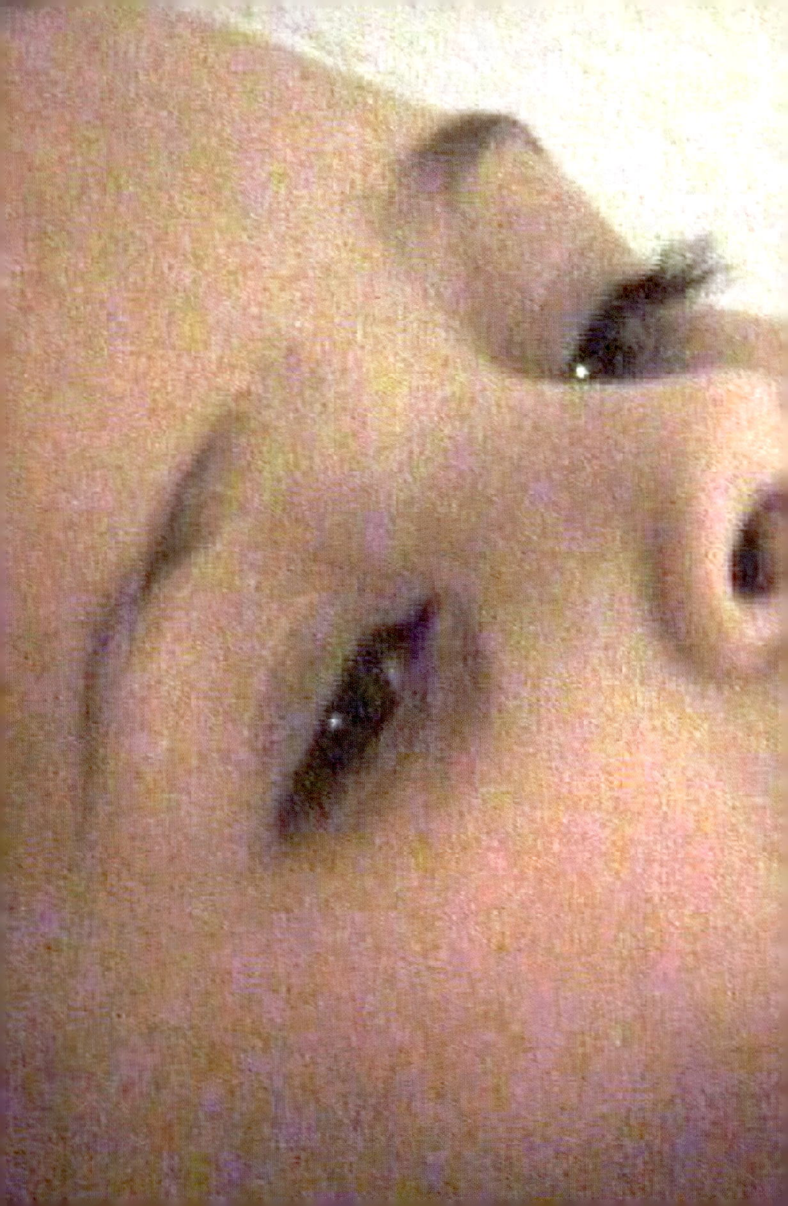

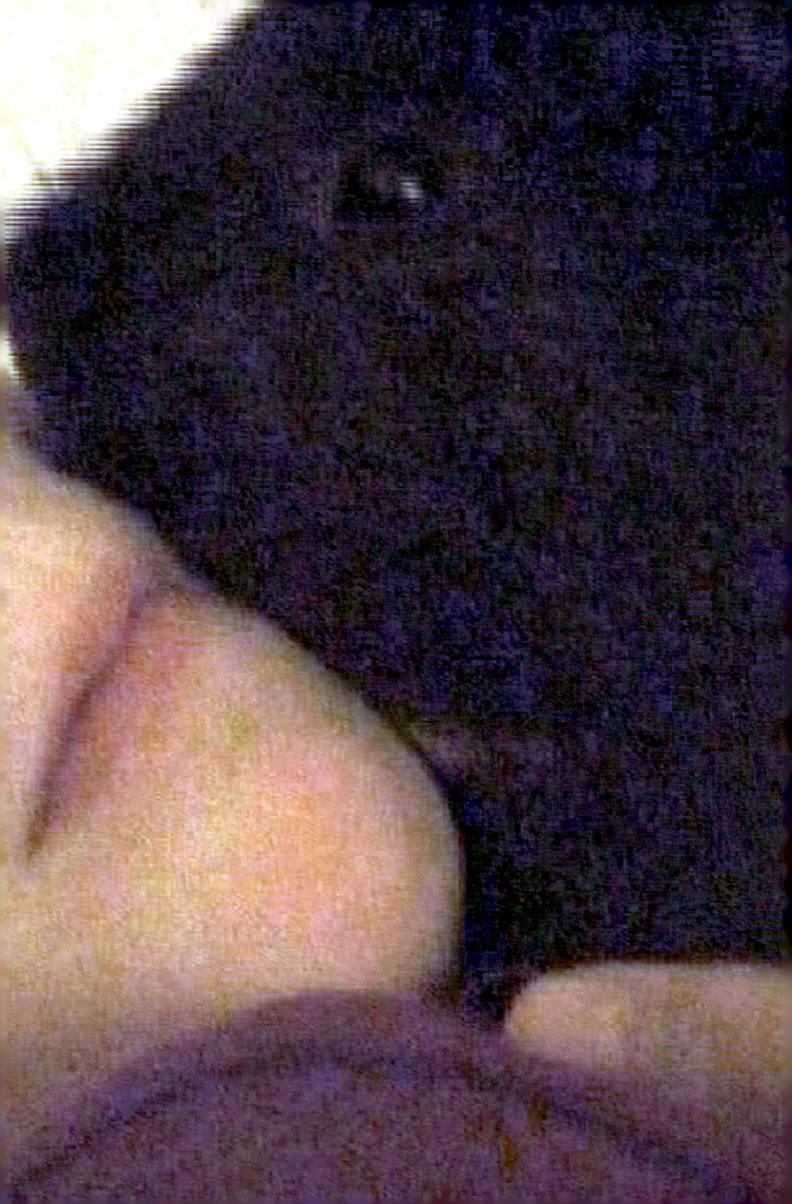

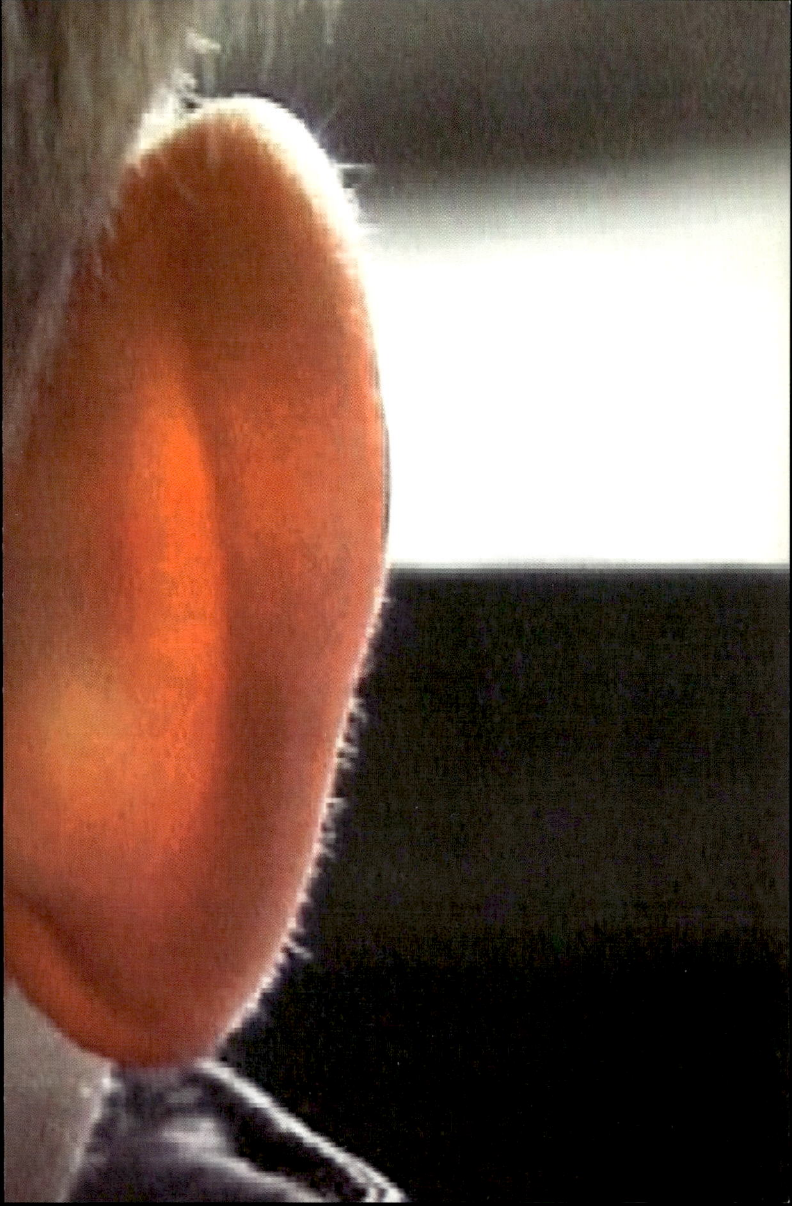

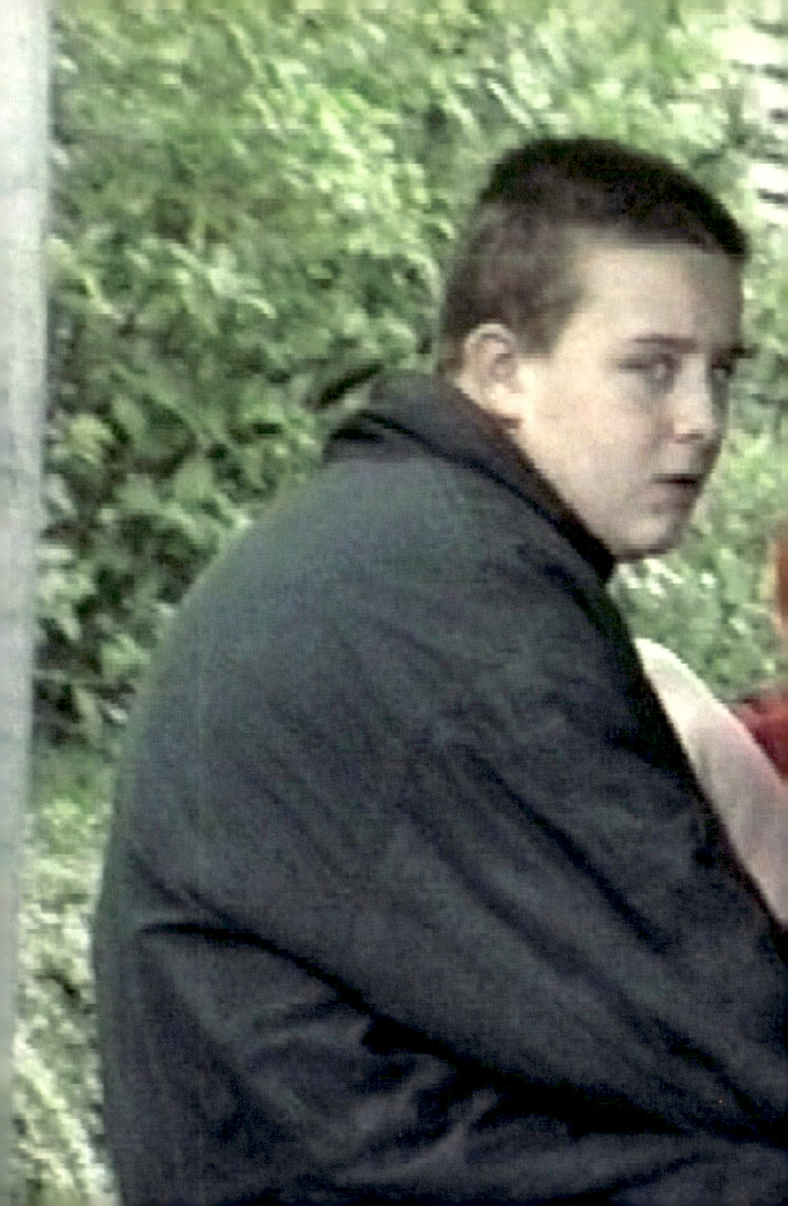

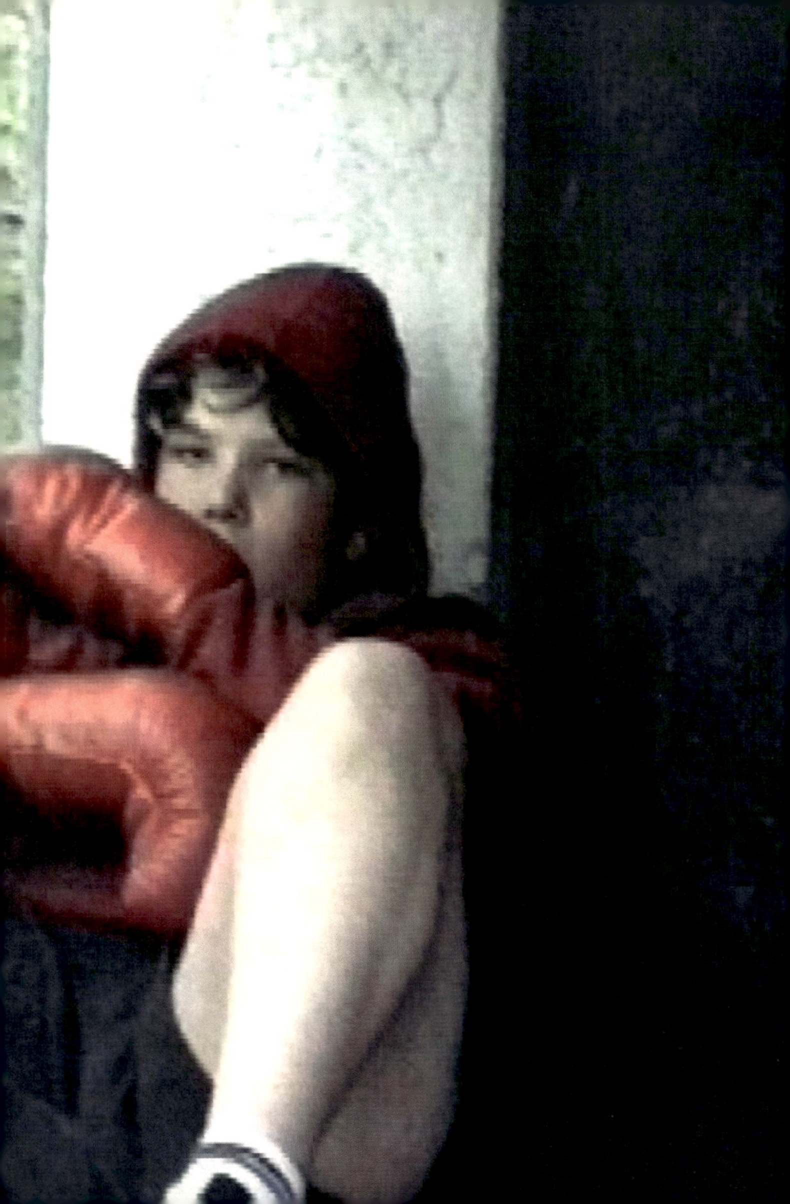

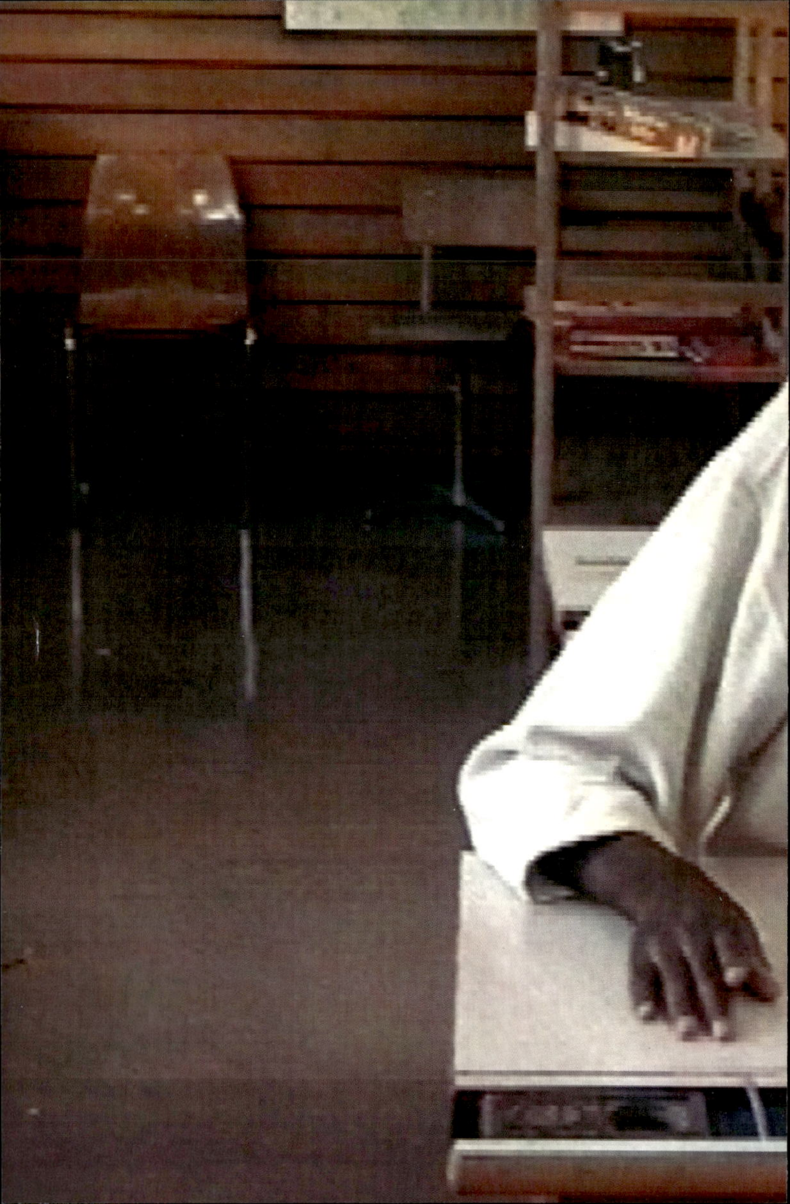

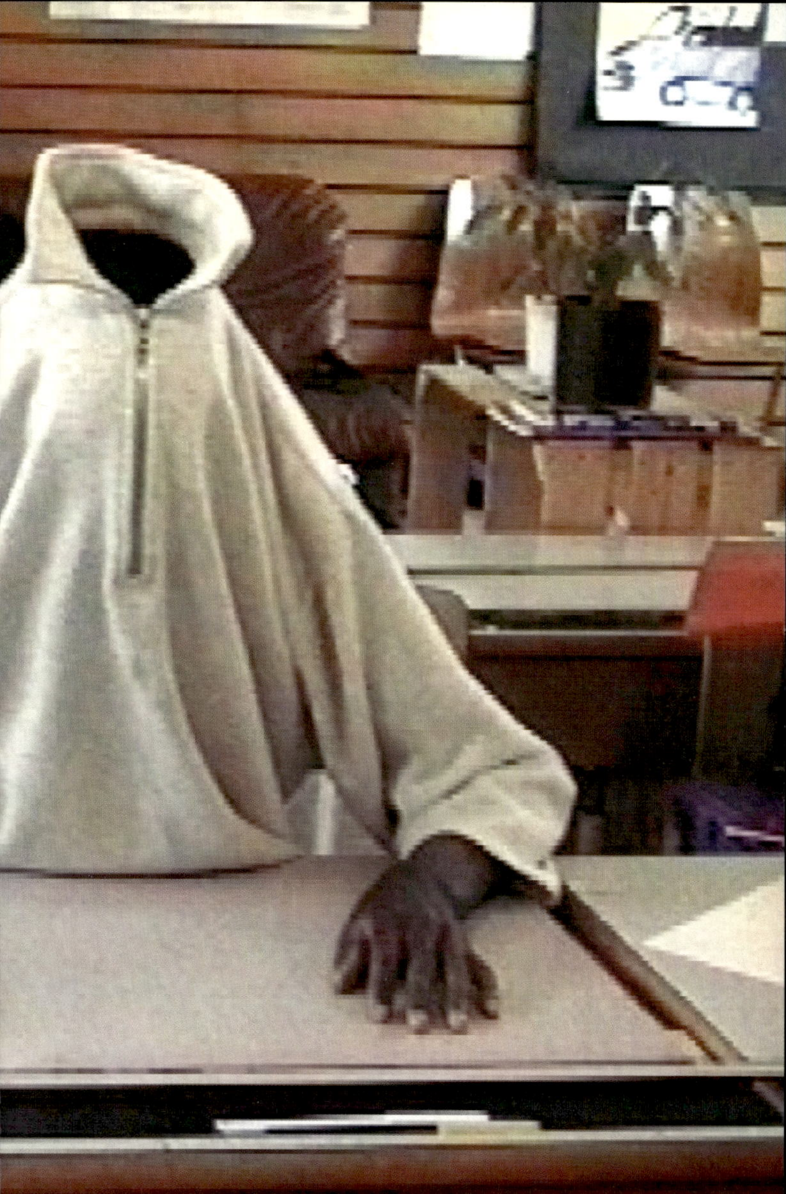

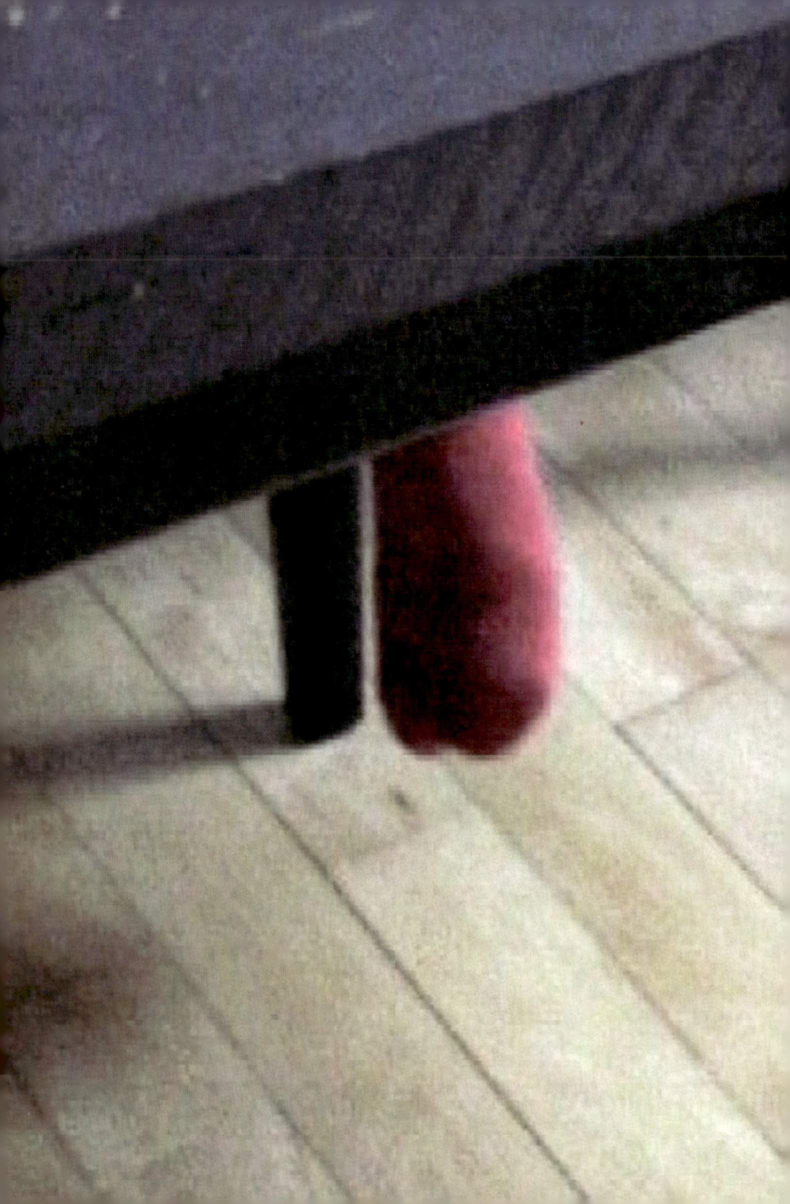

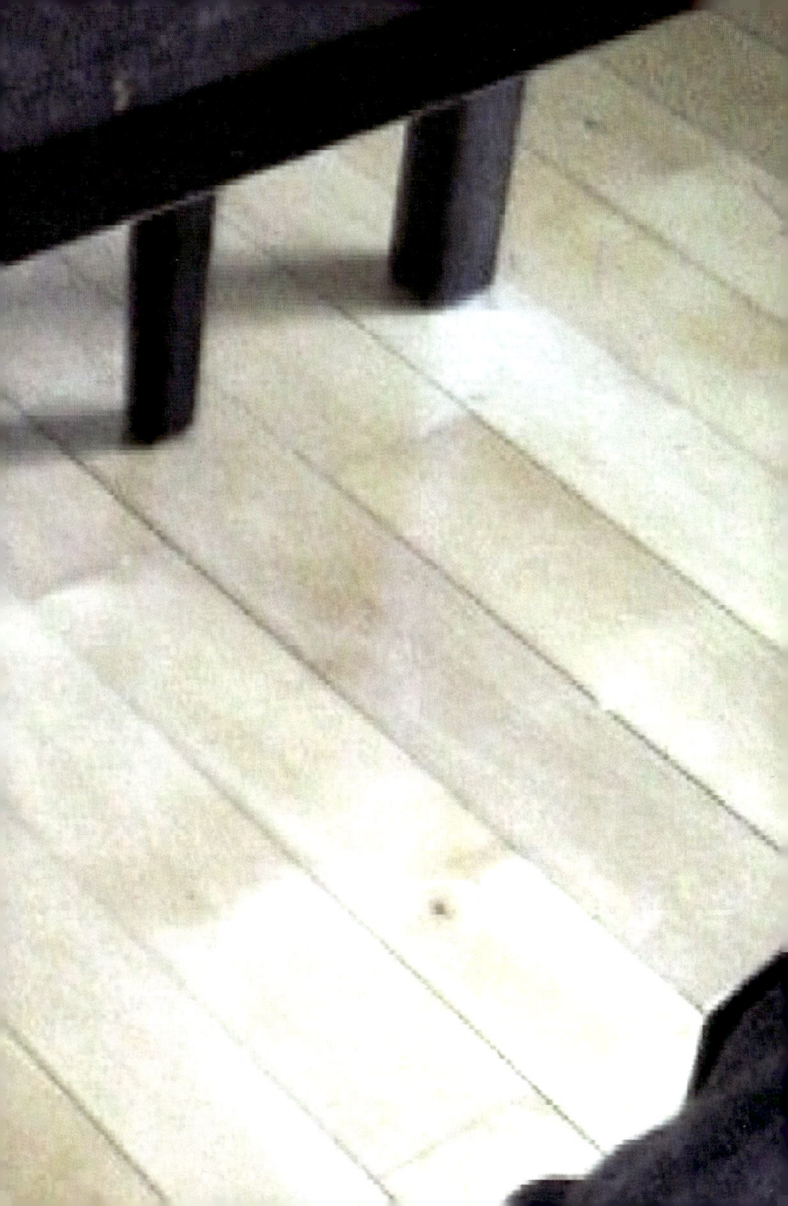

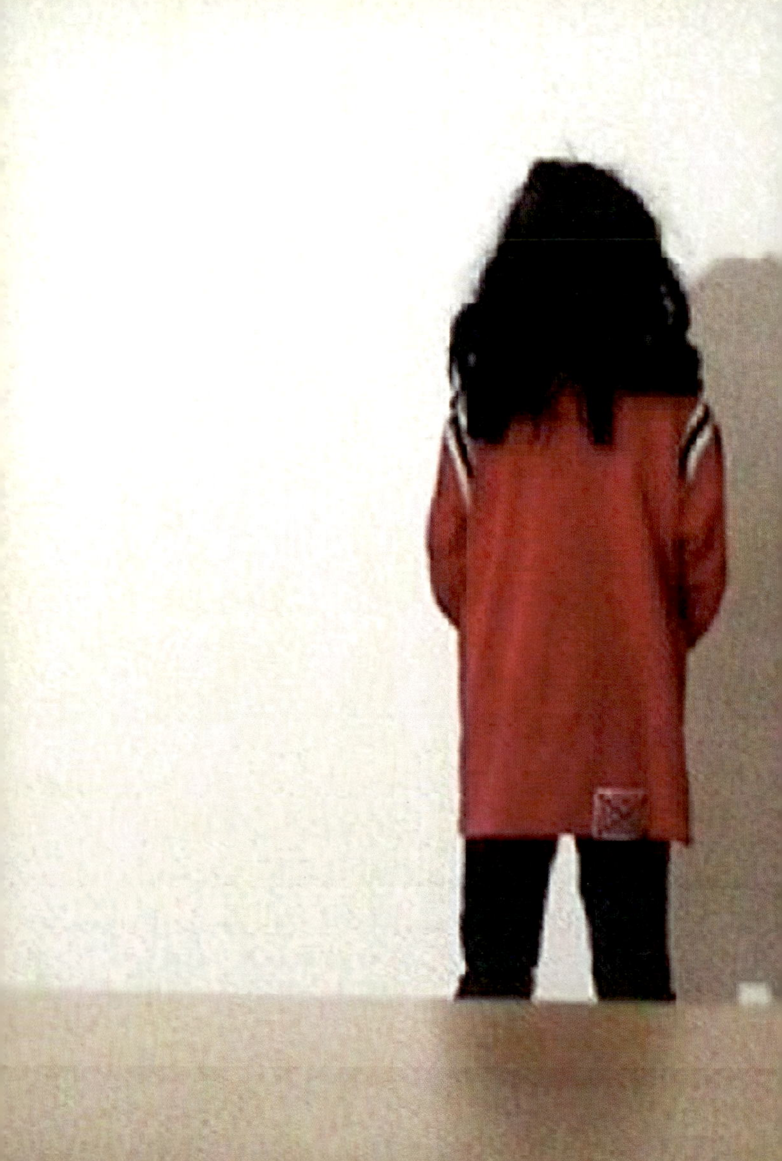

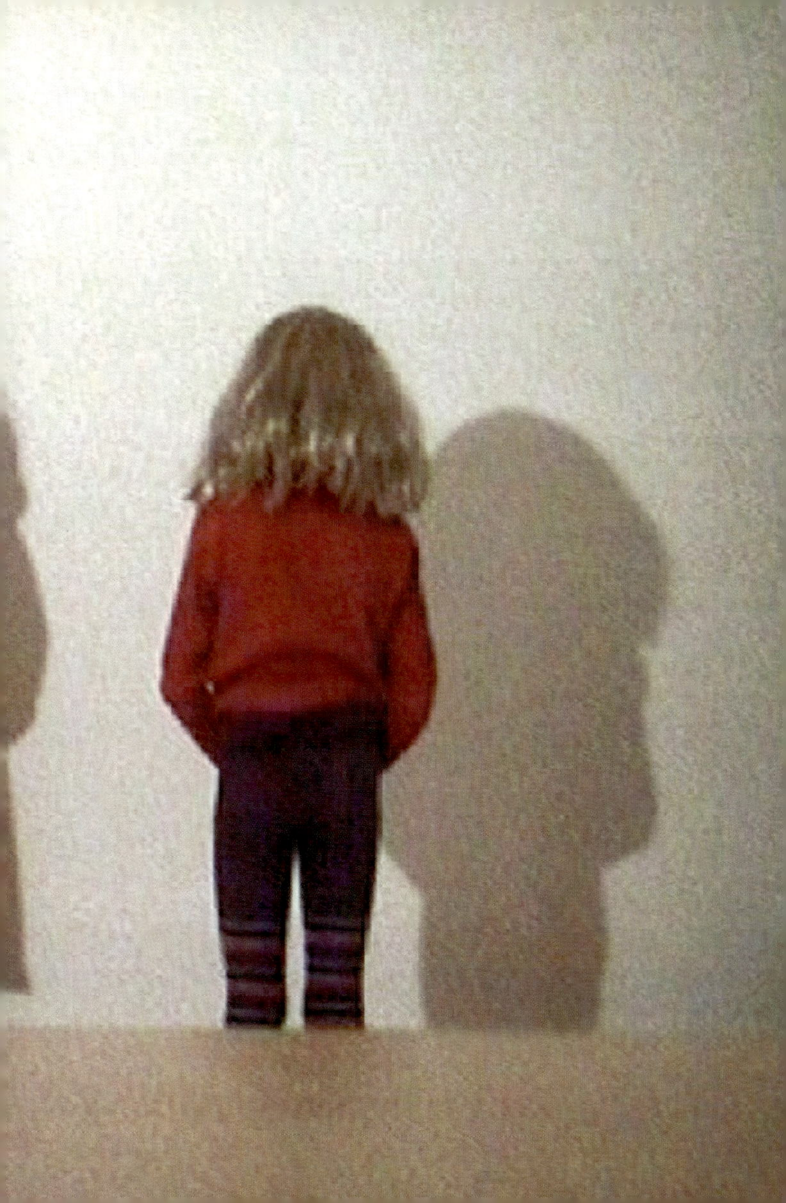

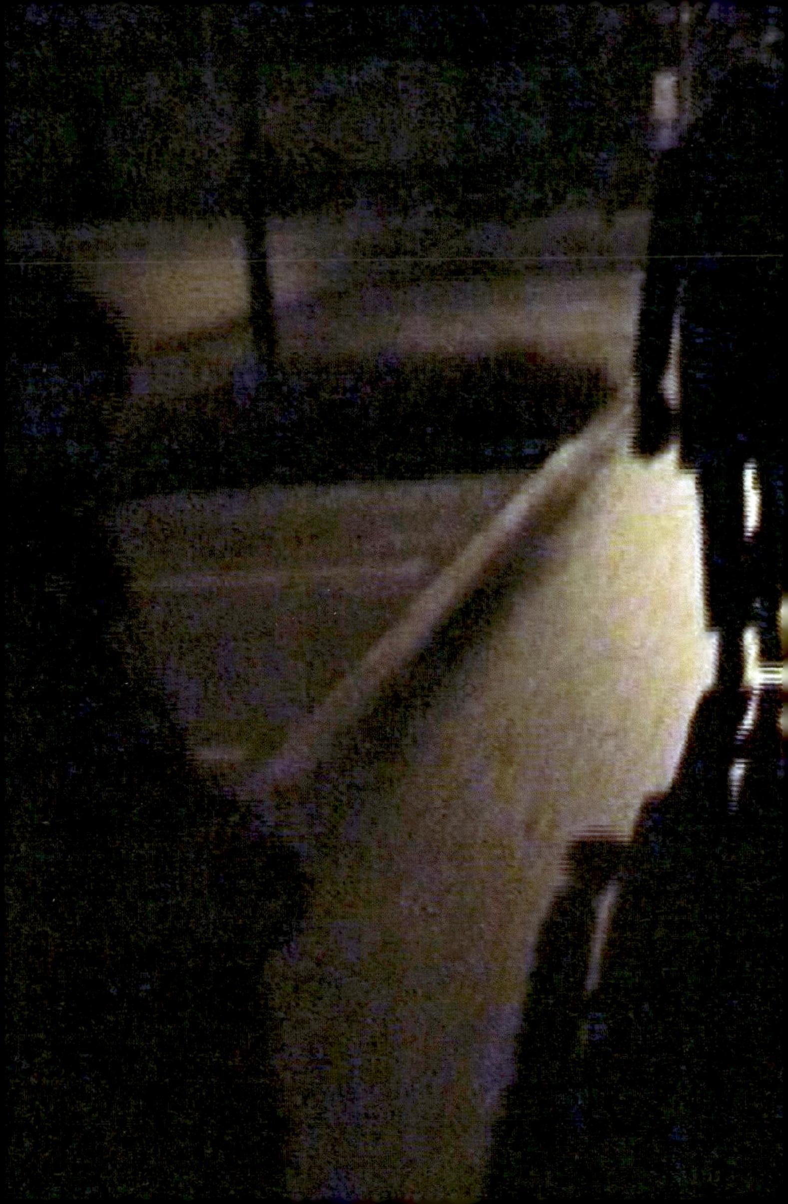

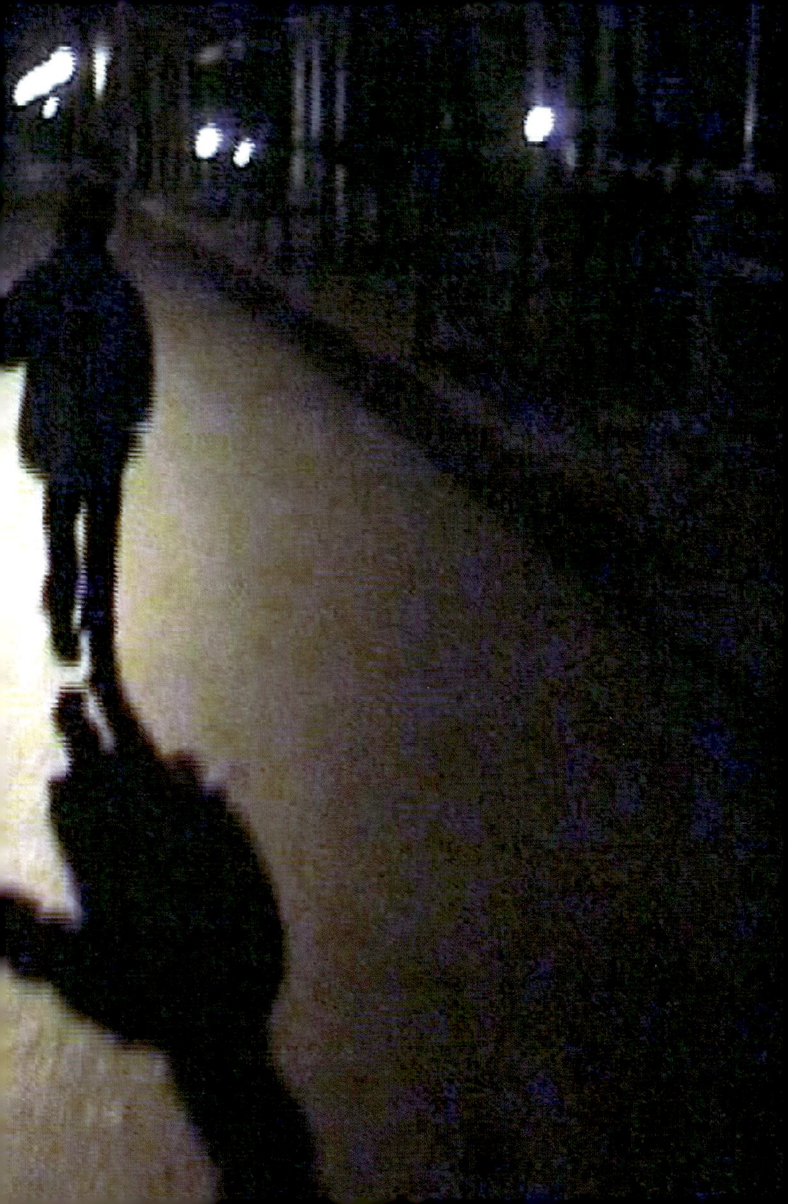

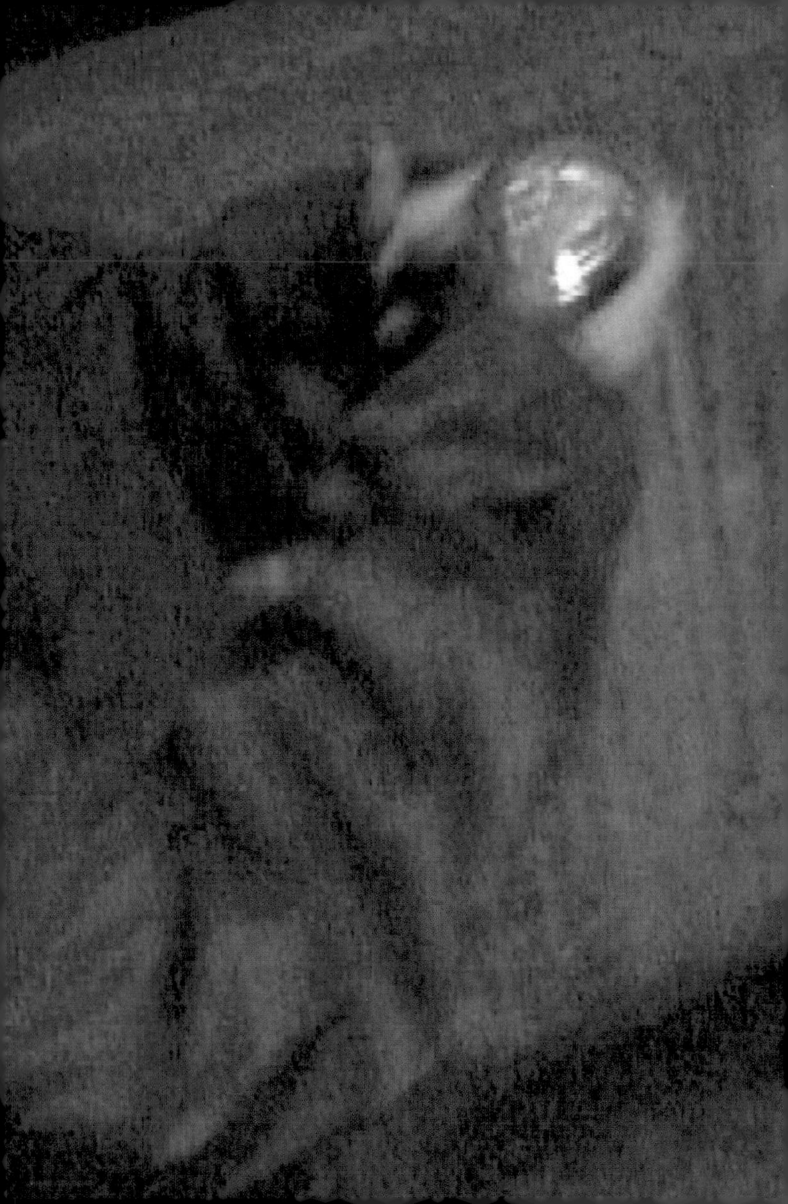

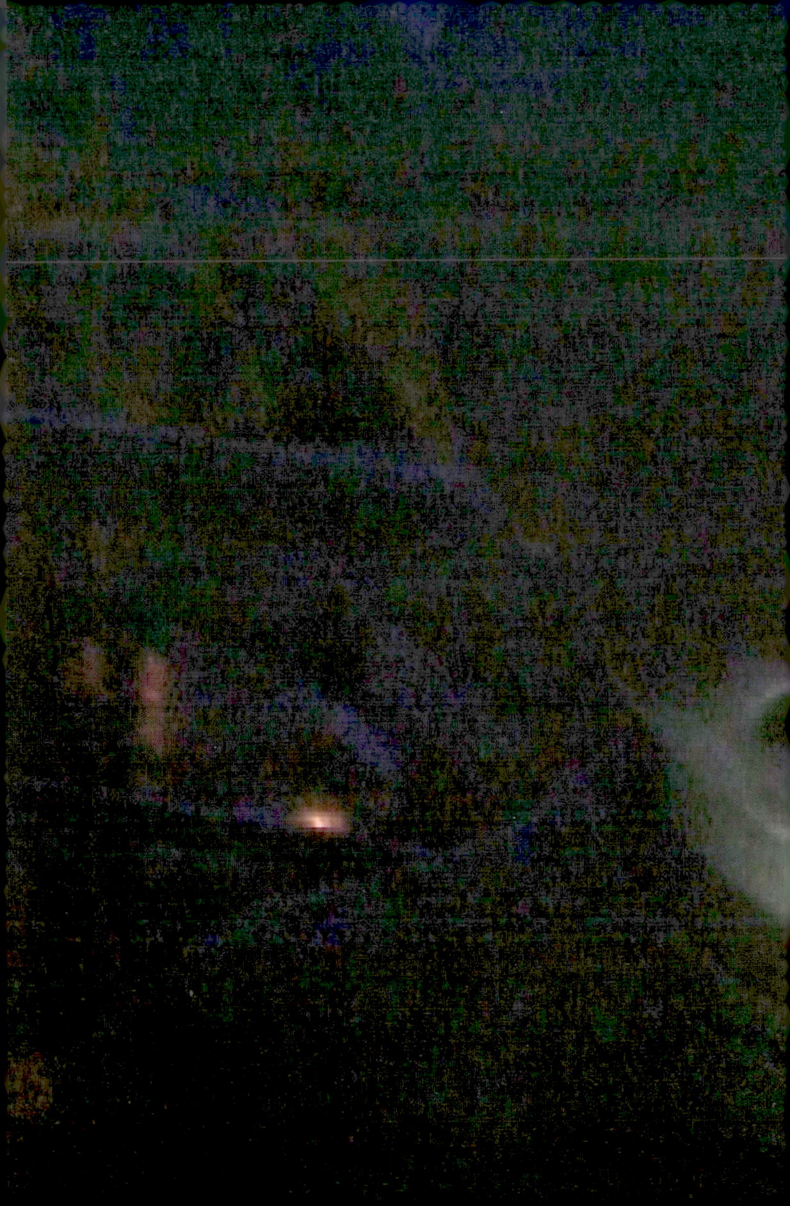

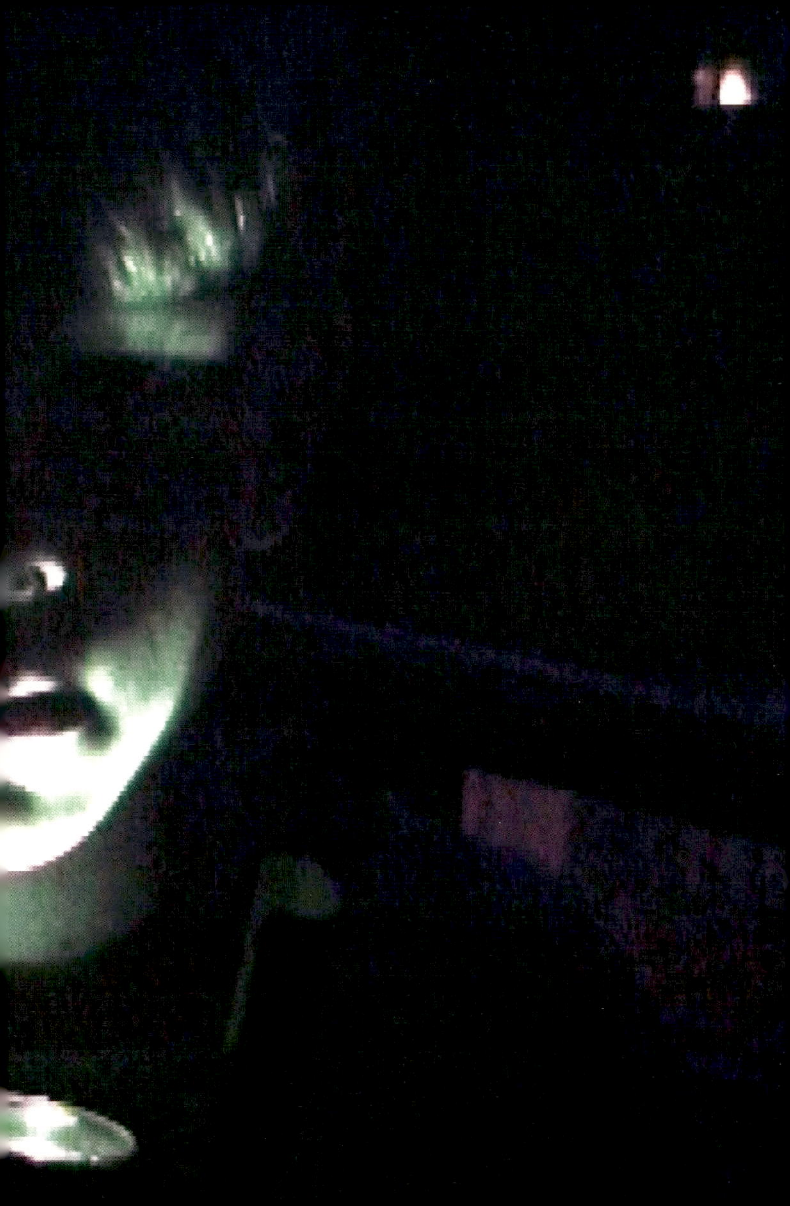

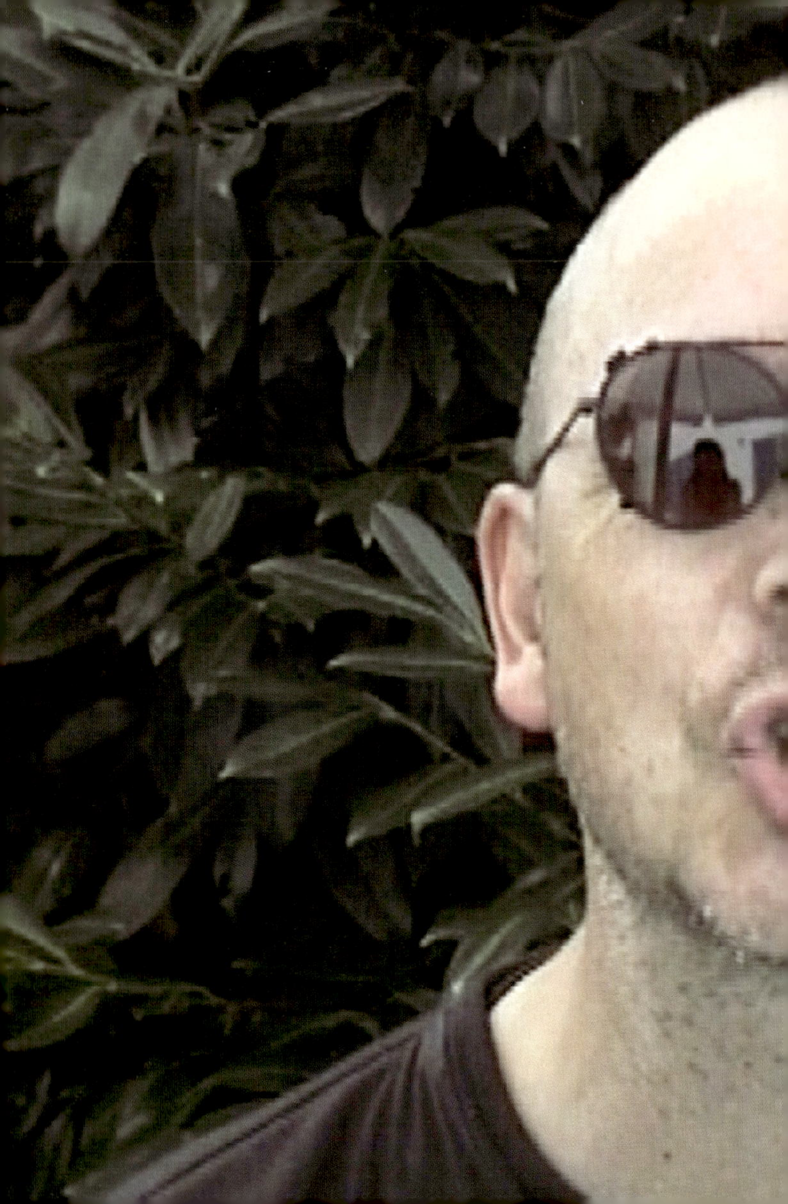

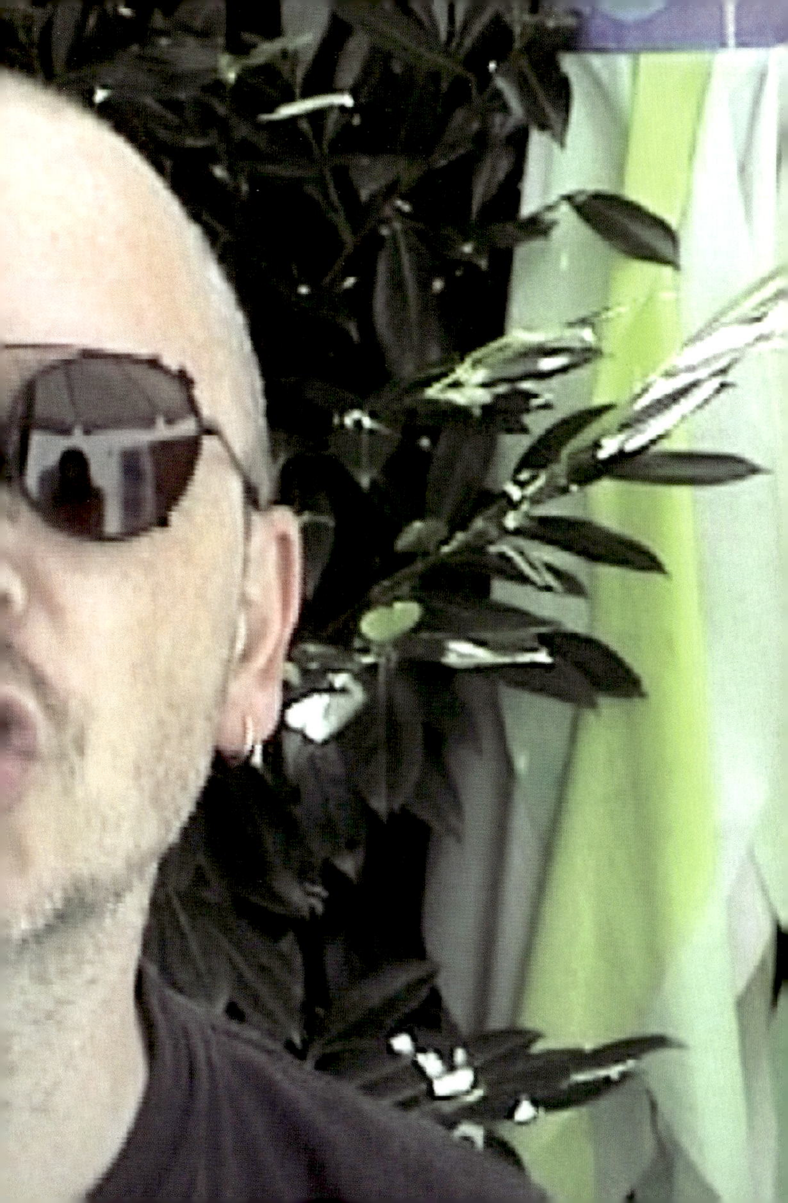

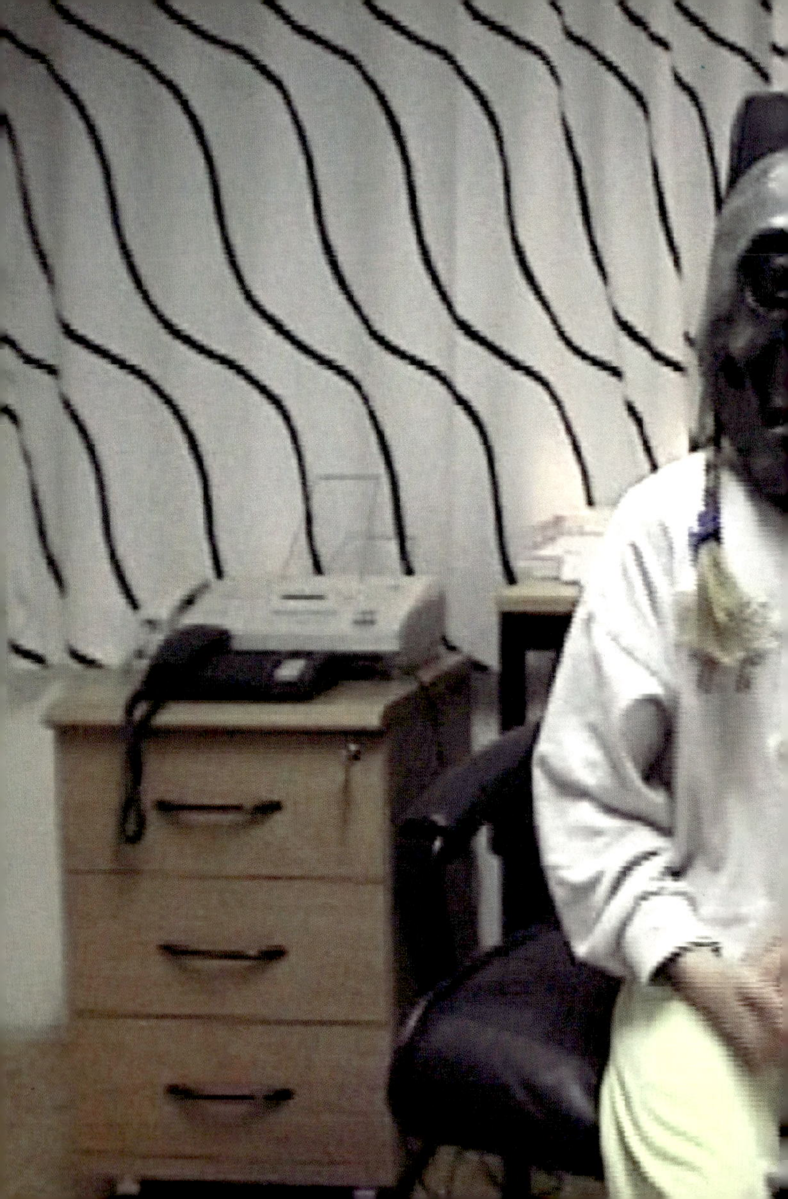

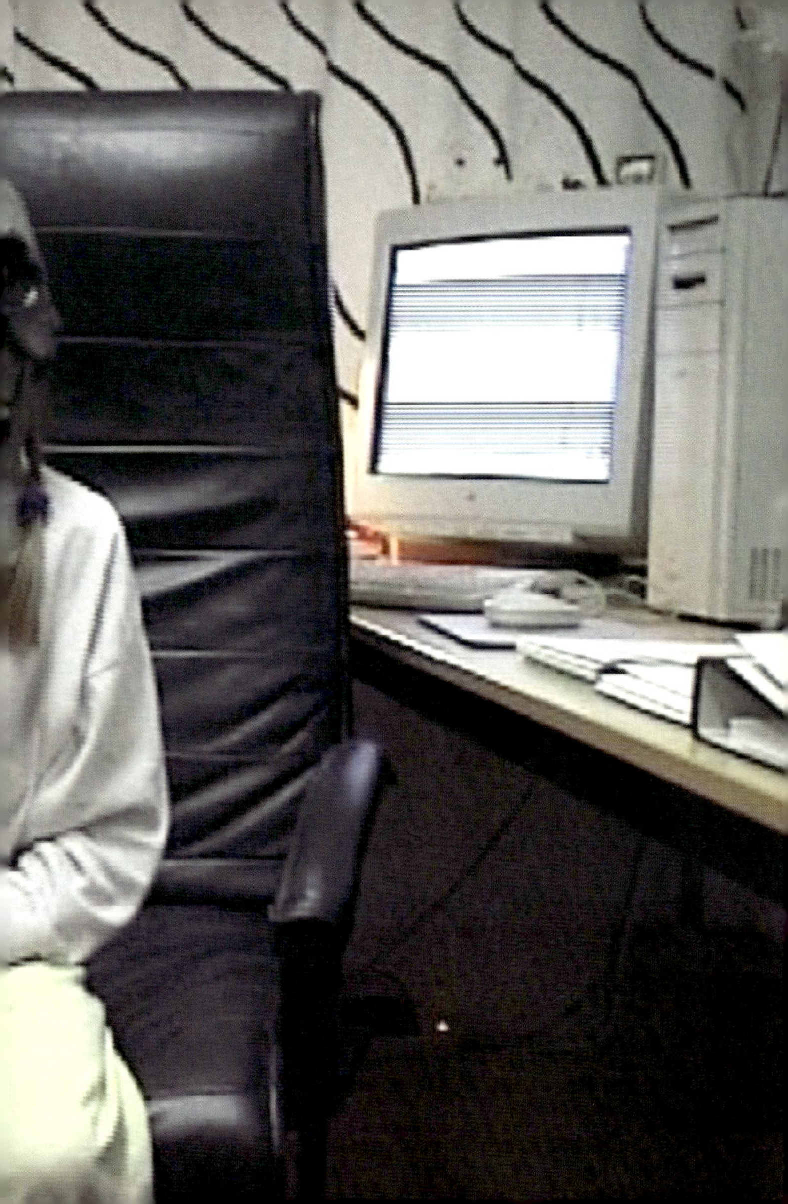

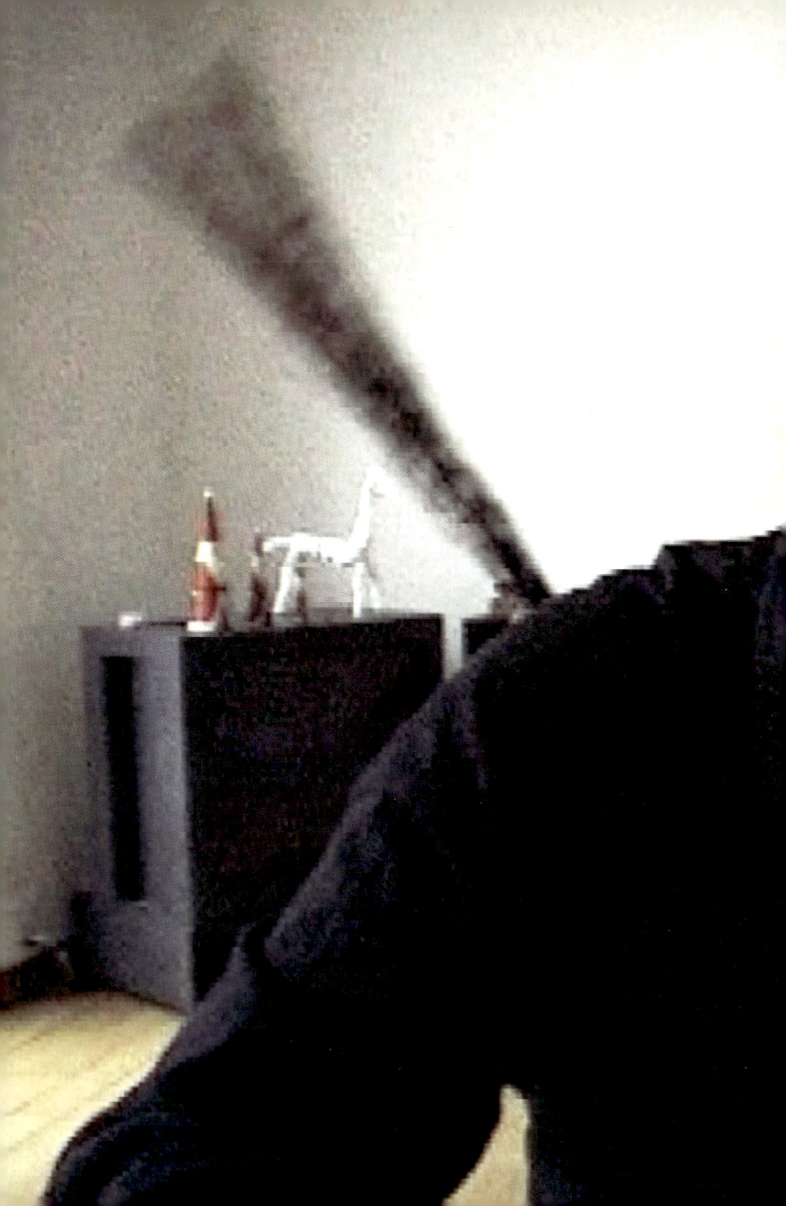

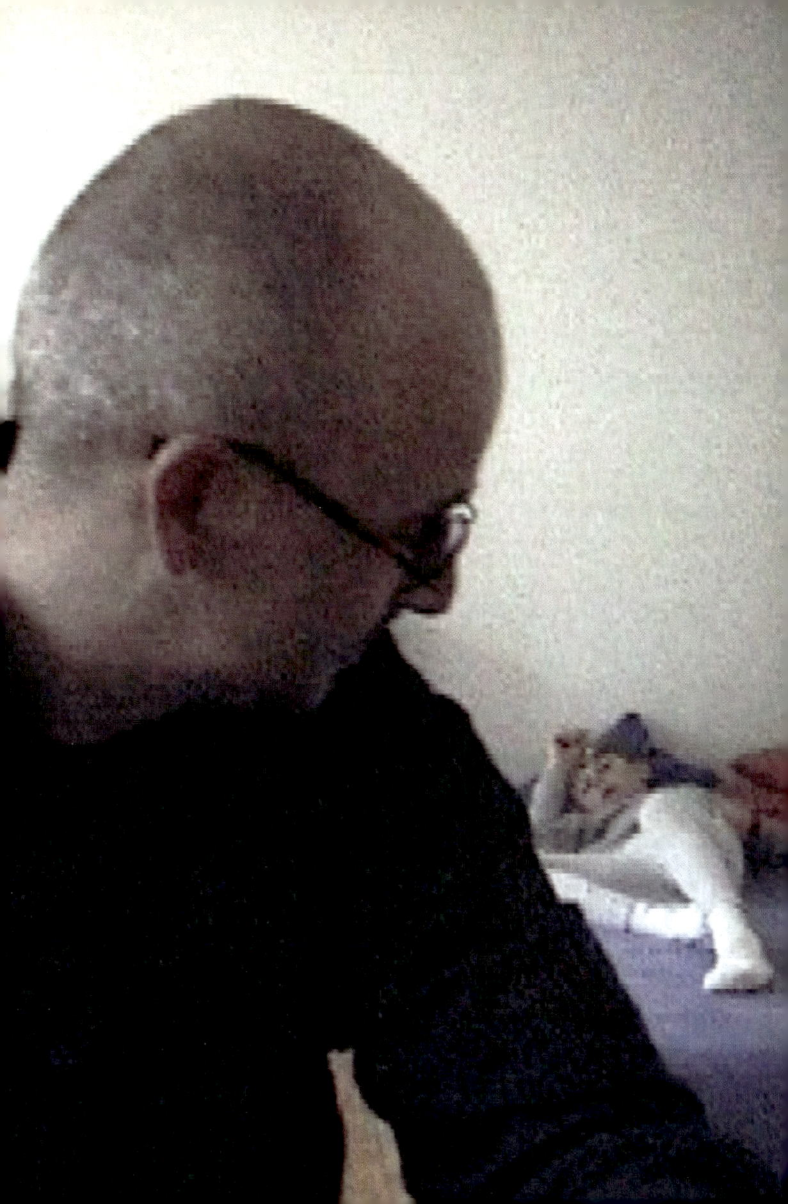

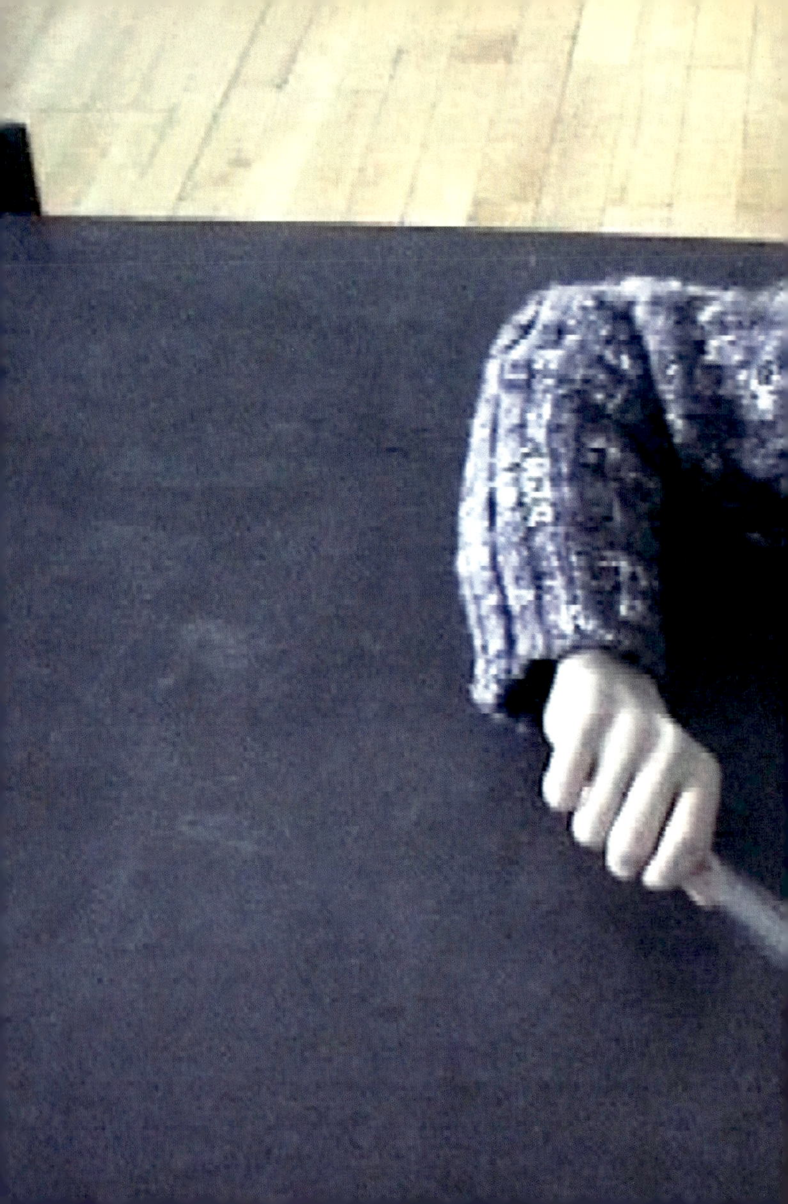

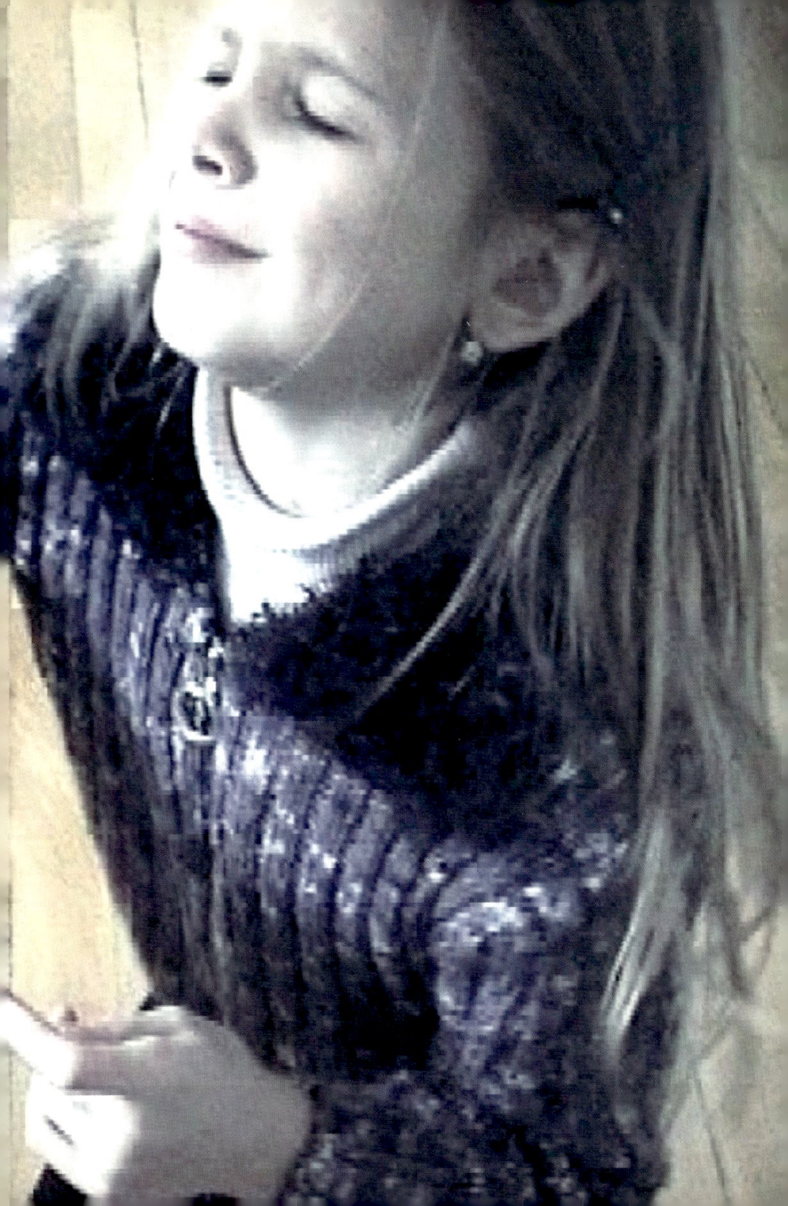

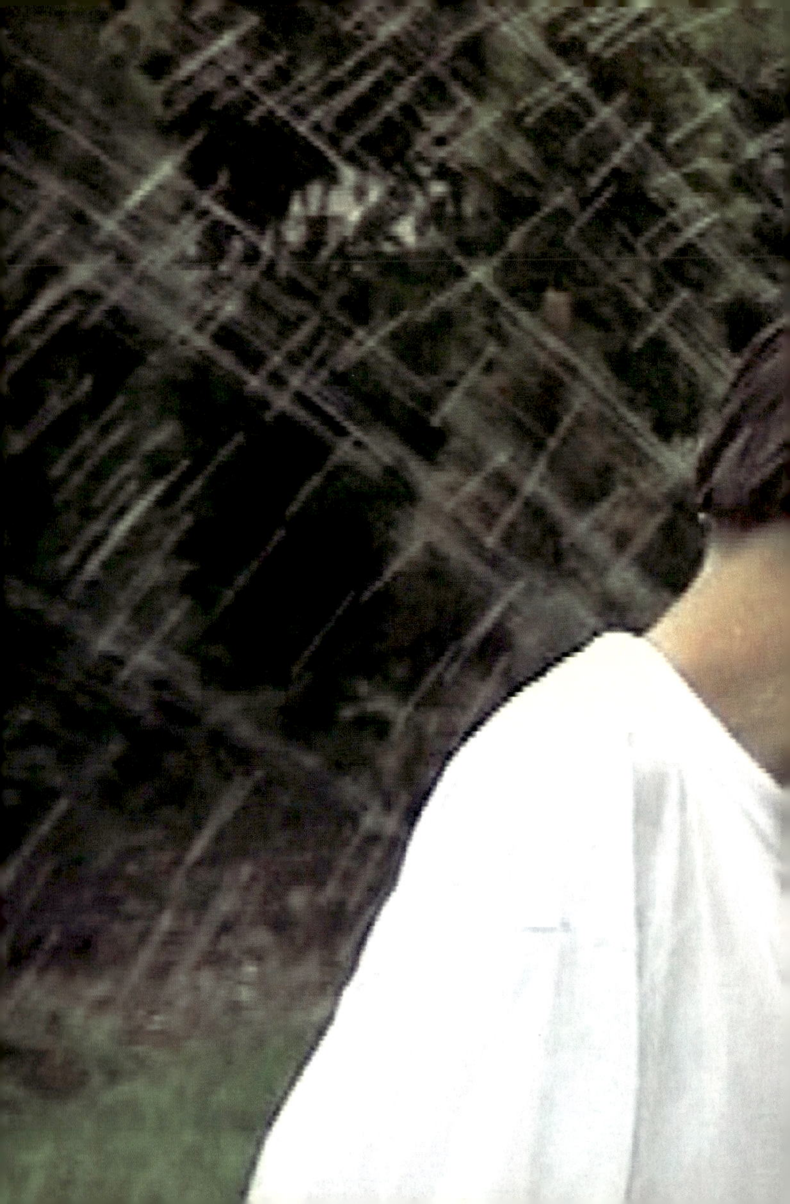

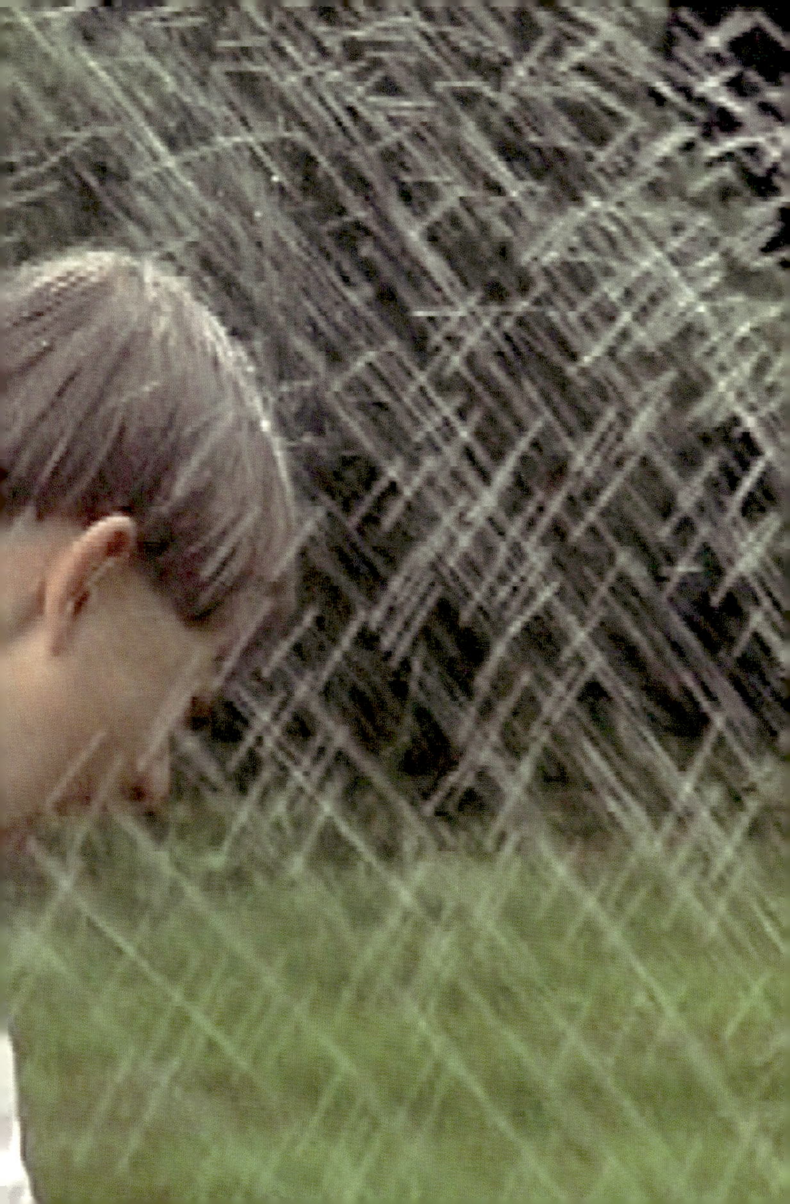

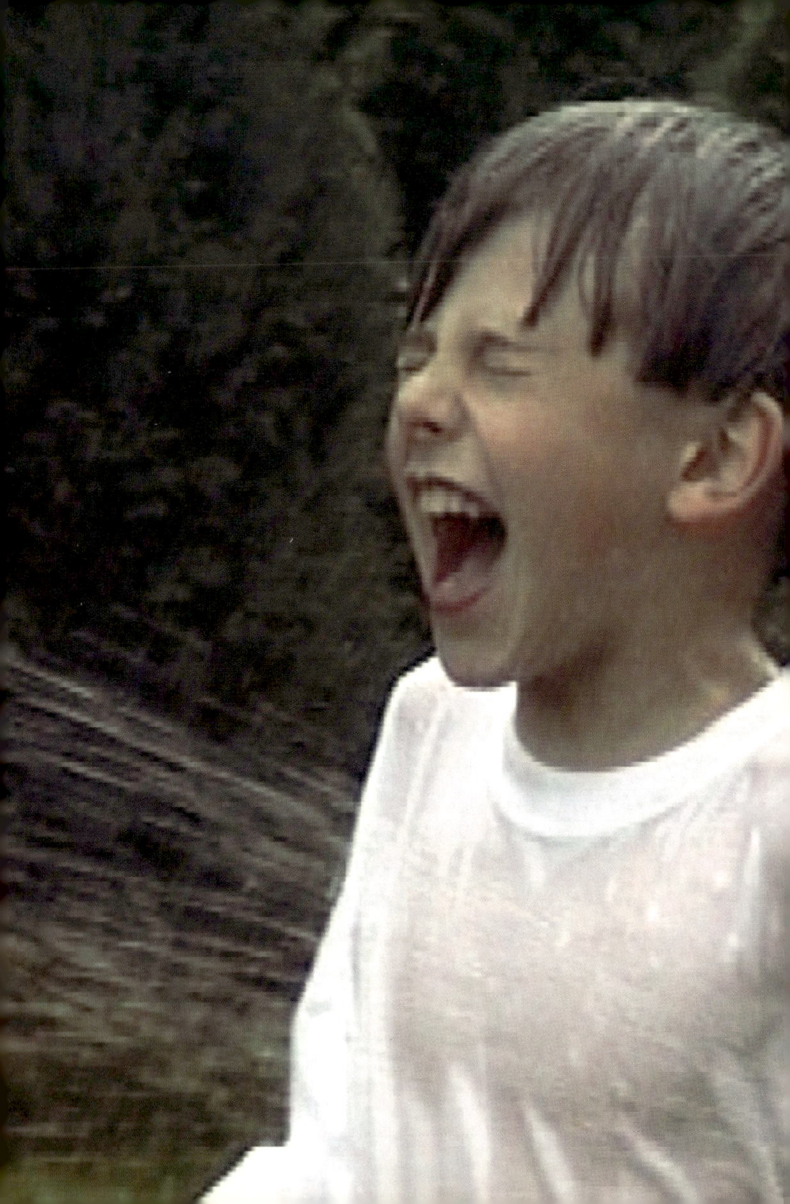

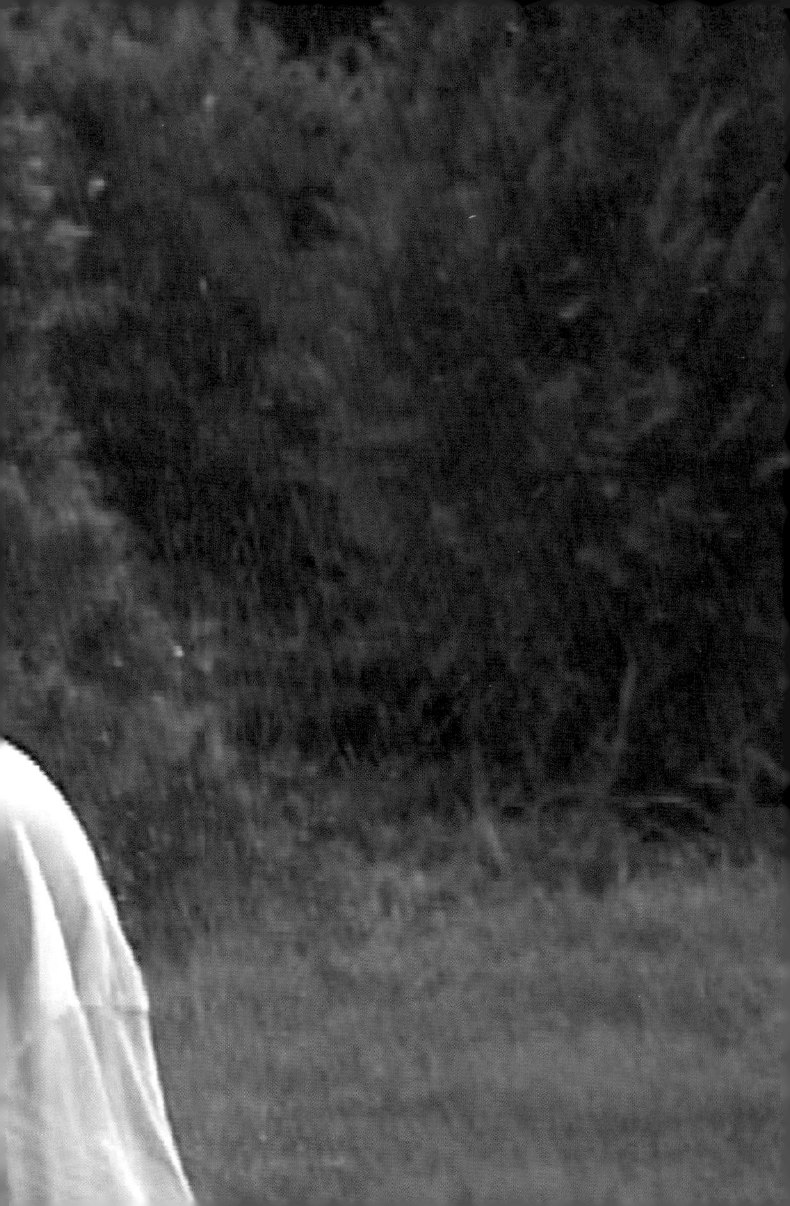

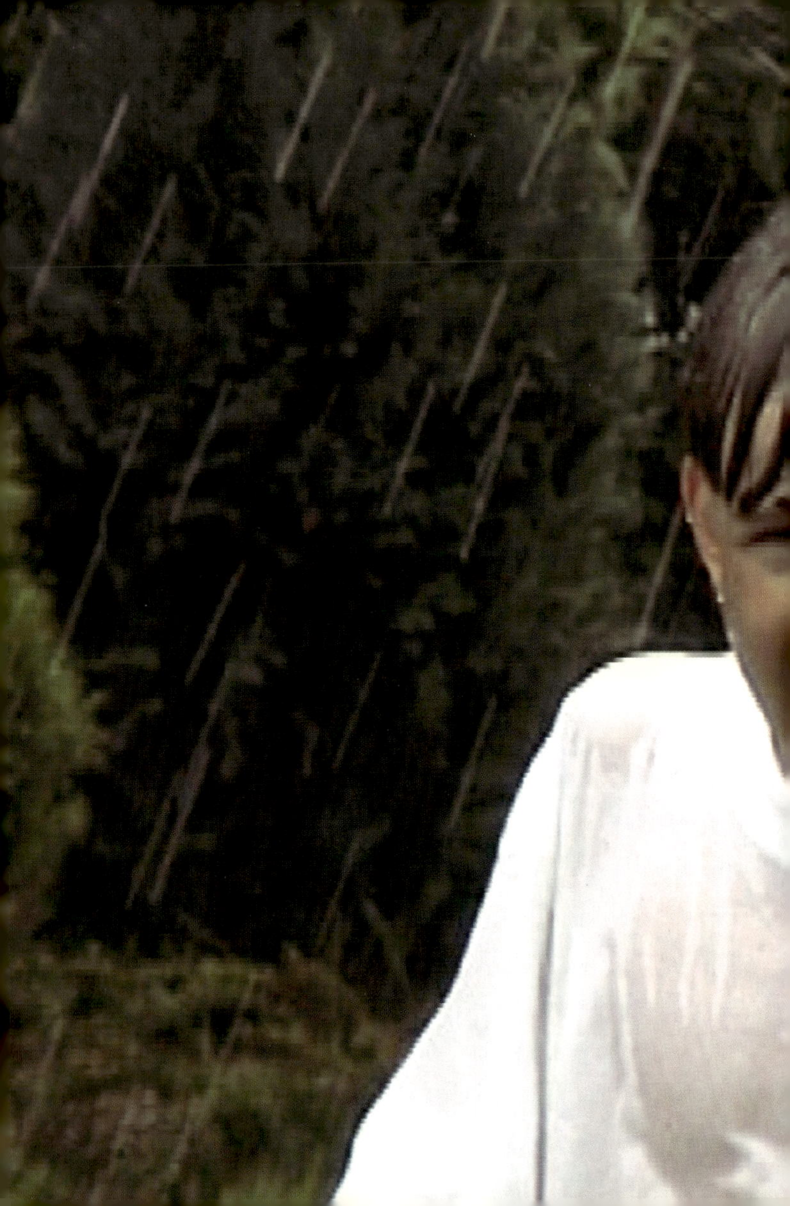

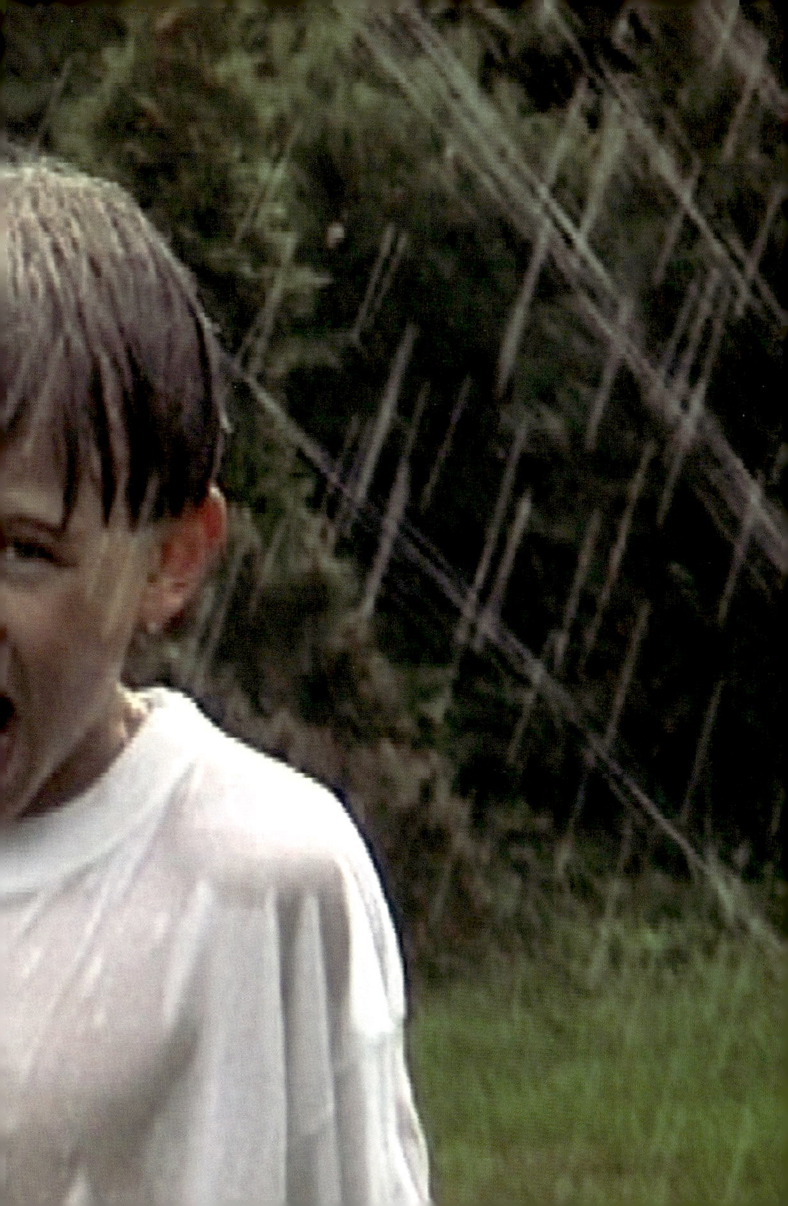

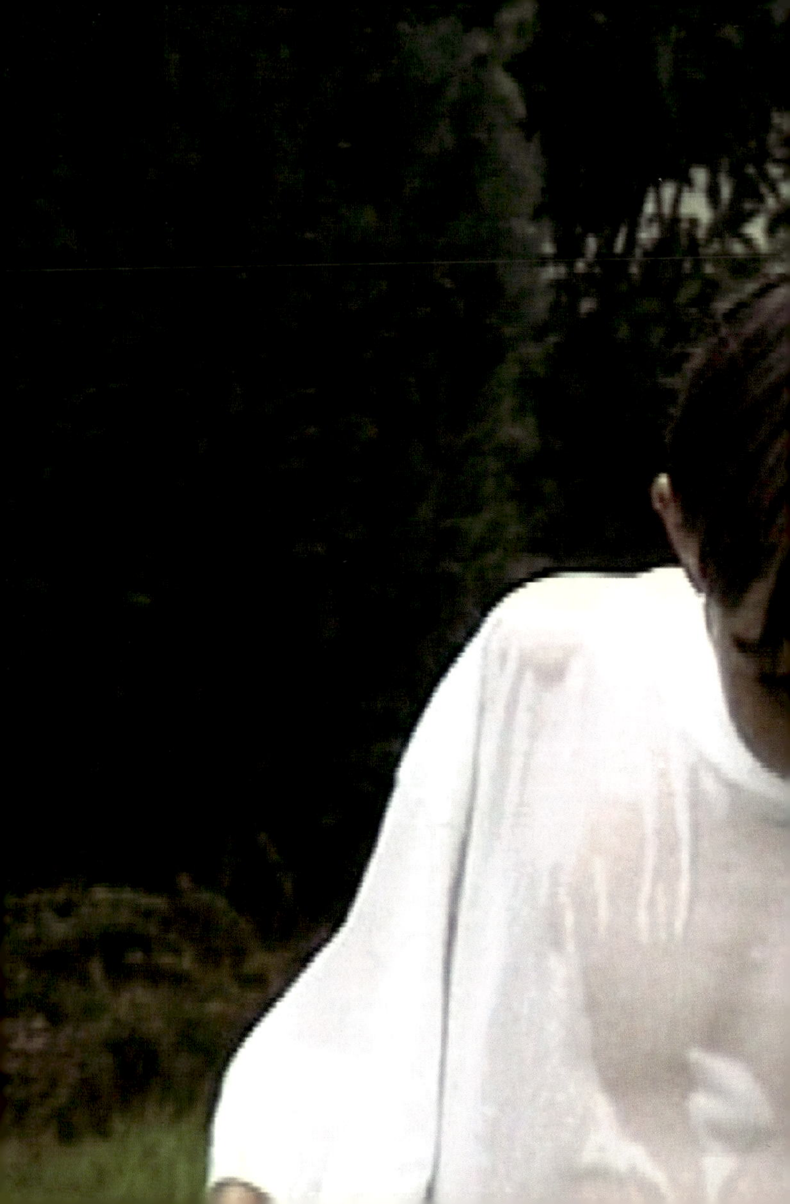

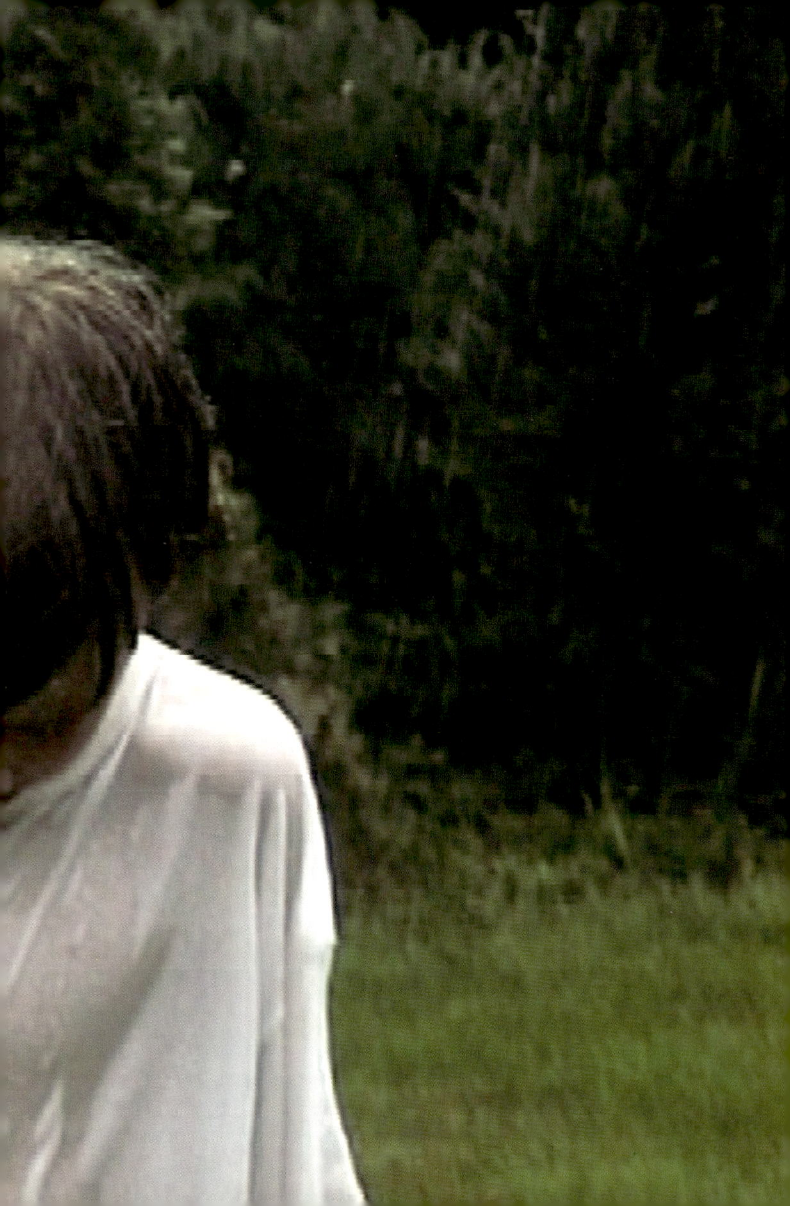

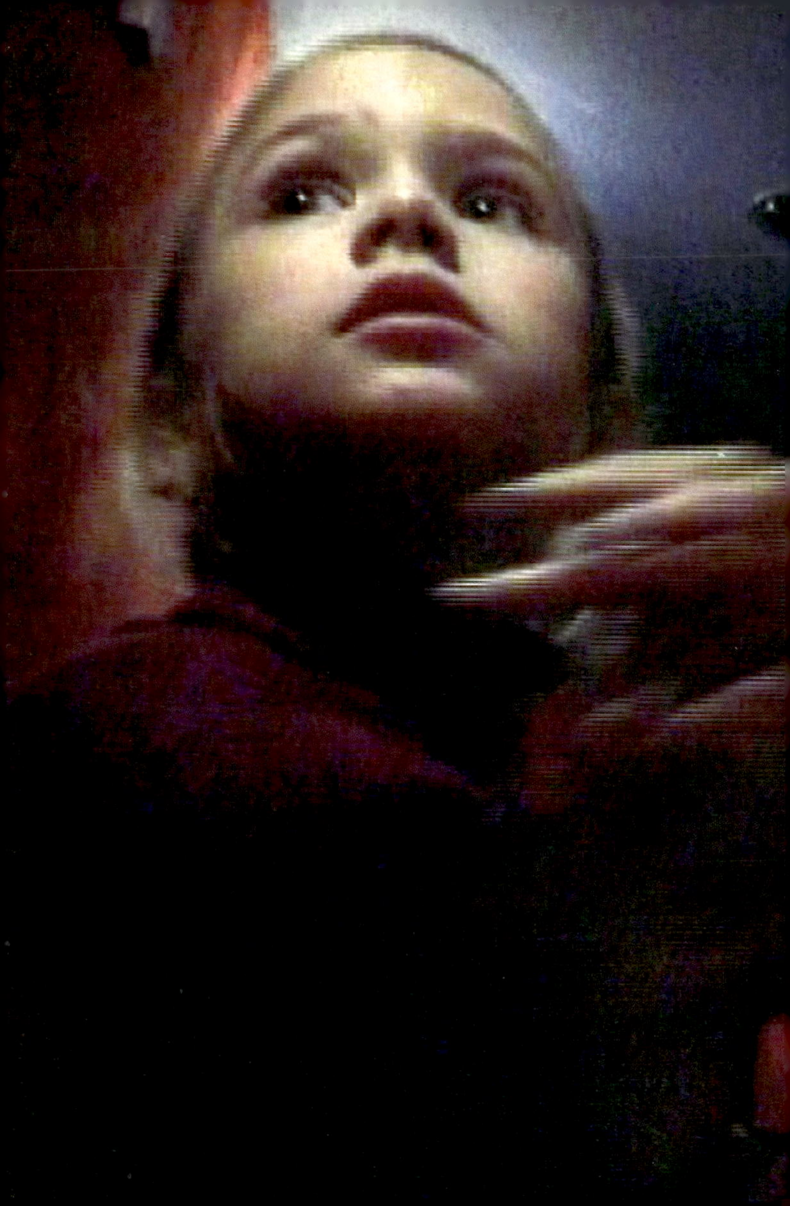

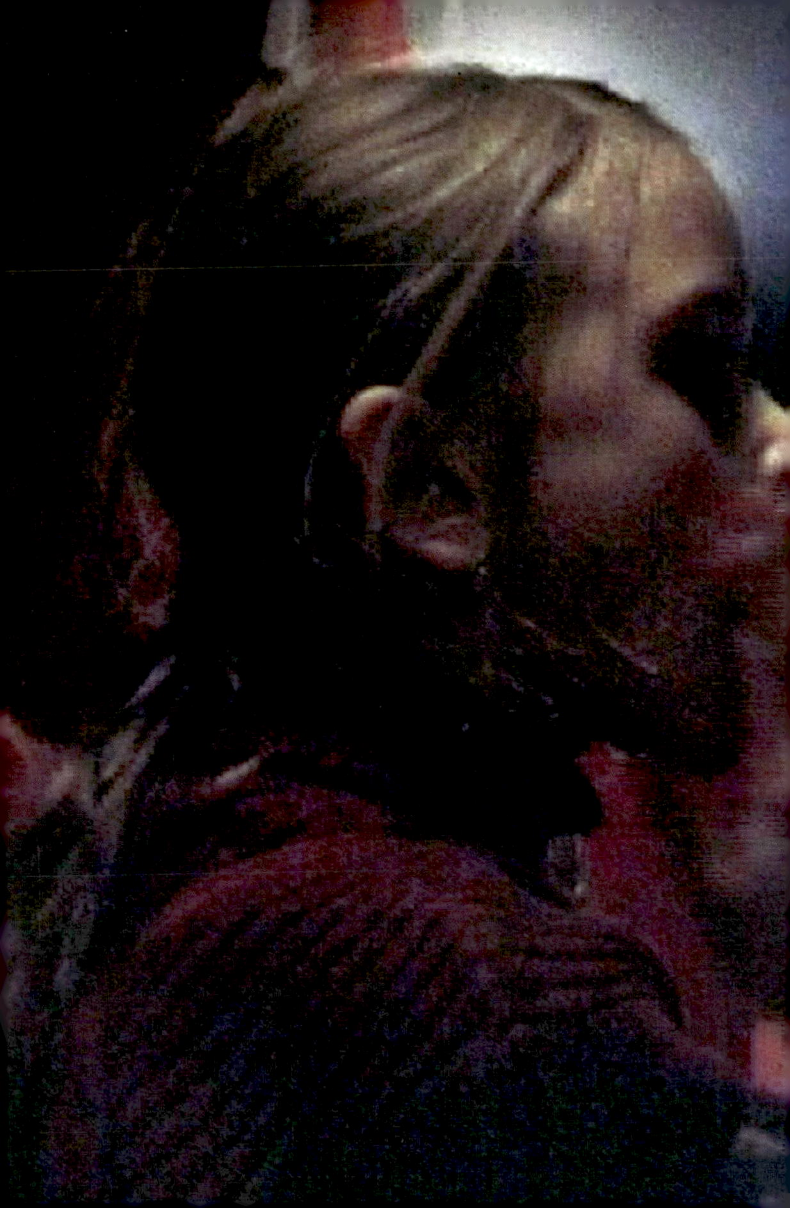

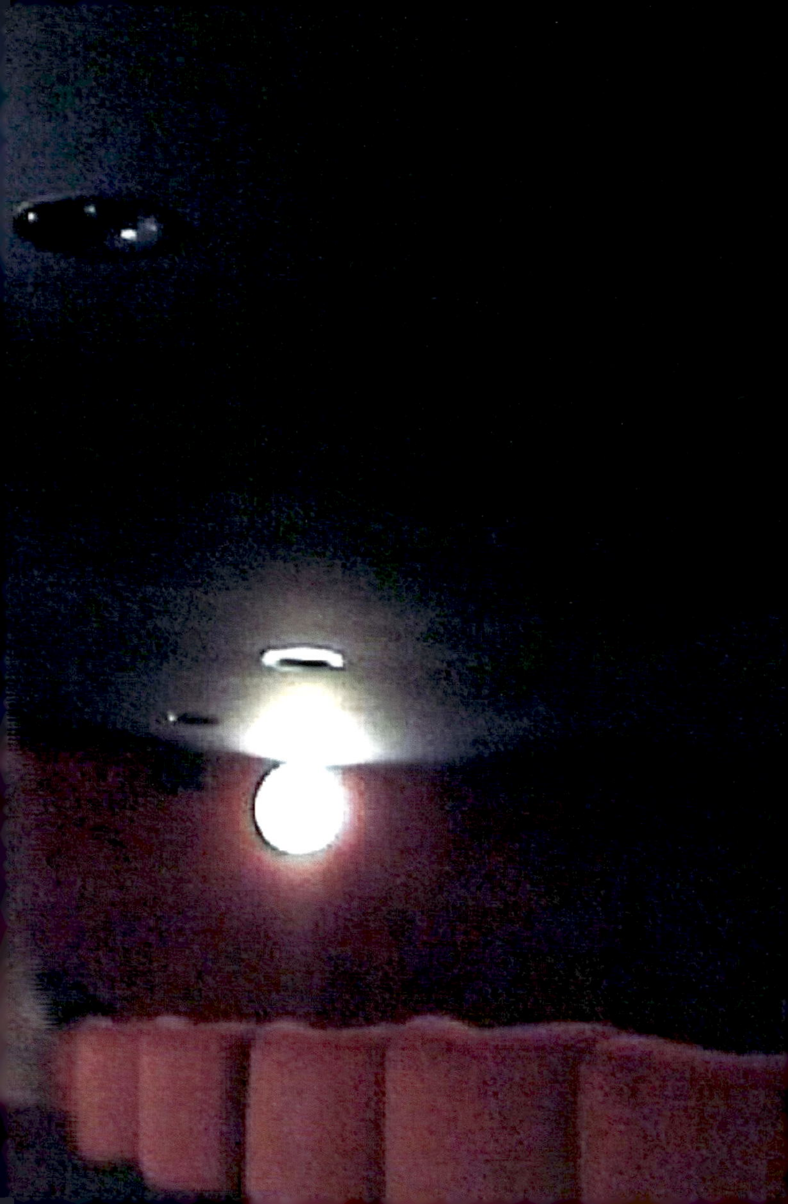

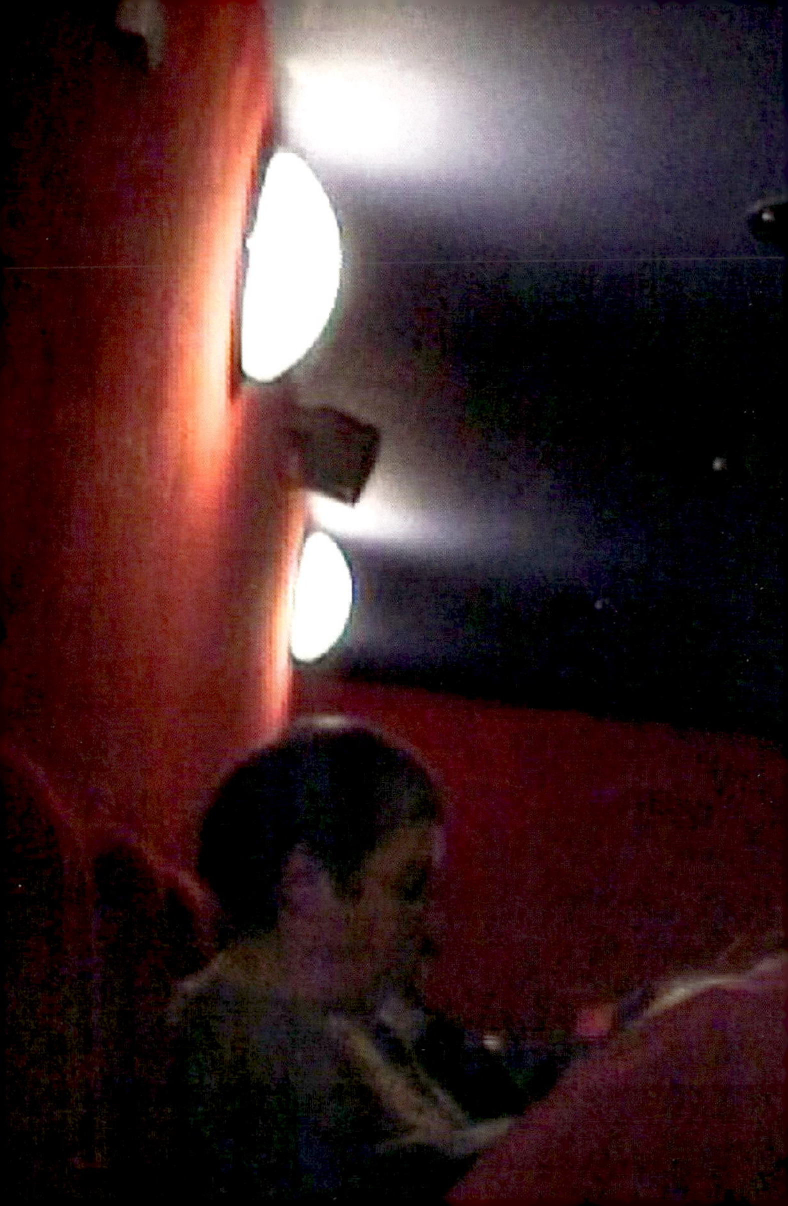

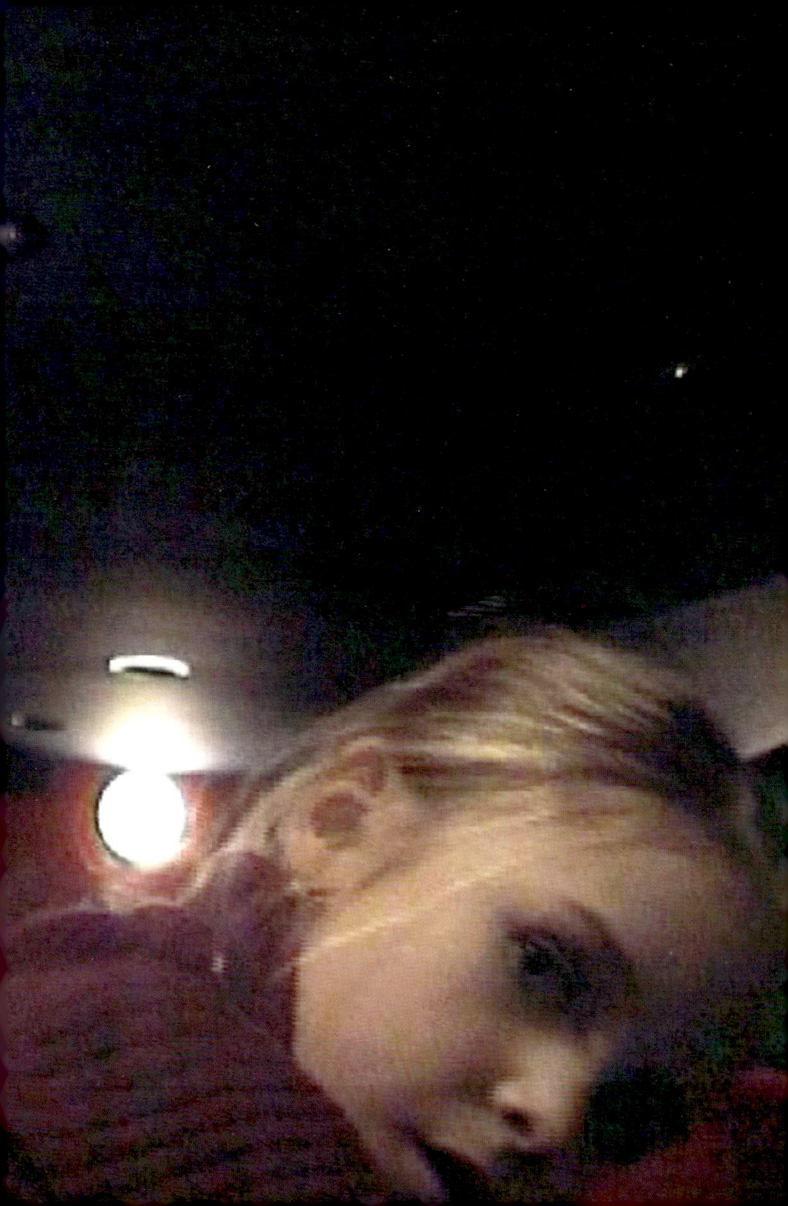

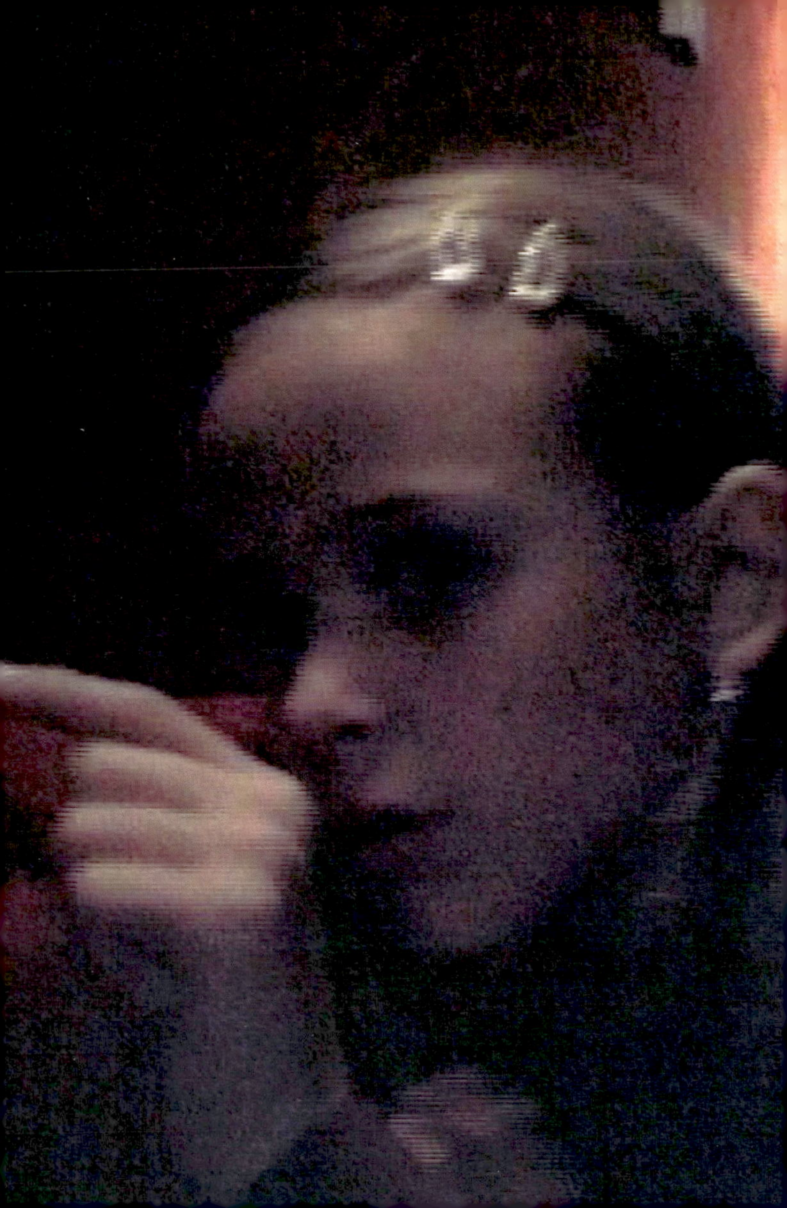

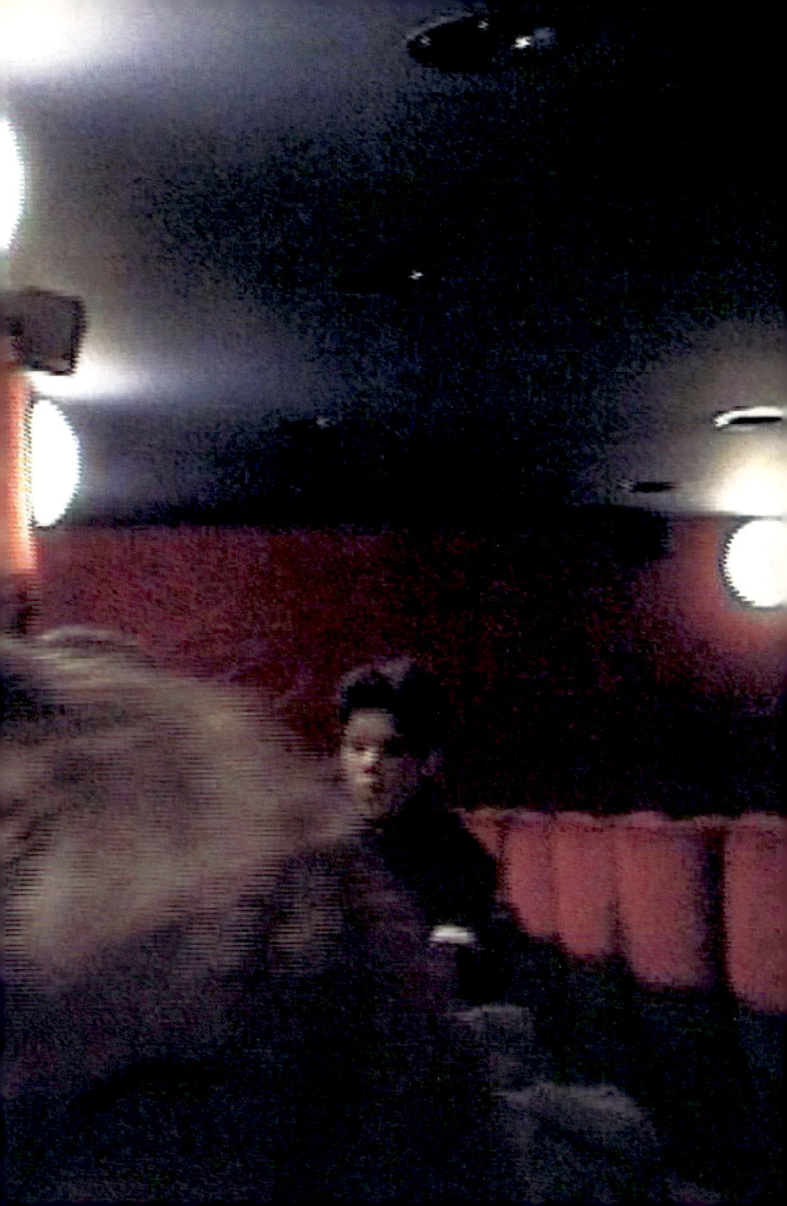

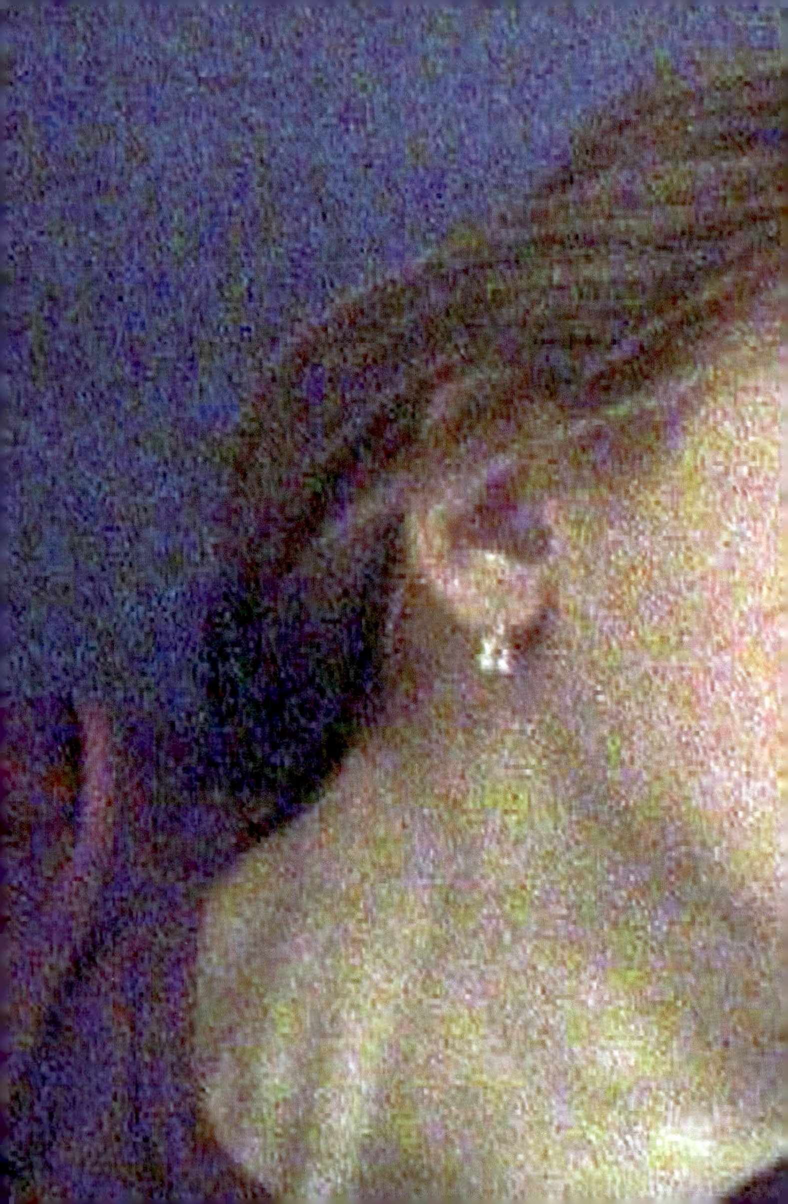

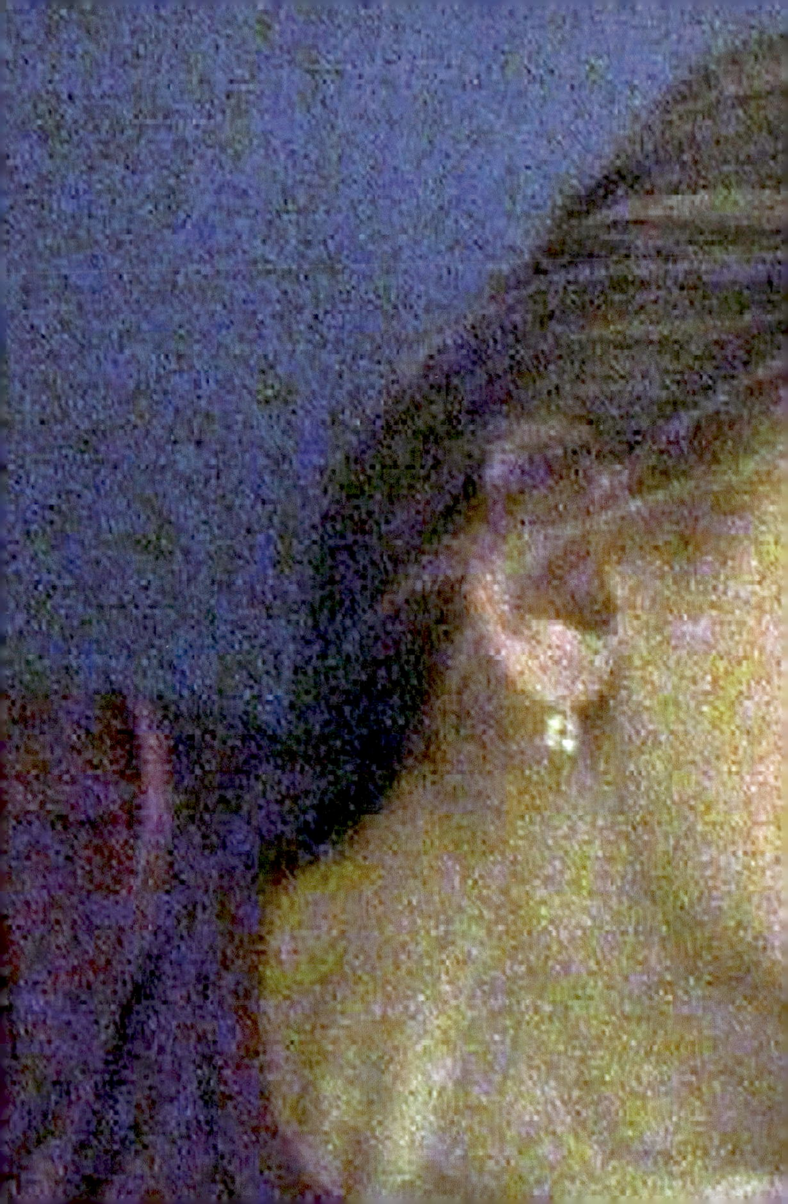

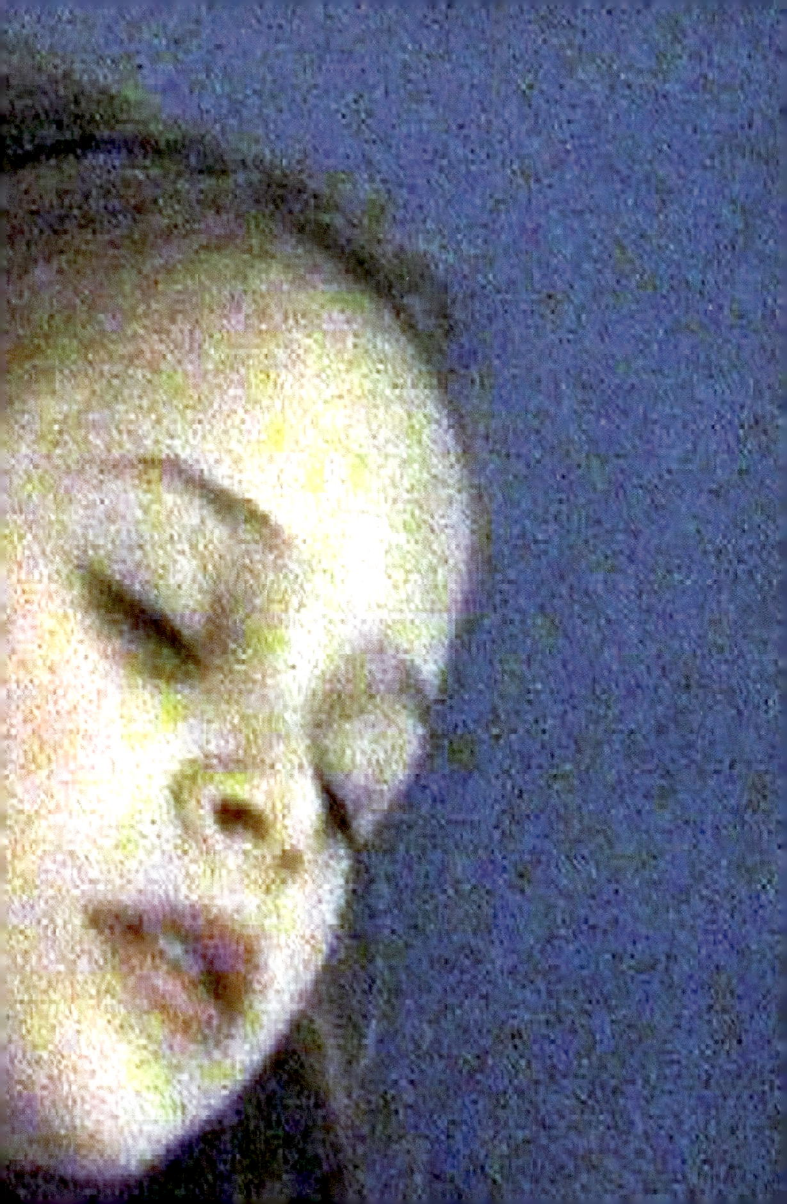

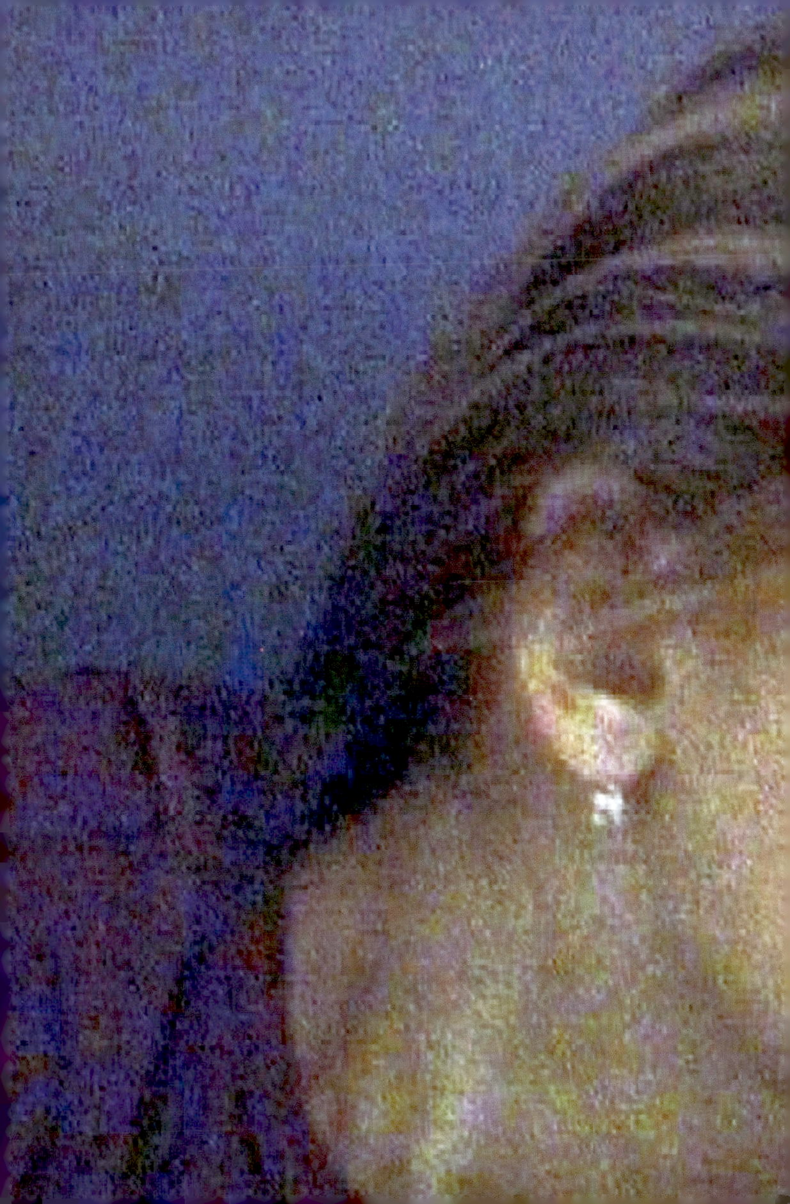

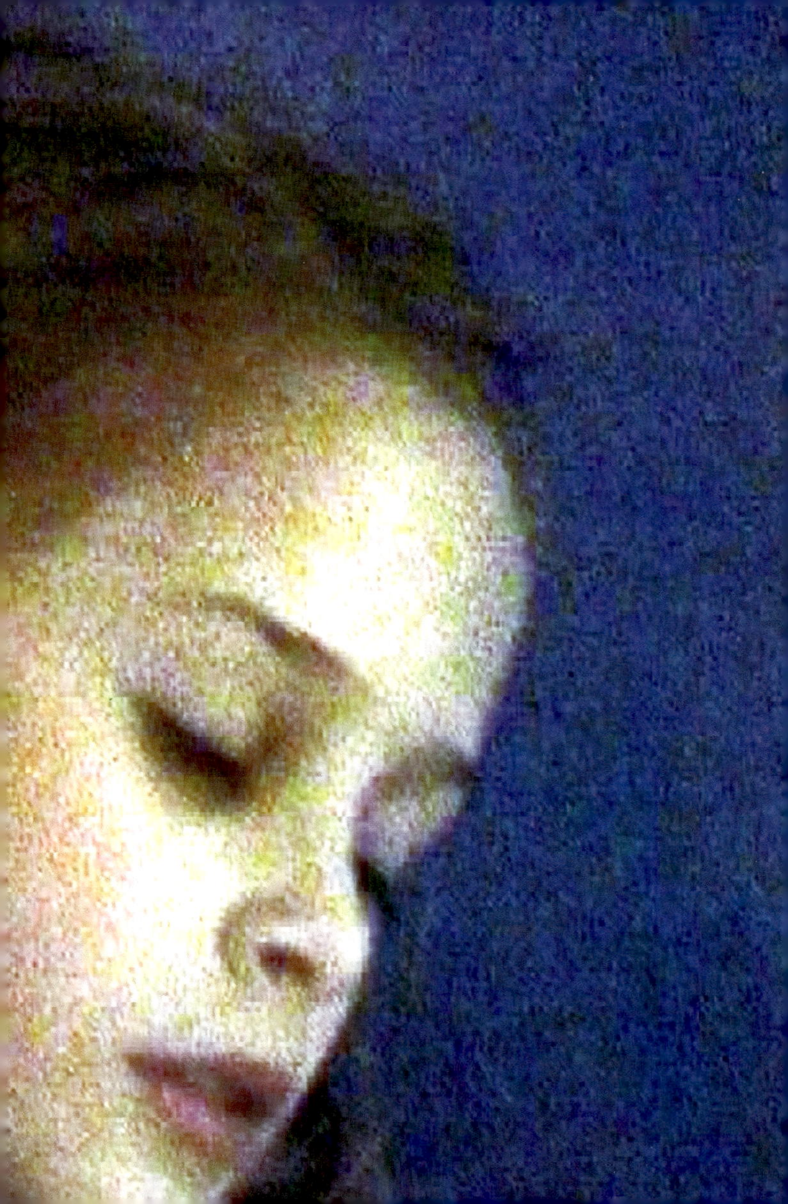

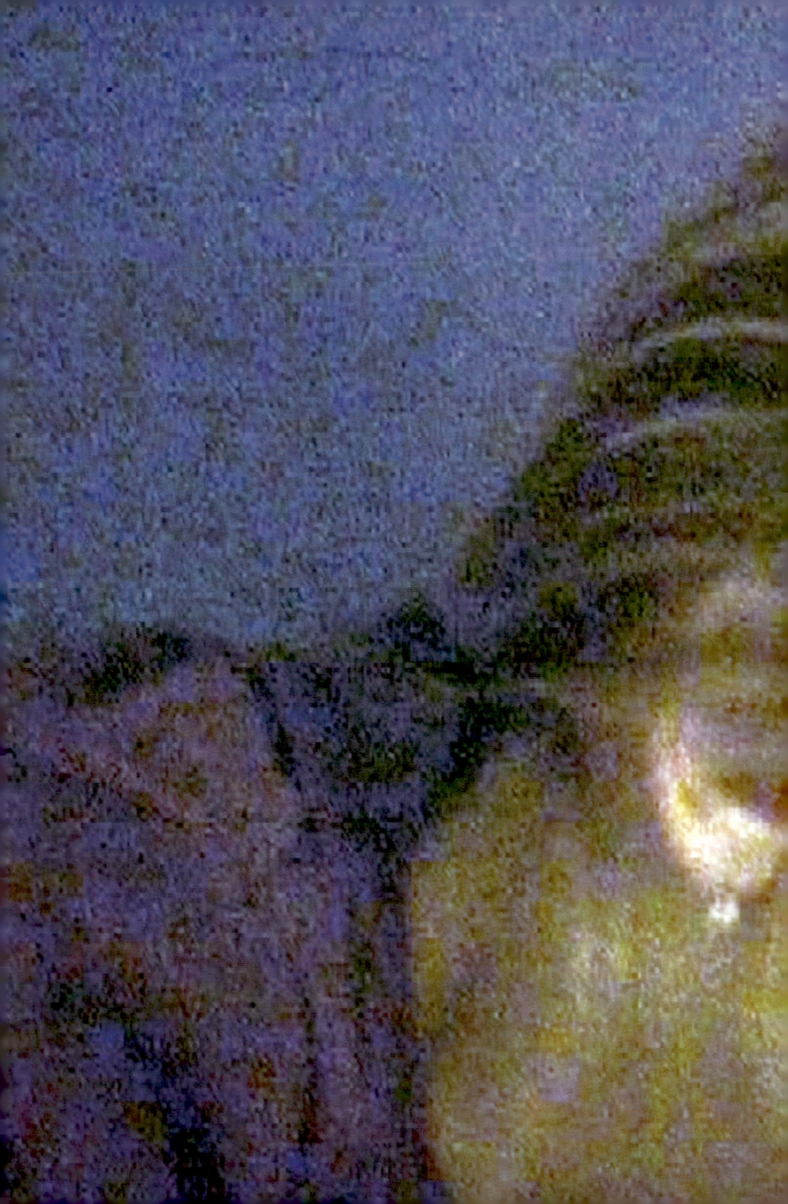

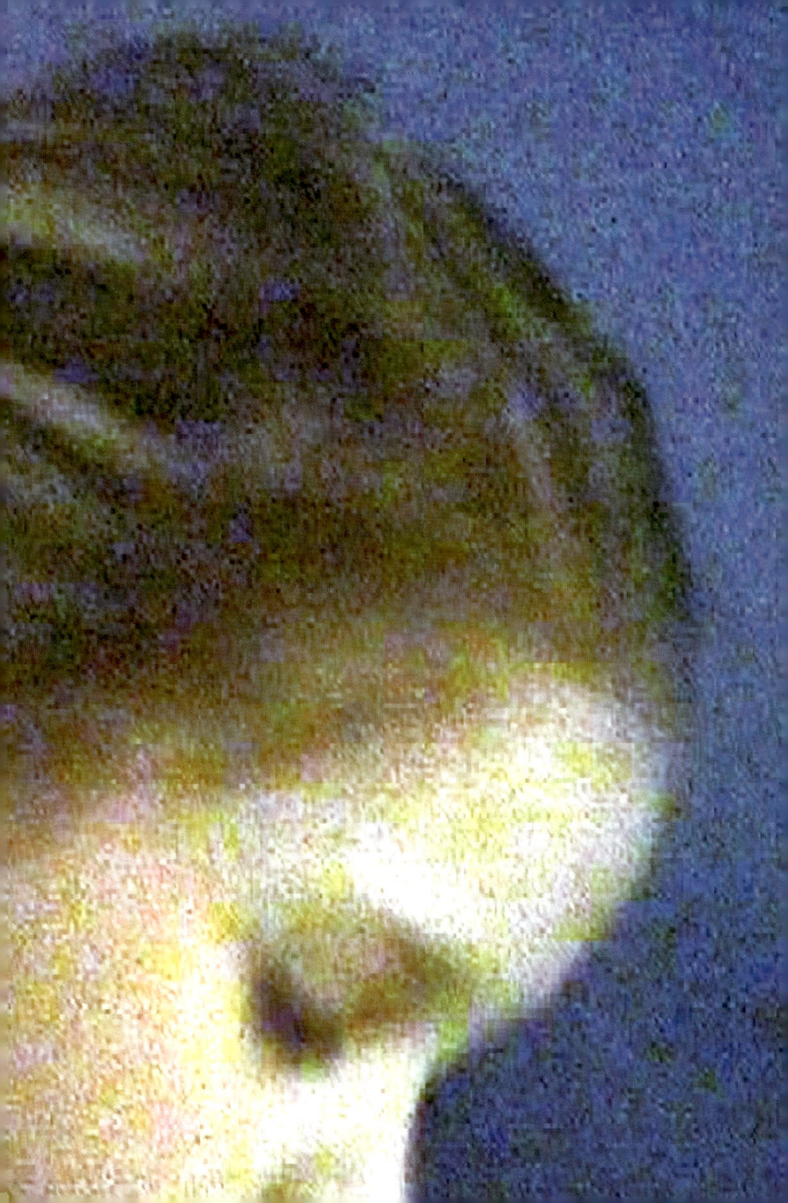

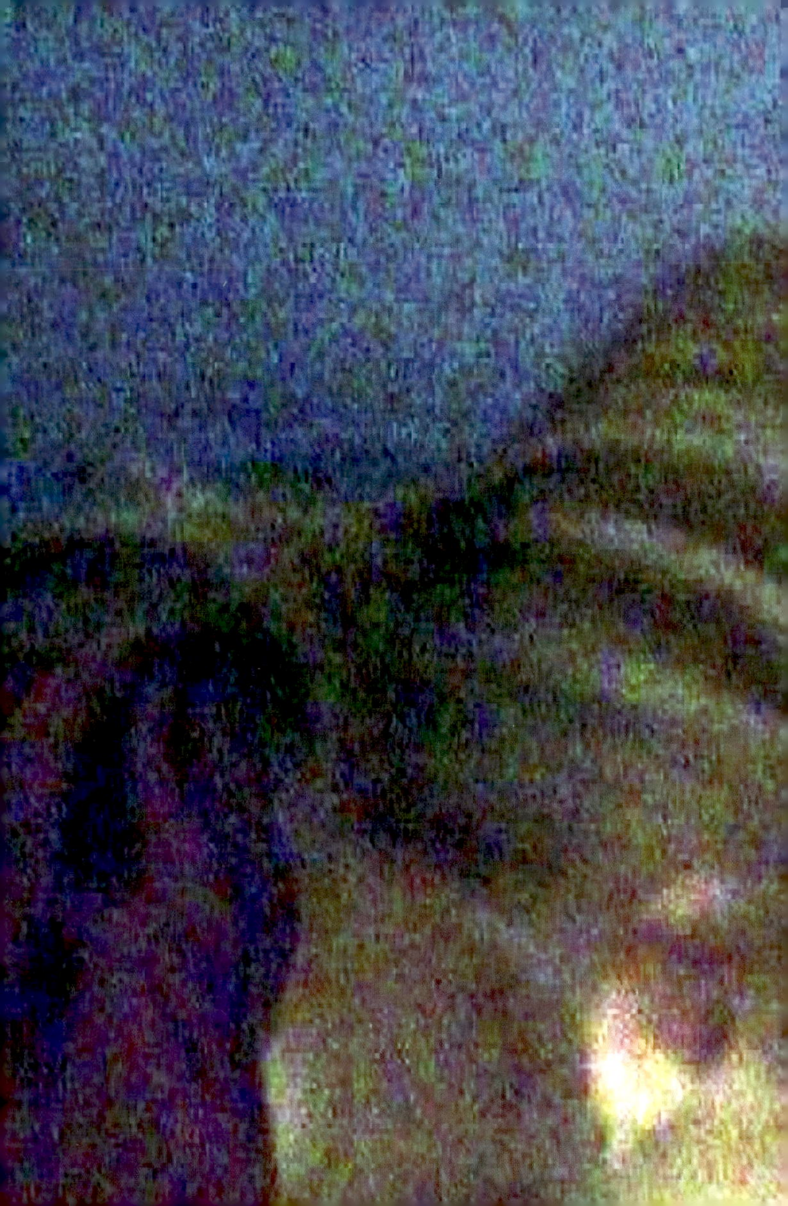

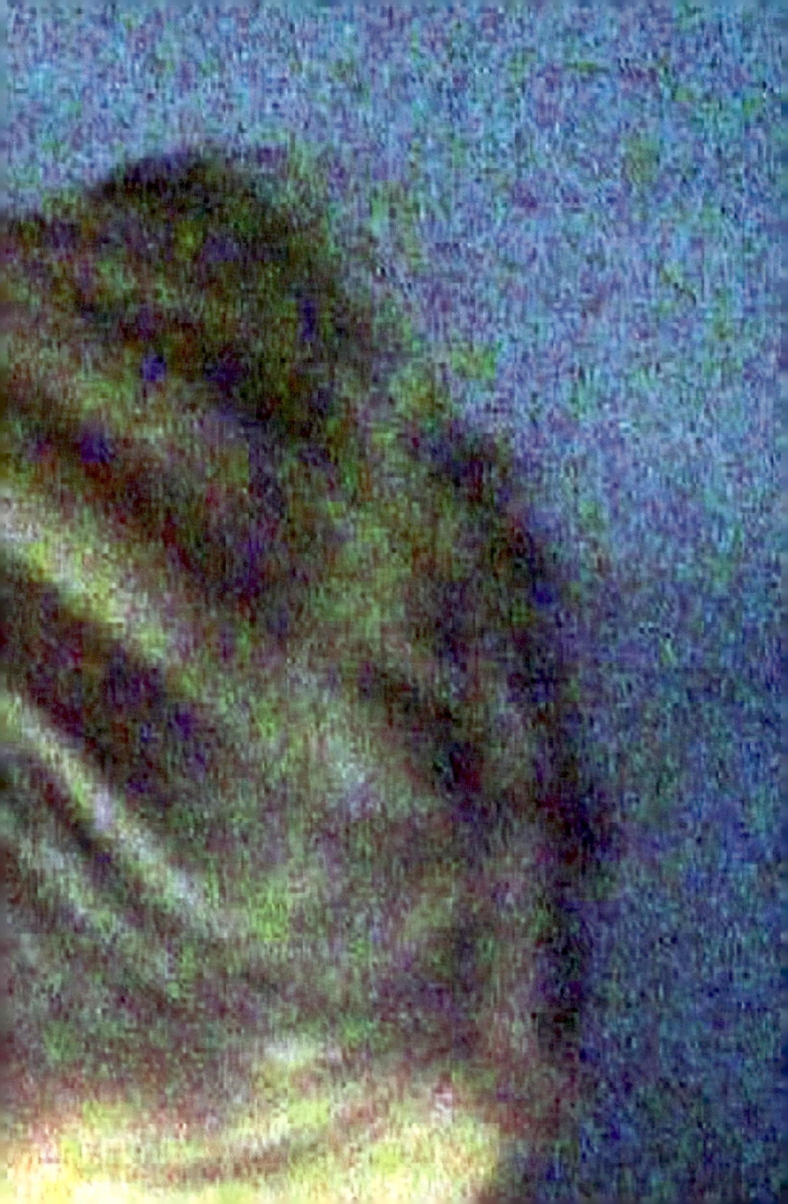

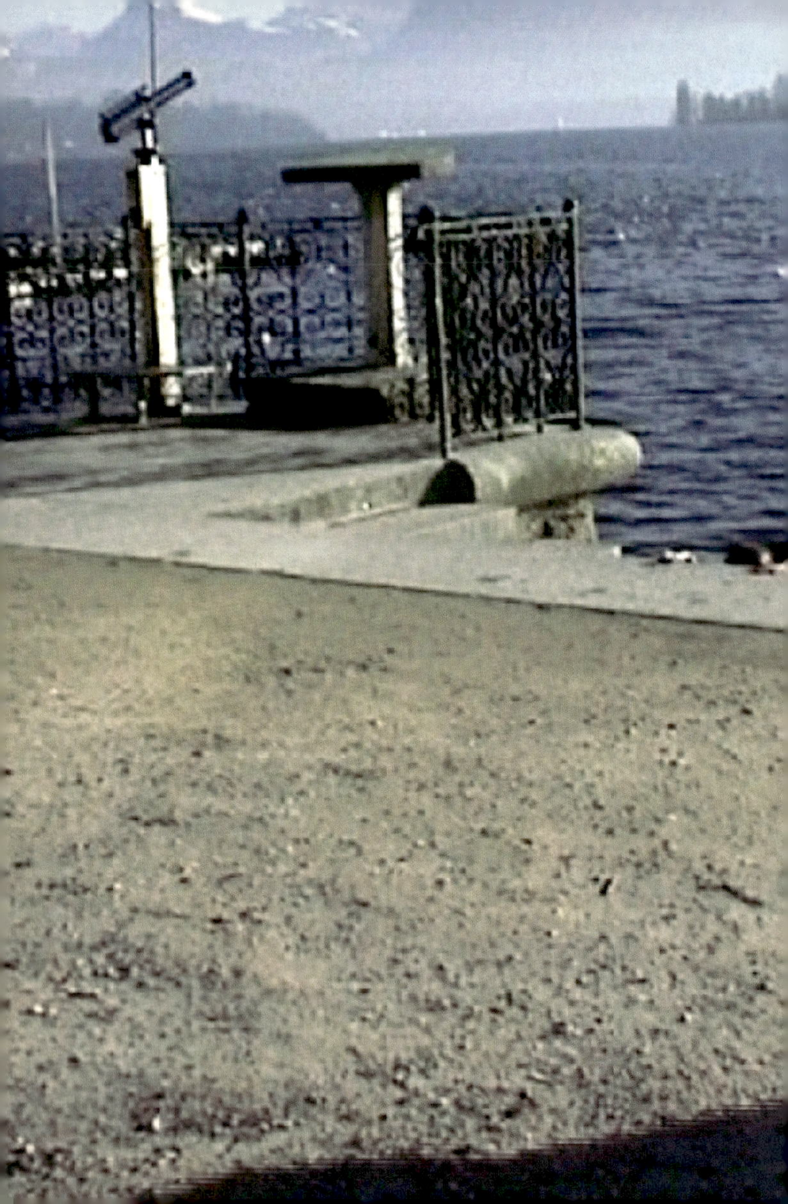

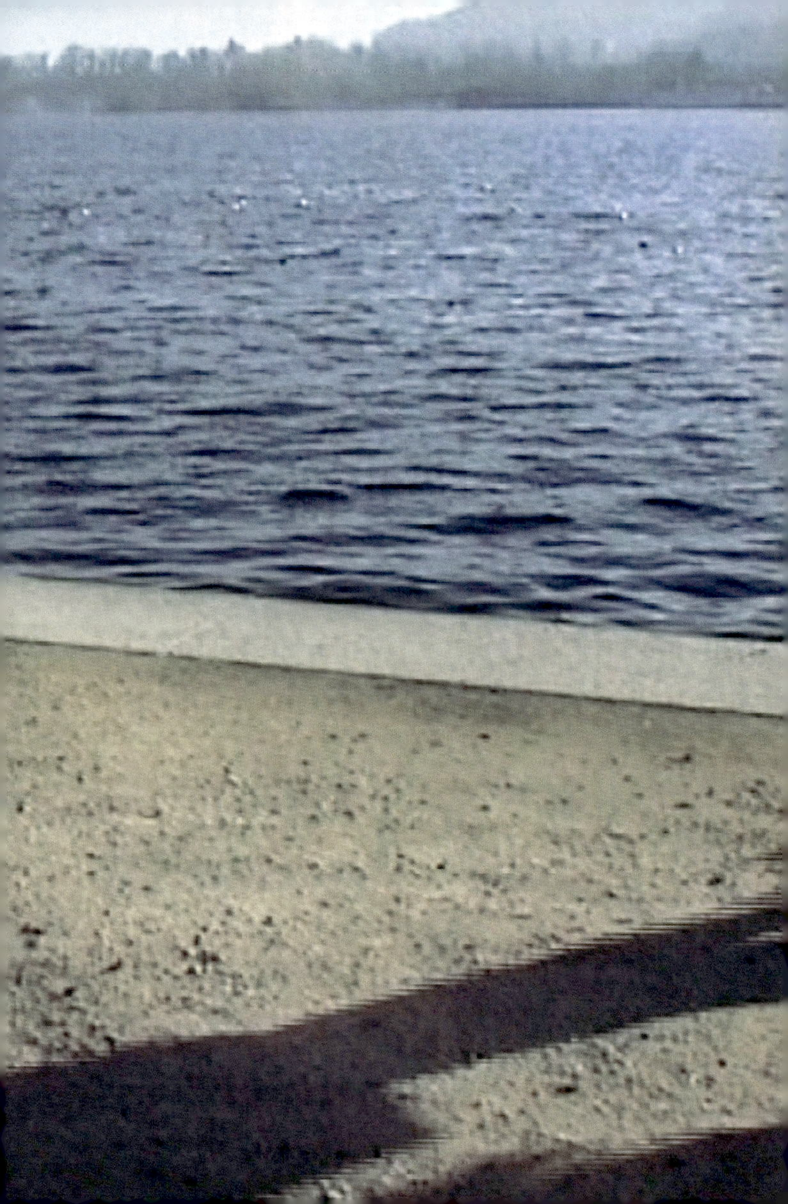

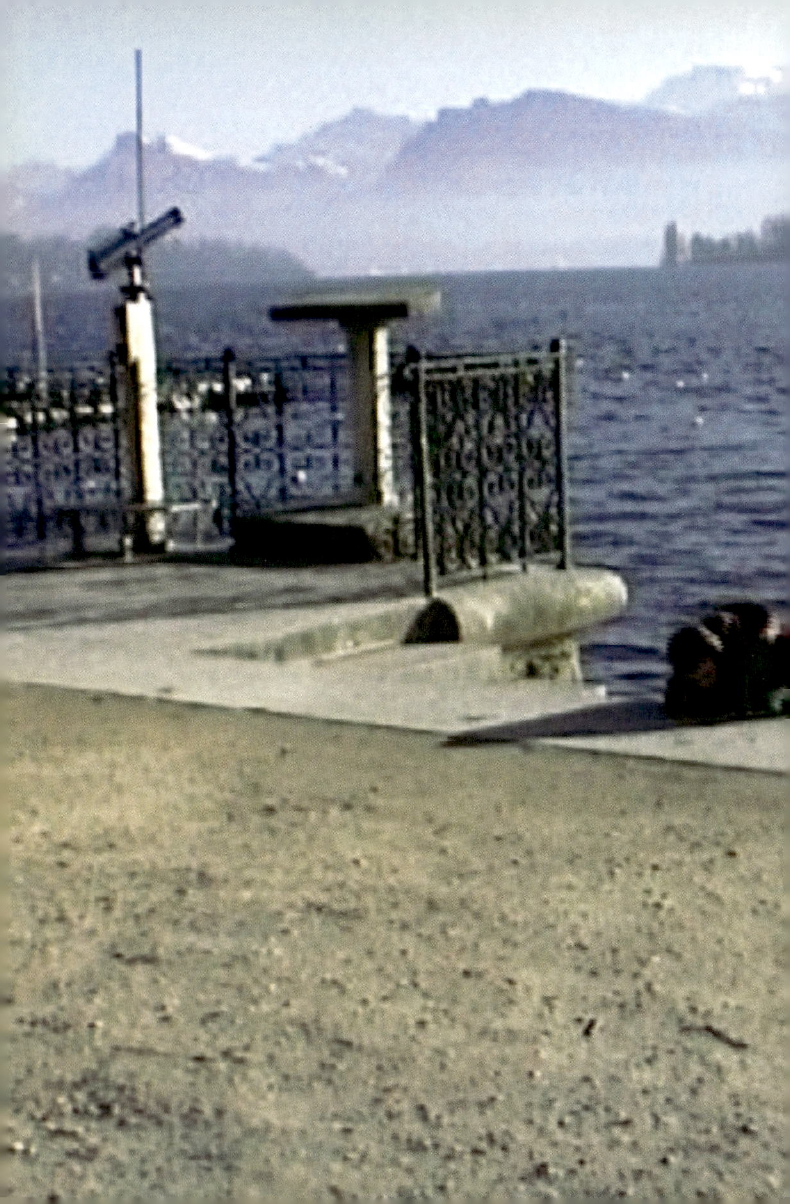

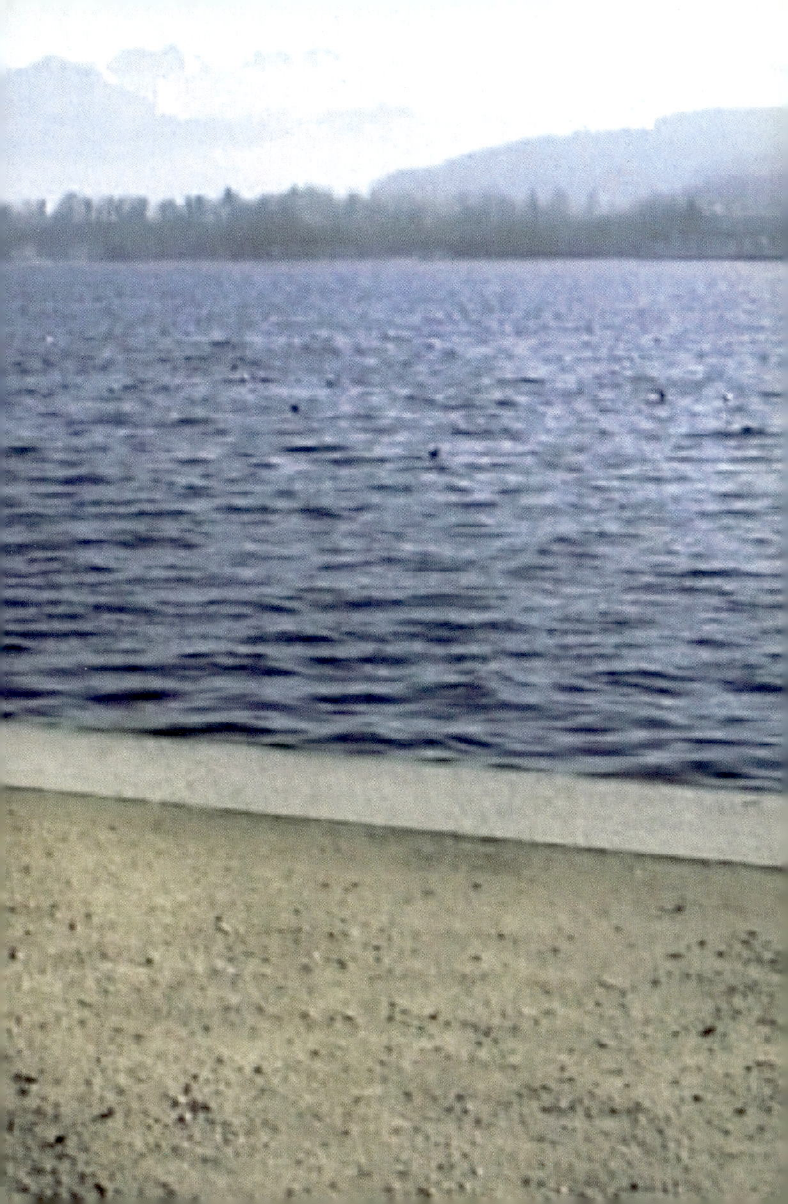

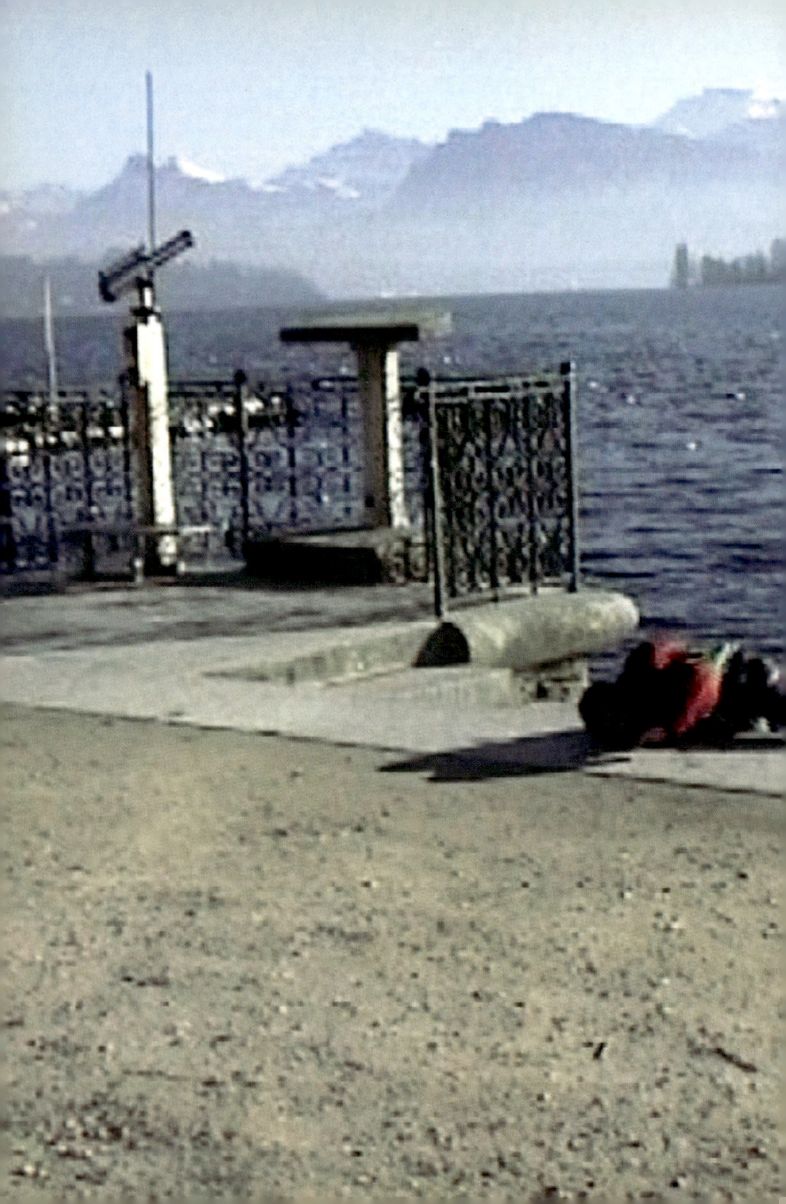

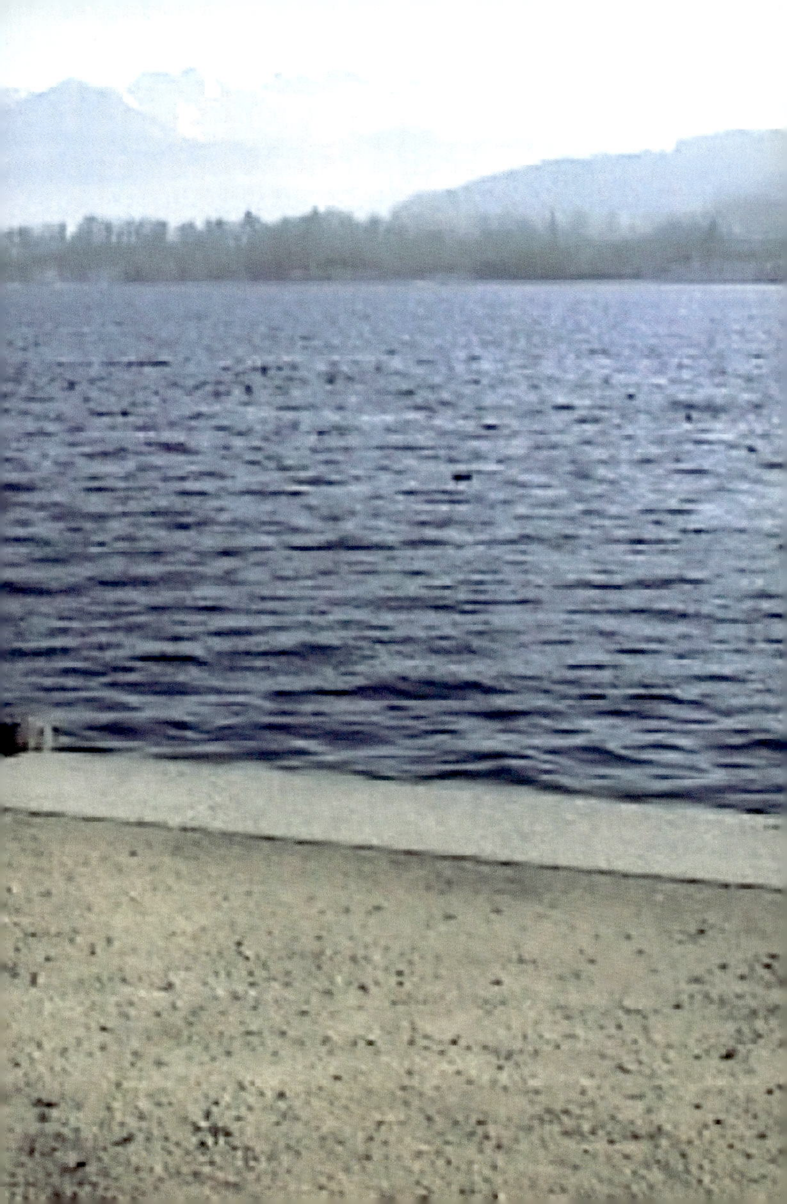

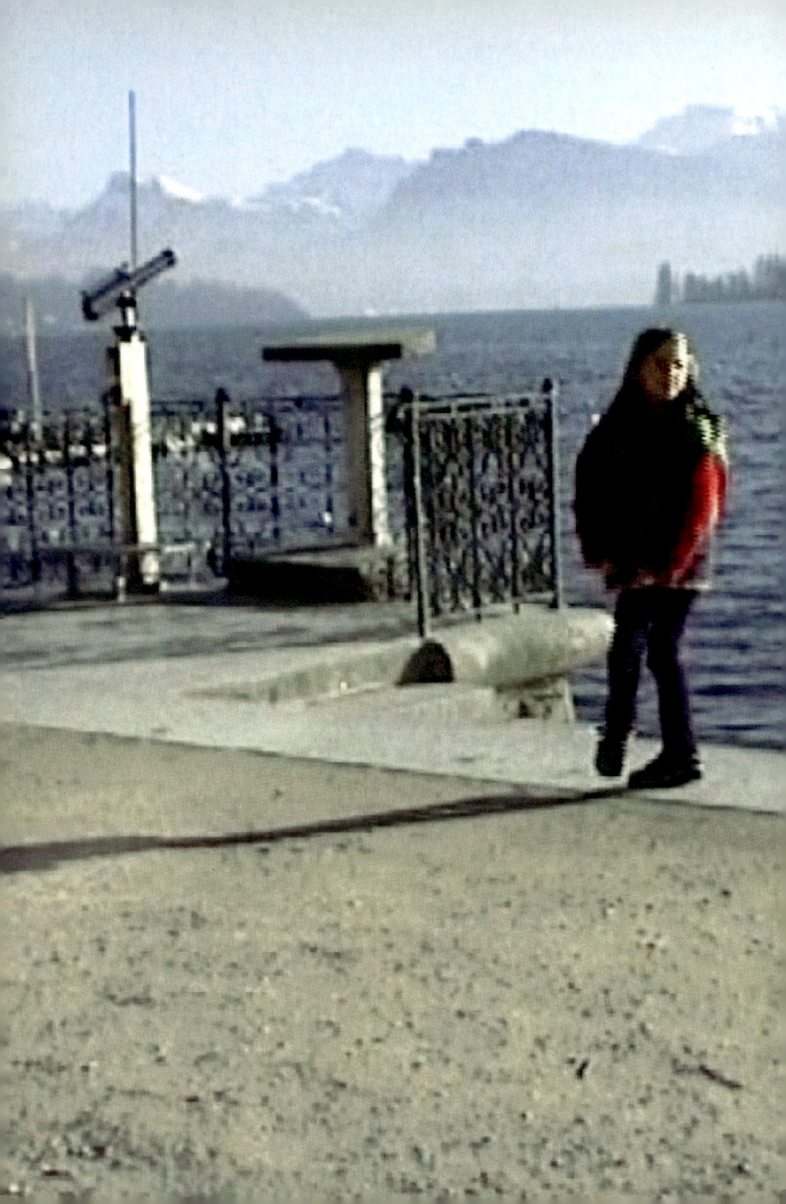

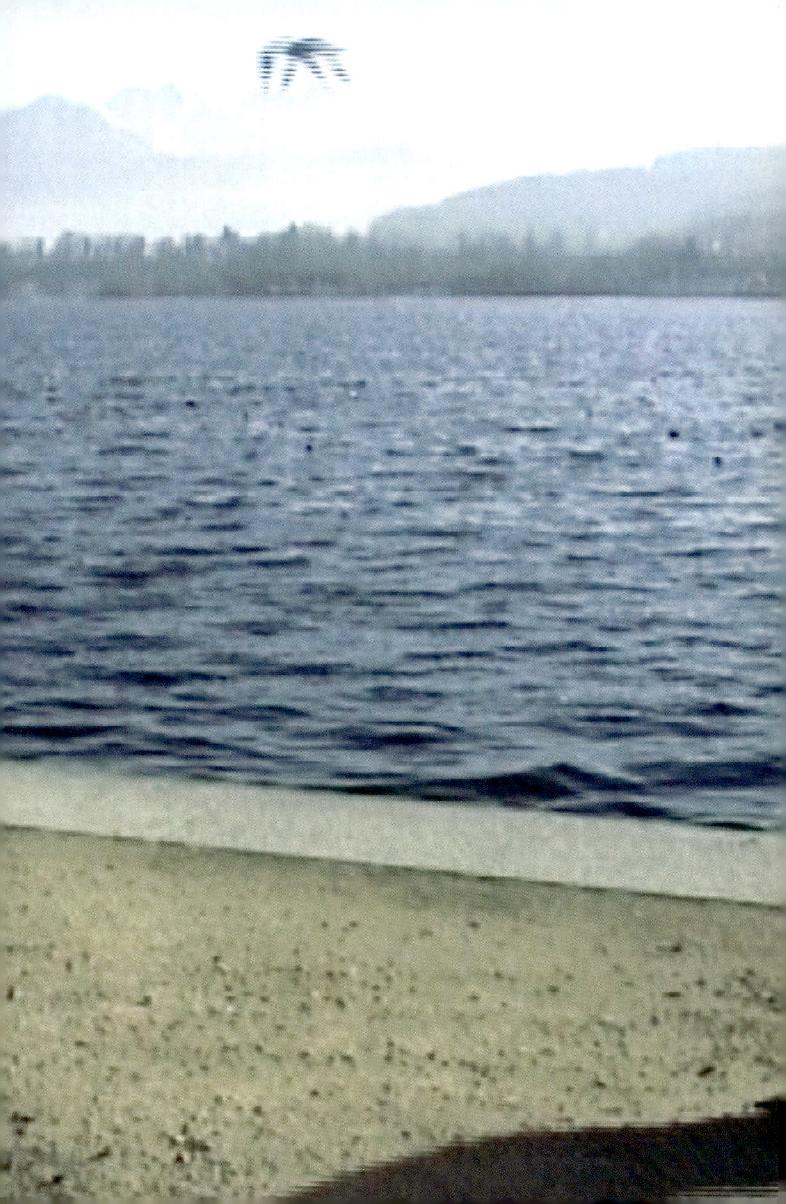

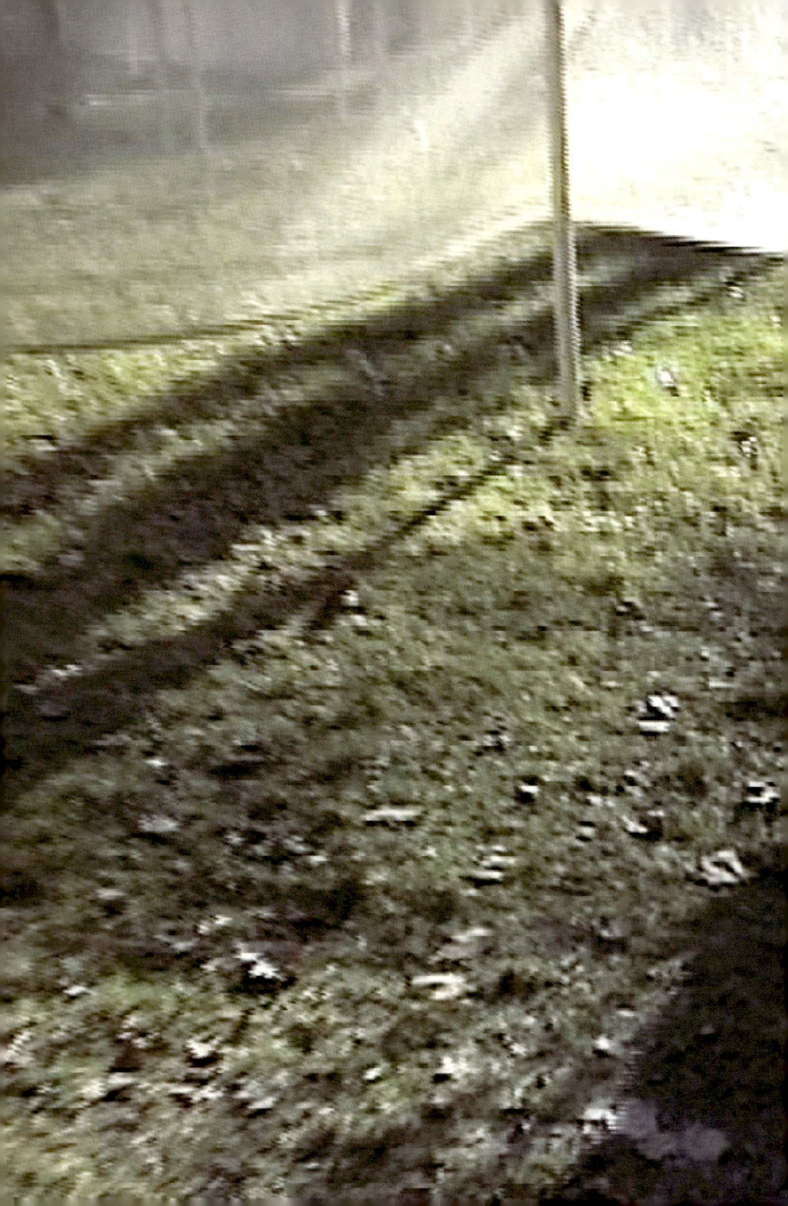

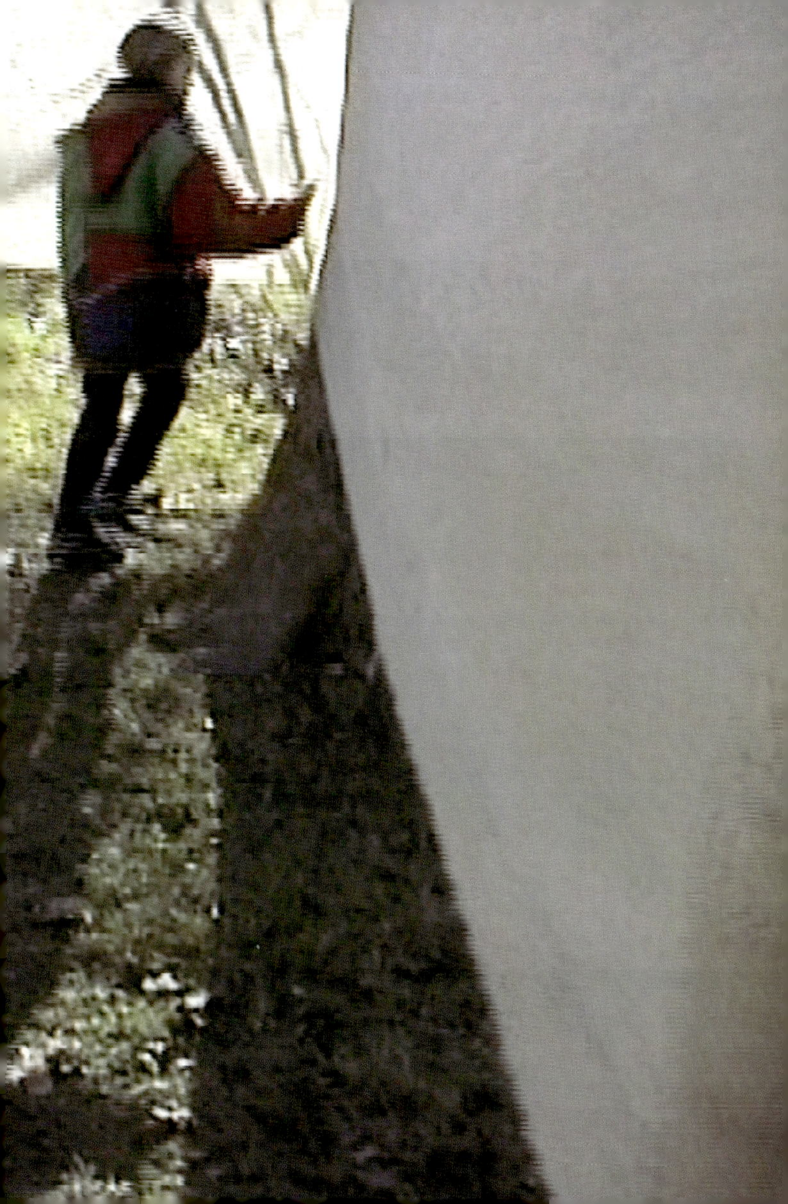

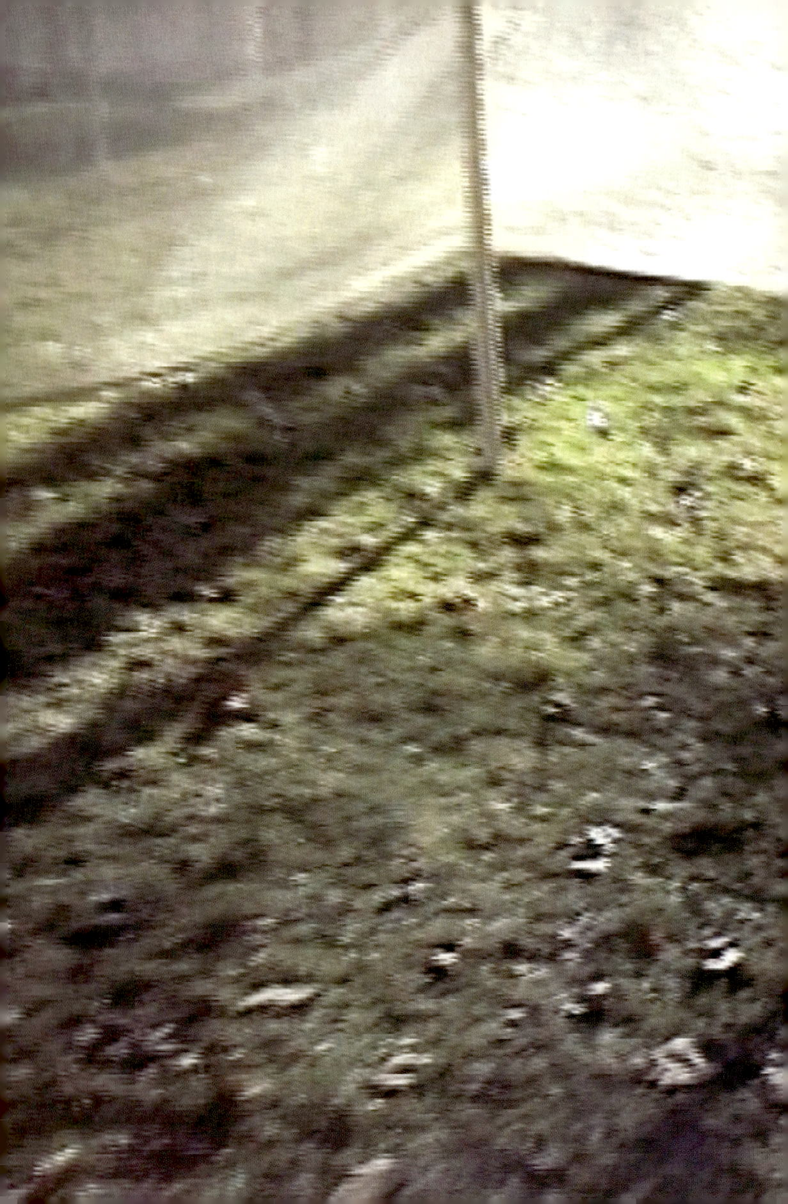

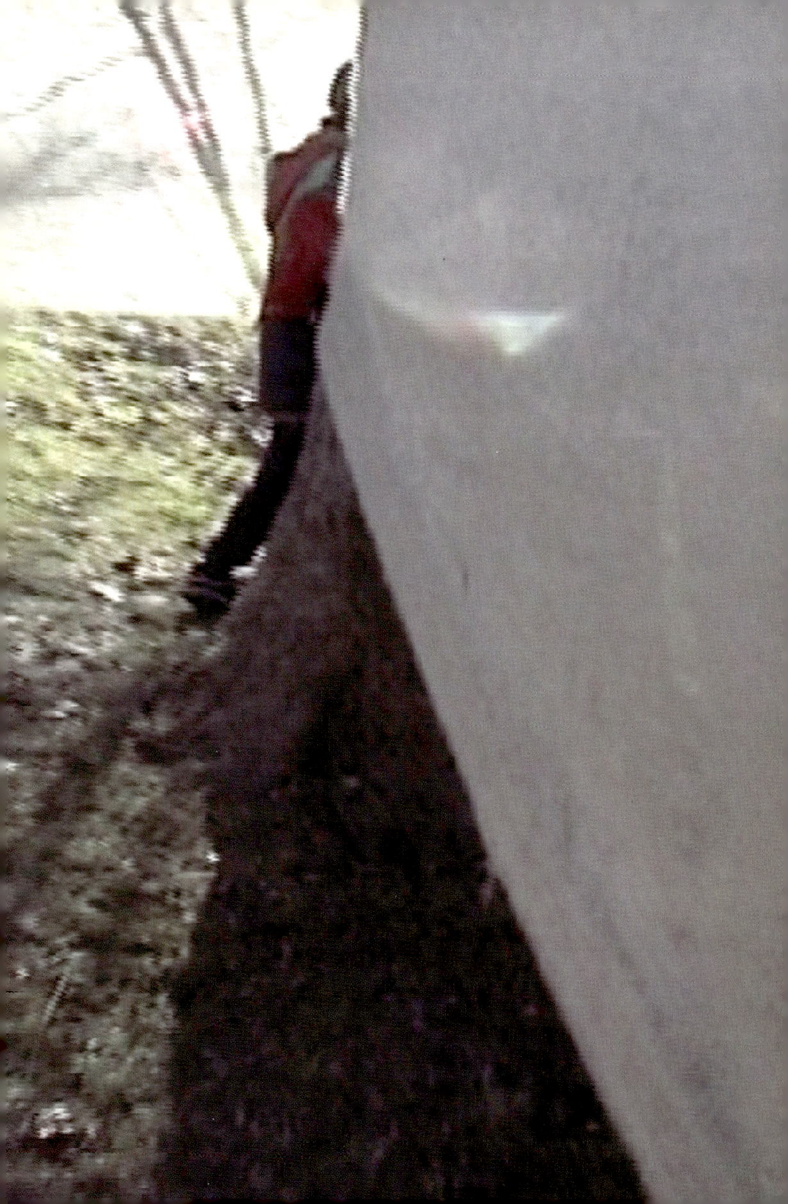

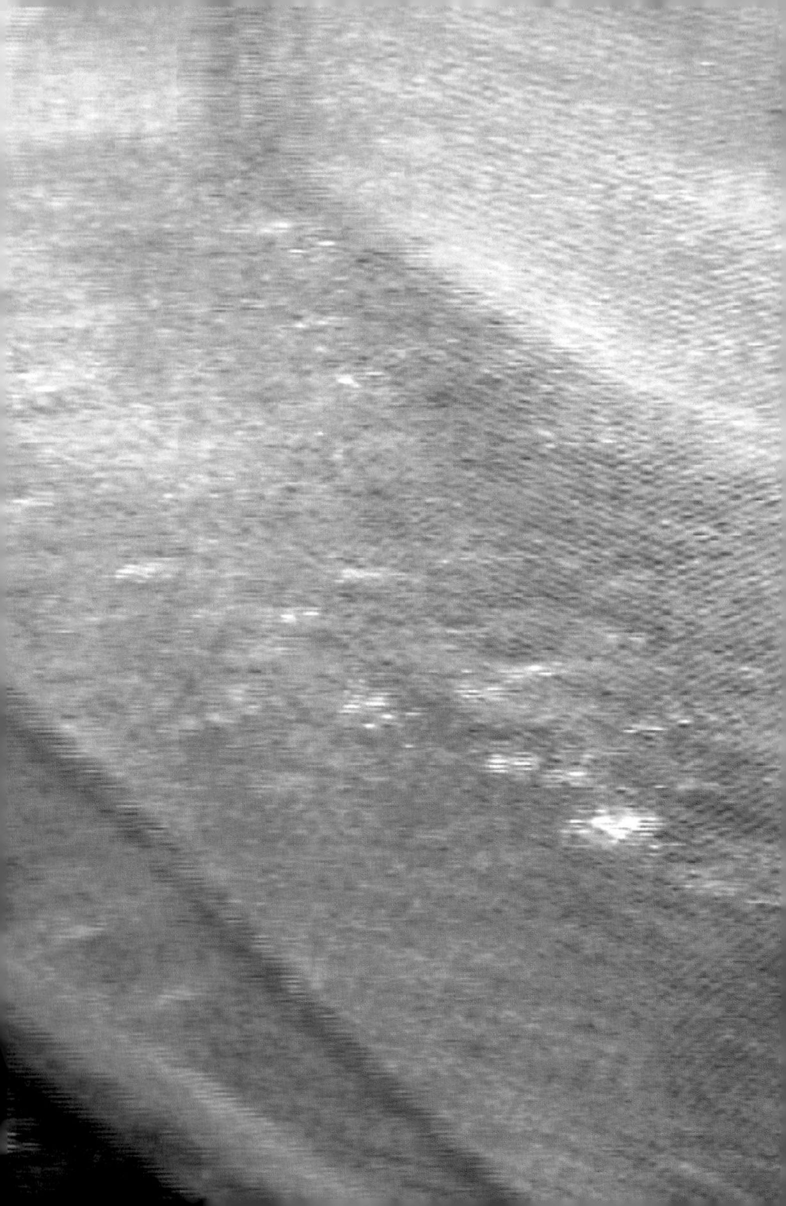

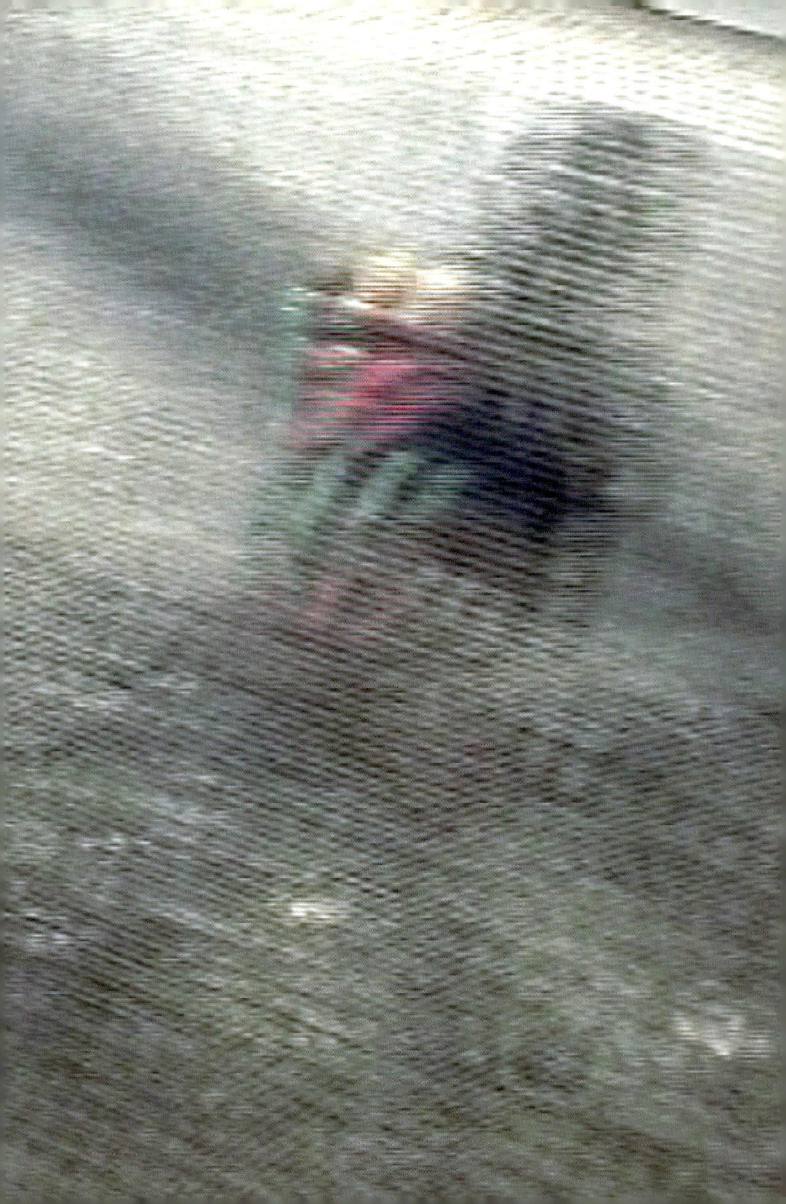

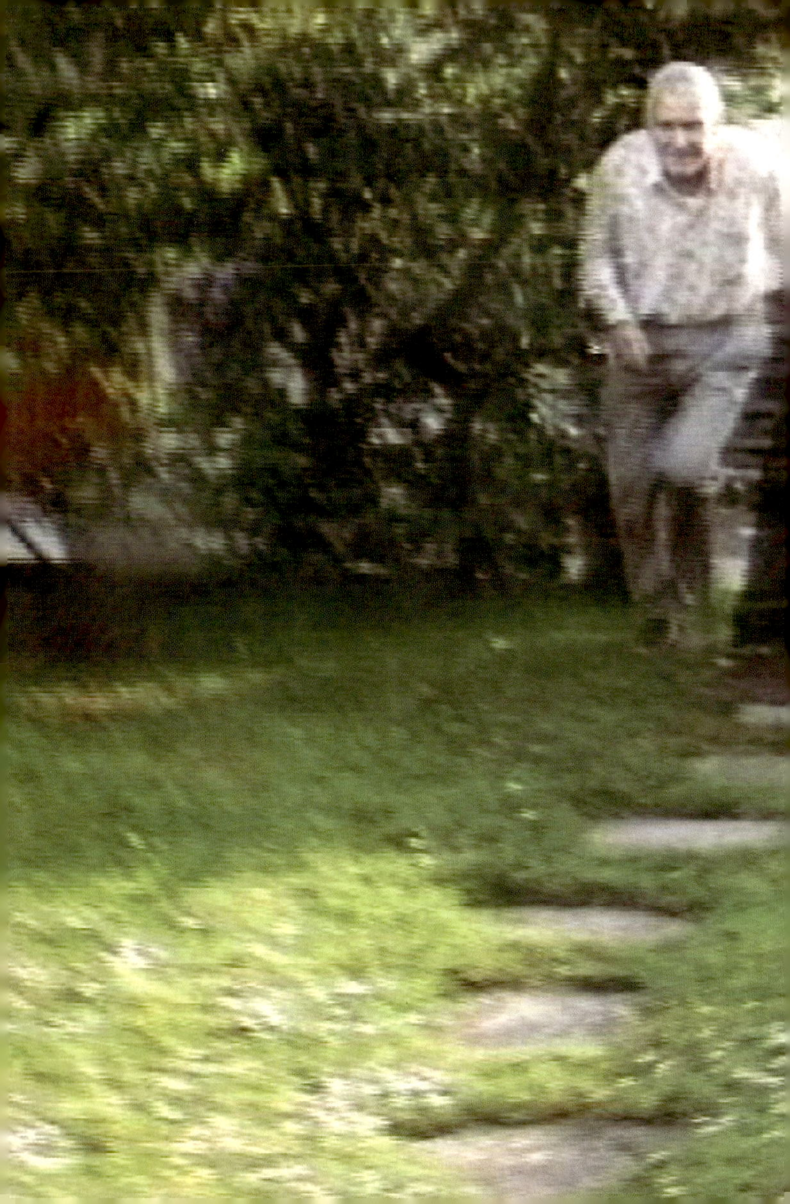

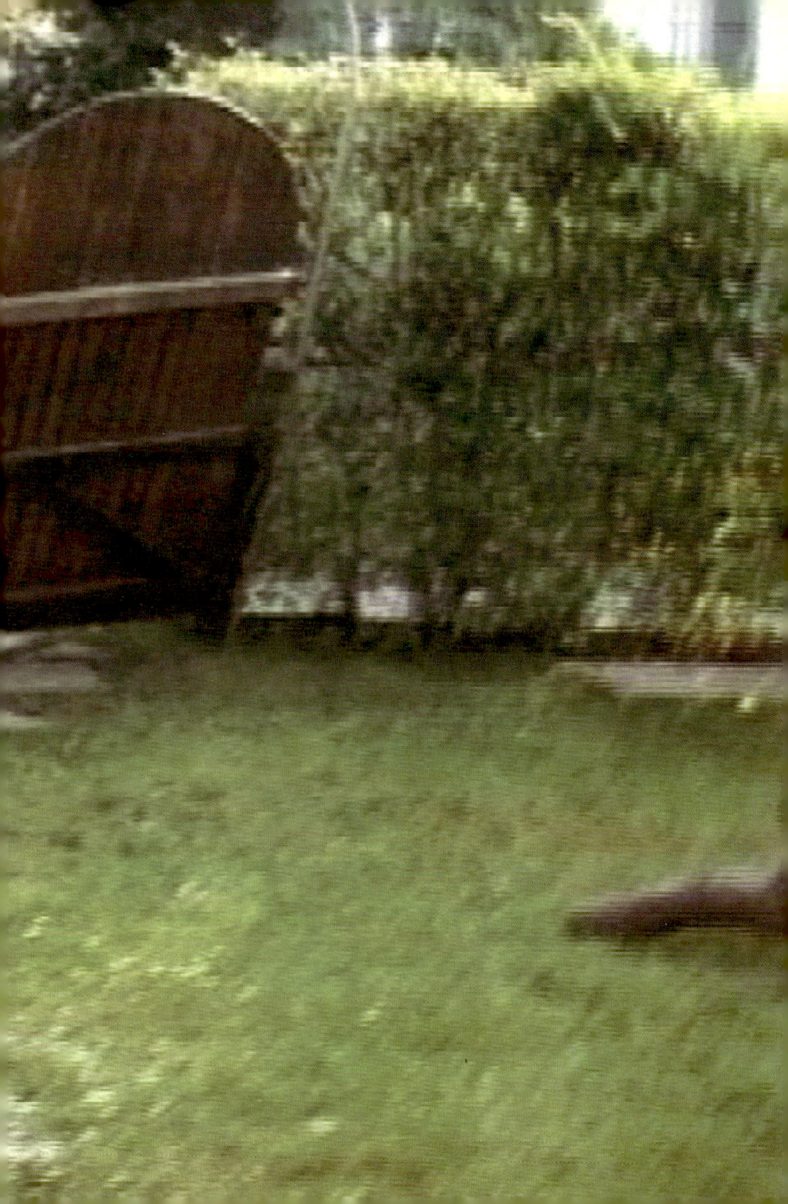

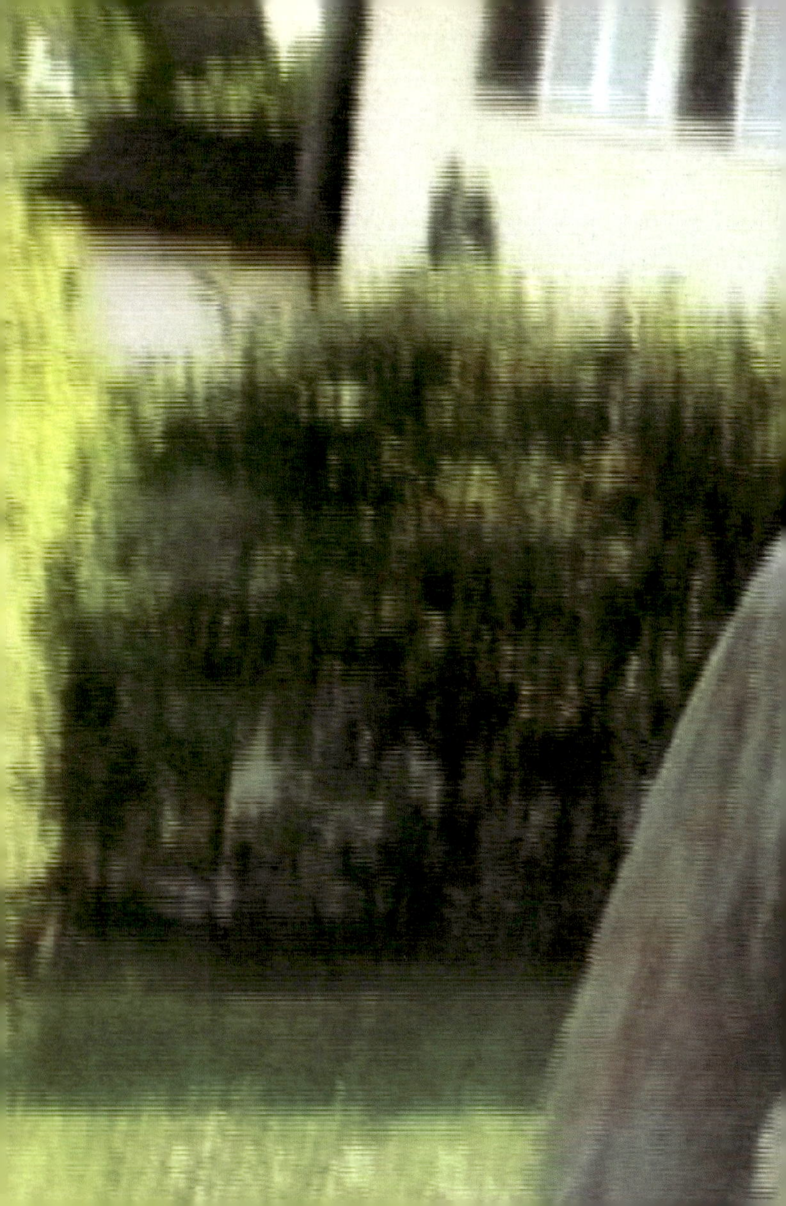

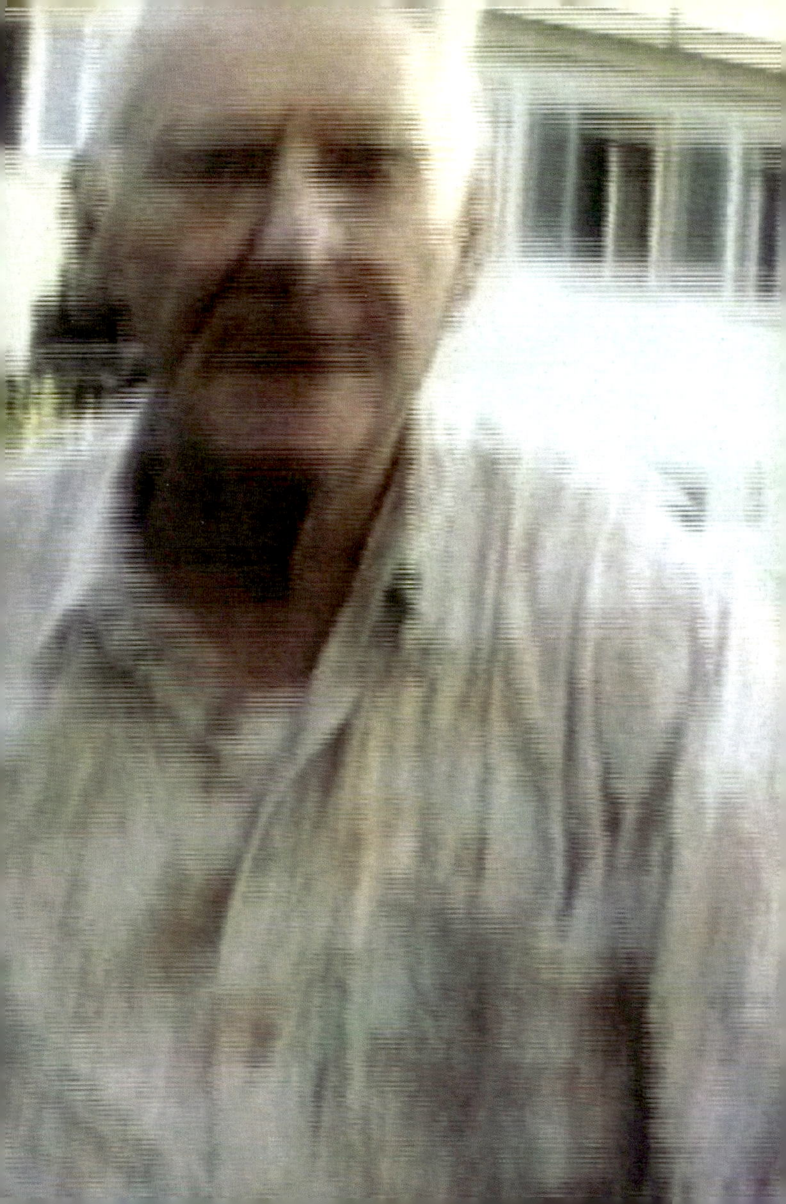

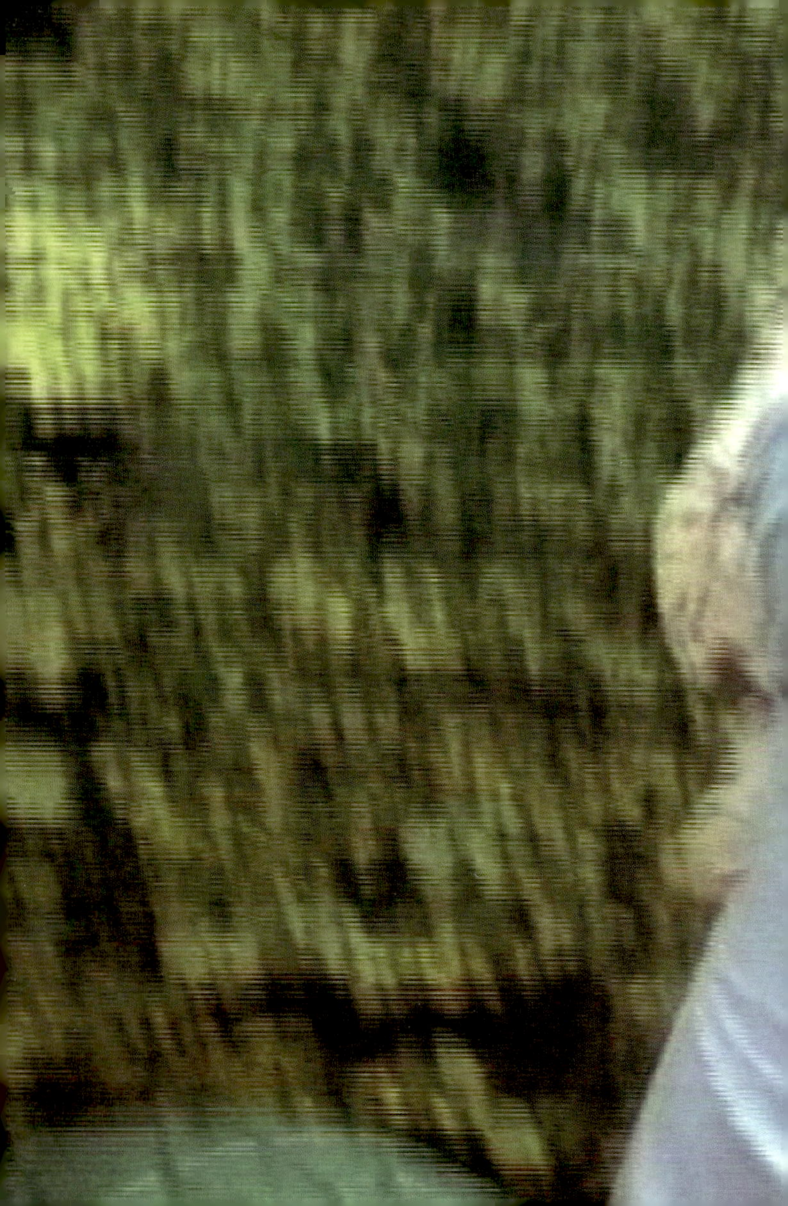

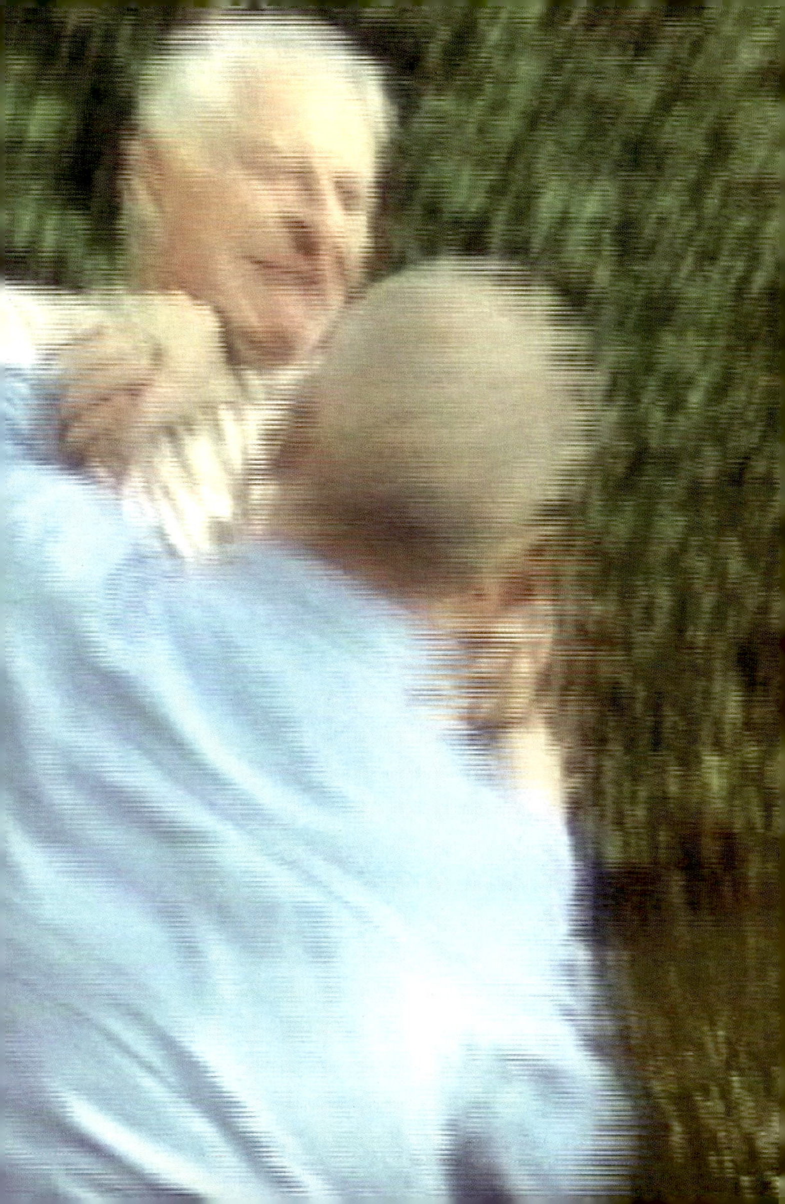

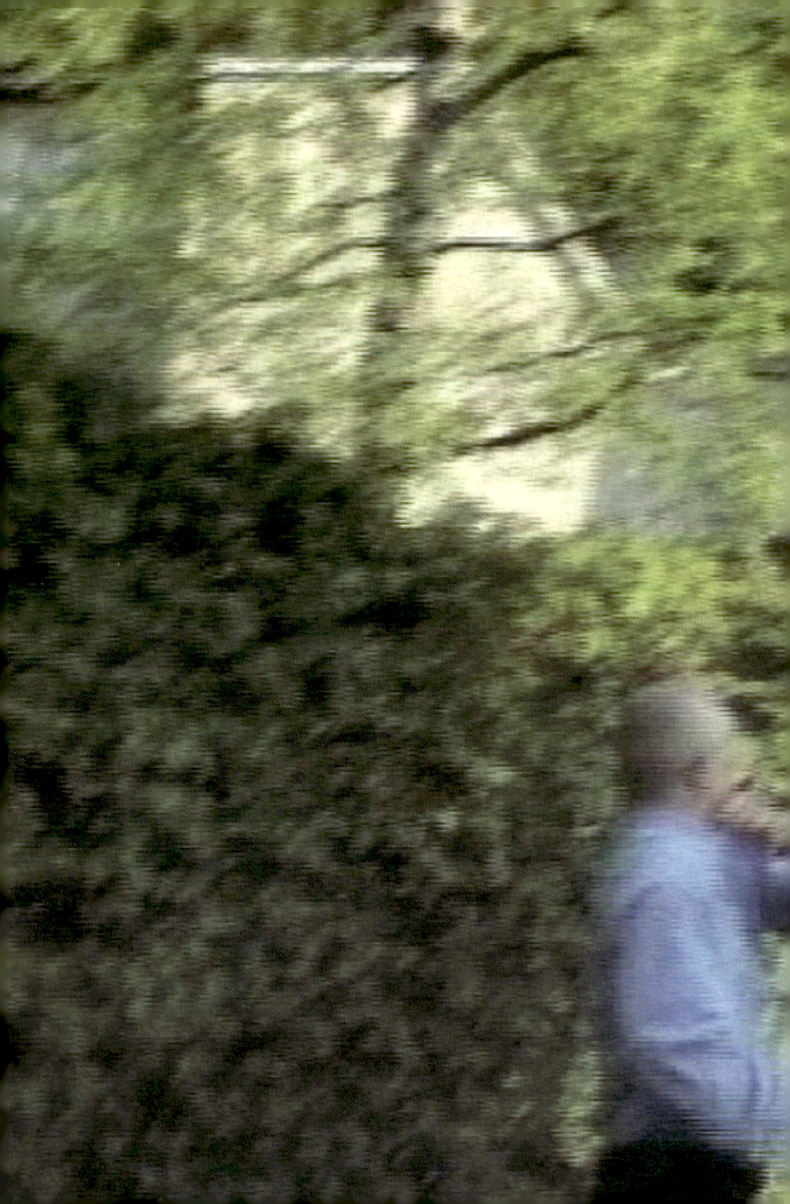

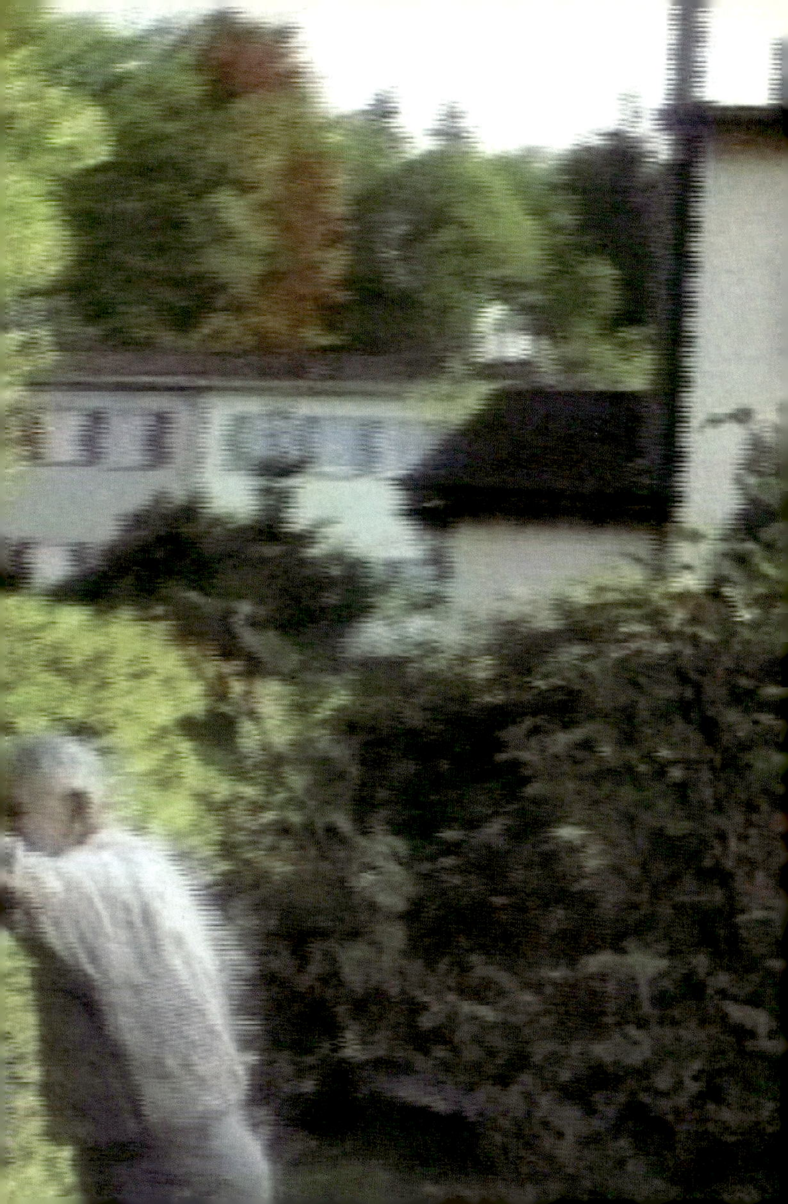

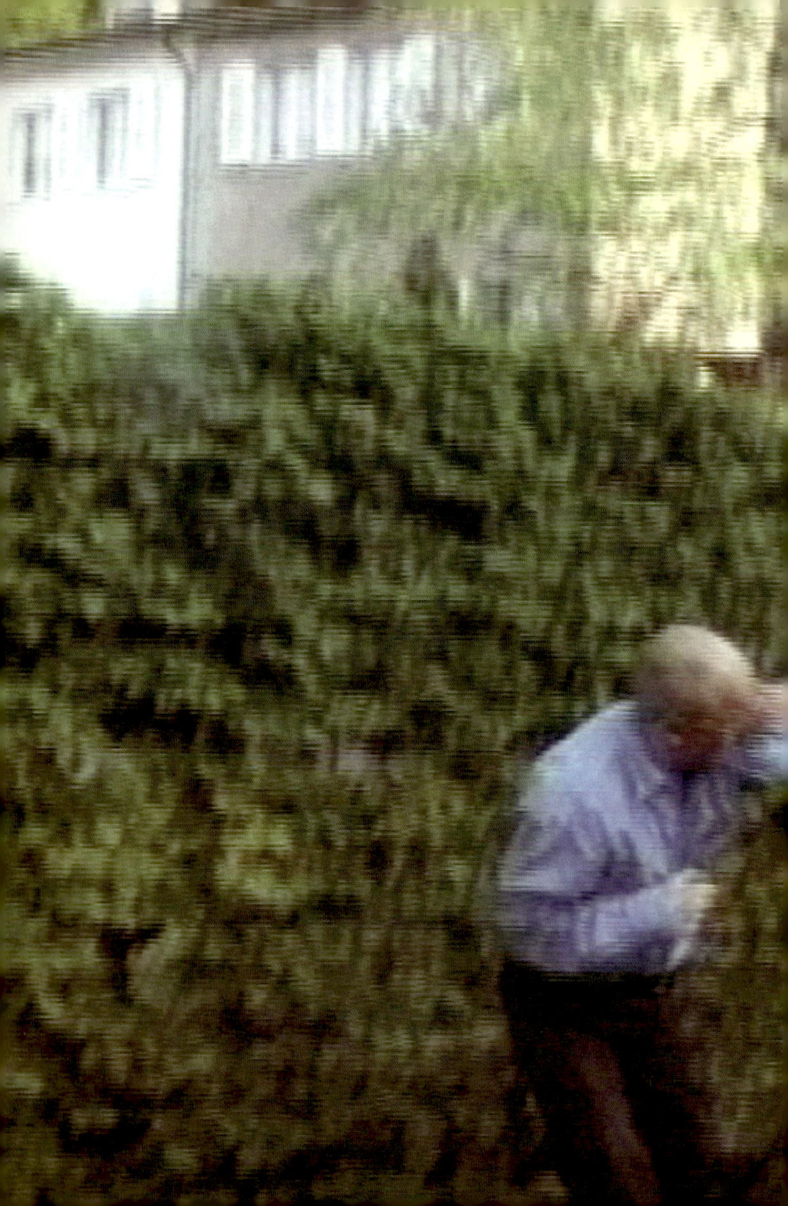

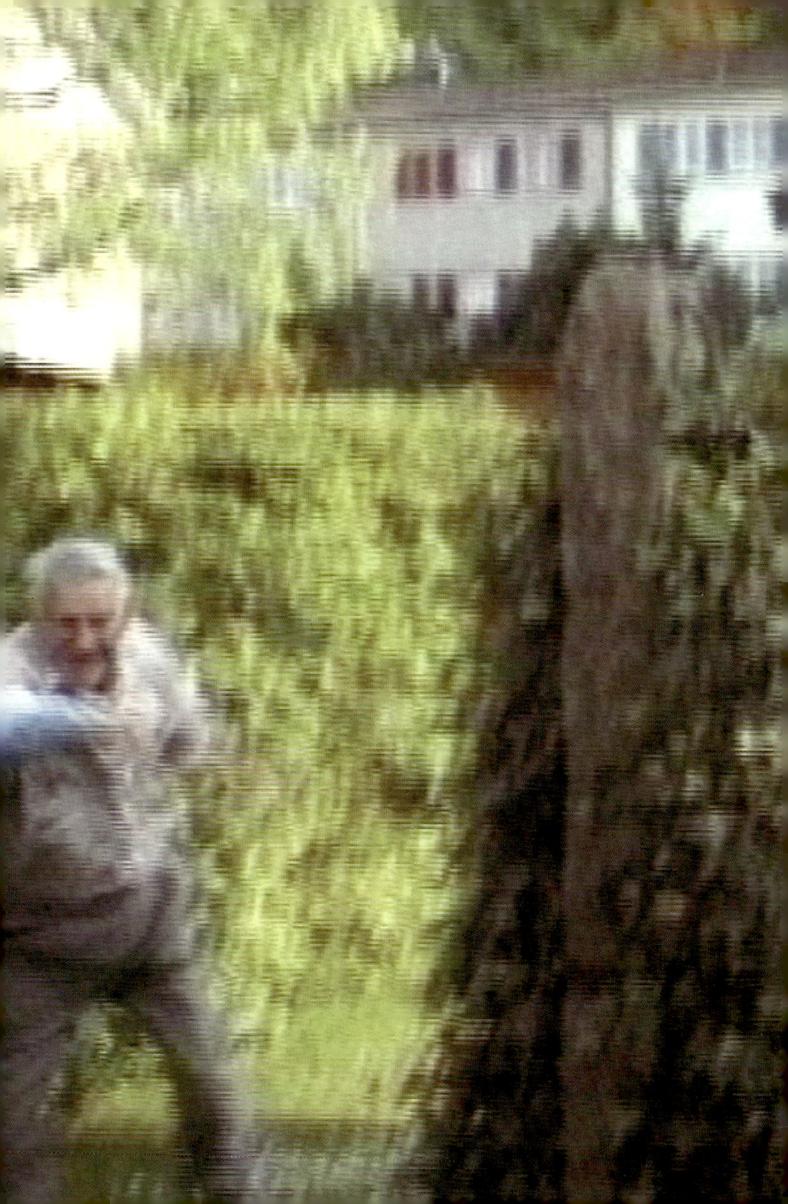

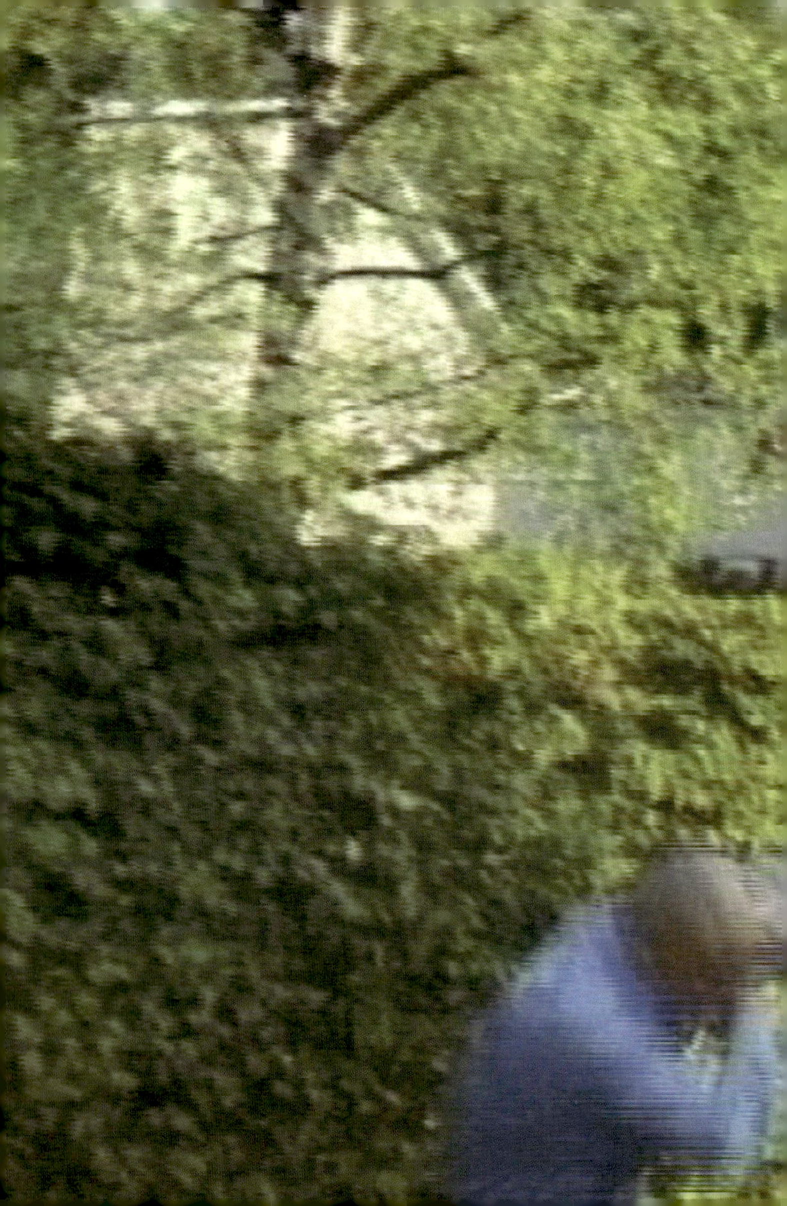

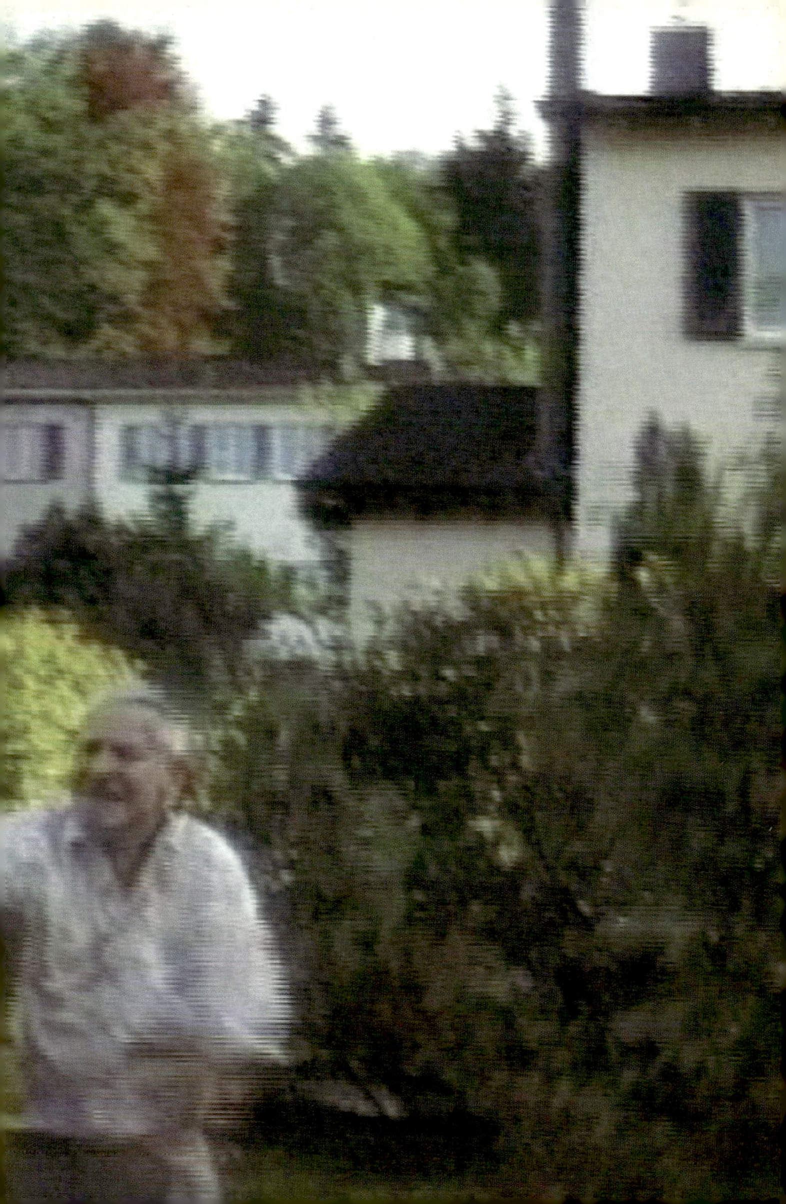

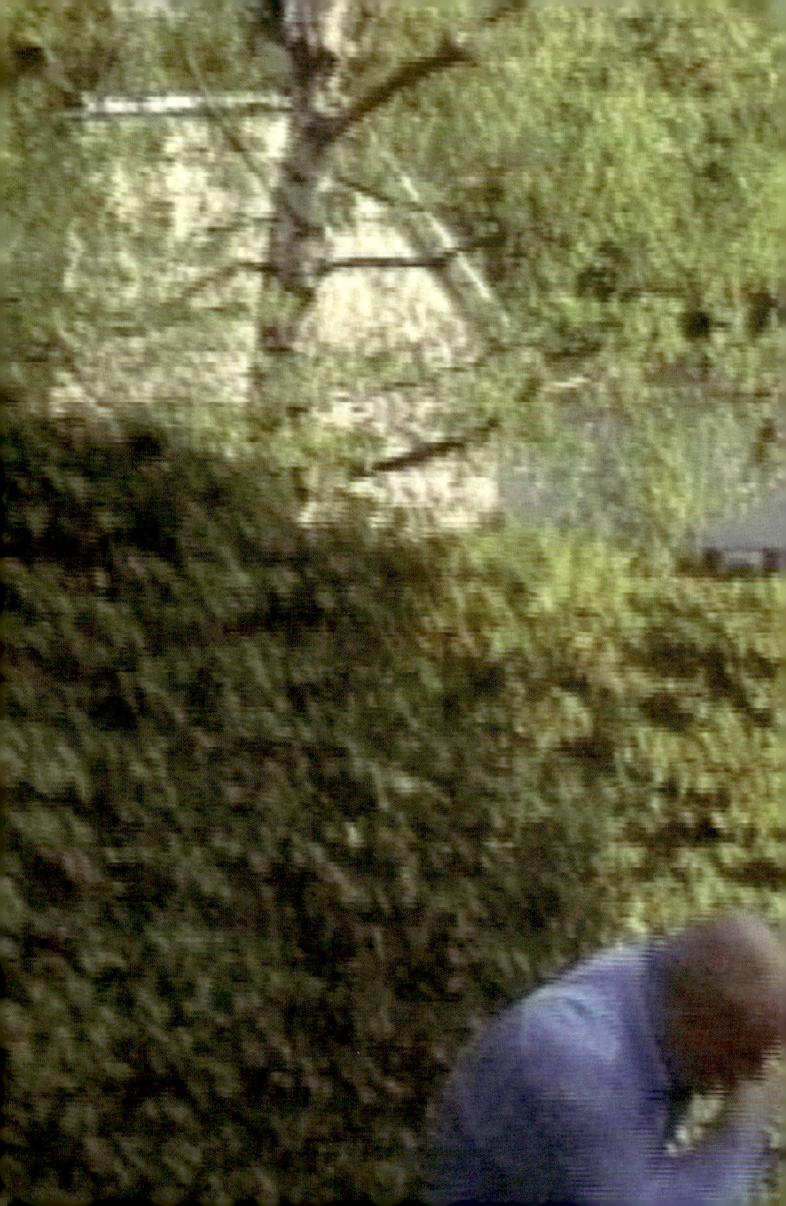

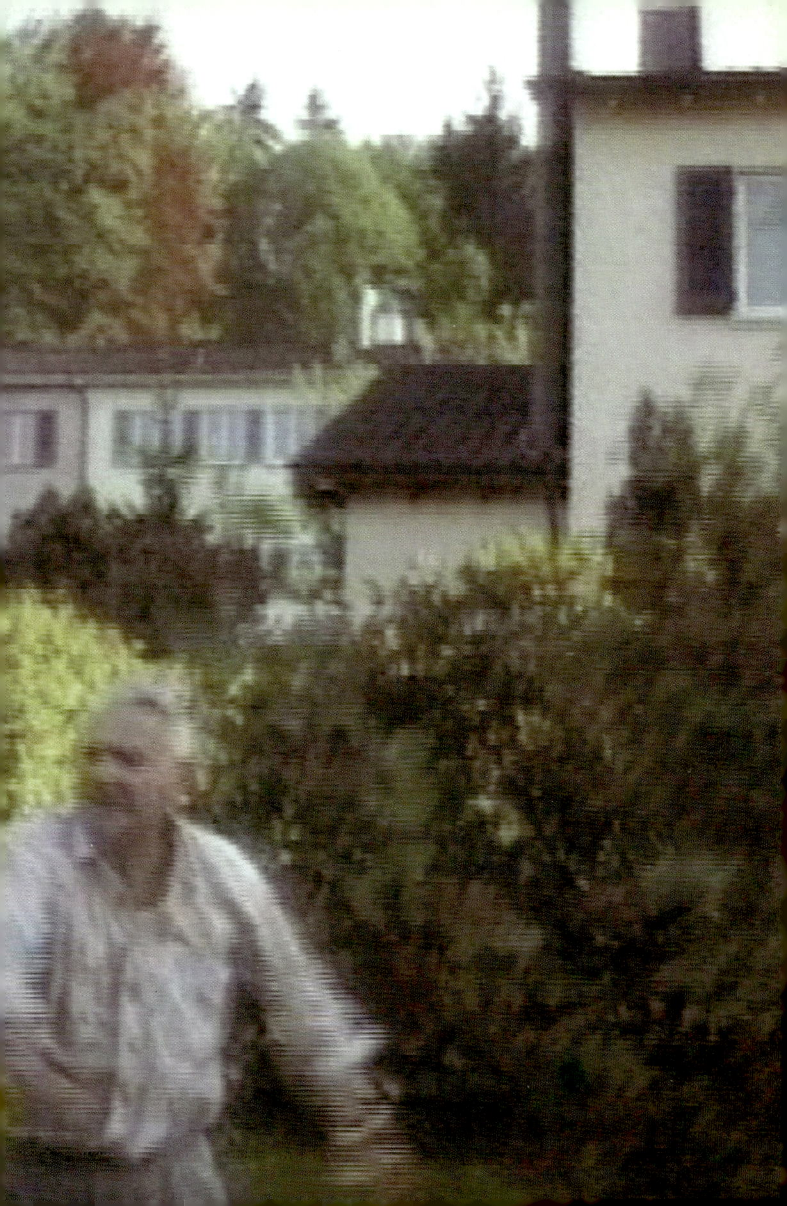

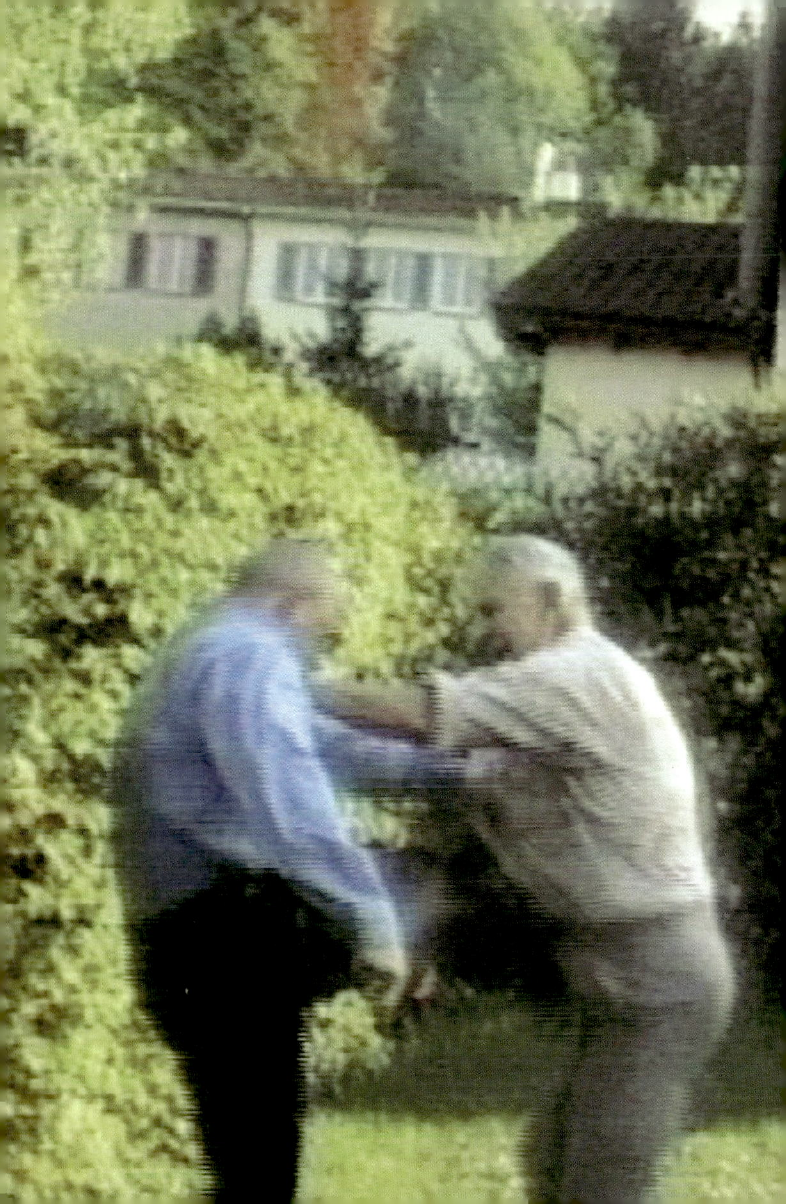

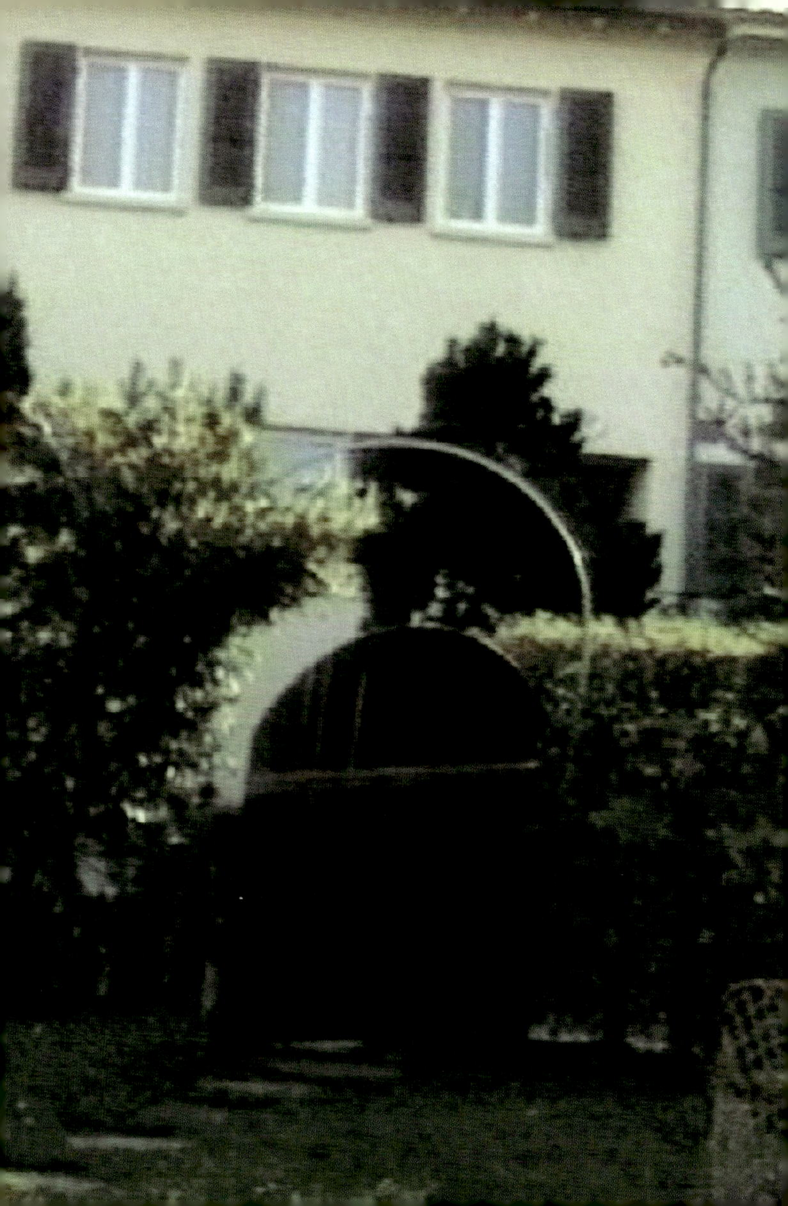

STEFAN BANZ – REAL REALITY

Christoph Doswald

"How real is reality?" – This was the question asked by the psychologist and communications researcher Paul Watzlawick as early as 1976, in the book of the same title, thus questioning any objective perception of reality.[1] Since then our image of the world and perception of reality have become even more radical, as all direct experiences of life have been translated into the media. Advertising, television, magazines, video and – more recently – the Internet are increasingly defining the framework and perspectives of our perception. The world is now largely experienced in images. We are aware that our impressions – that is, our perception of reality – cannot be objective, just as reality itself cannot be turned into anything objective. We expected truthfulness from technical aids such as photography and video, but they have become suspect. We seem to have understood now that images are often deceptive substitutes.

Yet despite the increasing relativity of media reality we still carry that sentimental desire for authenticity in our heart. And when we look at an image, we do want to know whether a given scene really took place as shown. The same paradox also faces us as we look at Stefan Banz's photographs and particularly his videos. This insecurity of perception was especially noticeable when Banz showed his work titled "Door to Door" to the public for the first time.[2] The video, which lasts several minutes, is about an argument between the artist and his neighbour in a modern terraced housing estate in Lucerne. Although the dispute about 'badly behaved' children and 'antisocial' artists ends in fisticuffs, the scene is neither exotic nor absurd, but a day-to-day occurrence of a petty bourgeois environment. After all, in our supposedly civilised society, frustration and prejudice do erupt in the form of such verbal and sometimes physical acts of violence, although they rarely leave the confines of the domestic sphere.

When mundane things are placed in a museum and are given a special aura through artistic treatment and the setting of a museum, then the viewer is faced with the essential question: artificial or real? "Door to Door" is a prototypical example of the discourse on this delicate difference.[3] Viewers who are unfamiliar with quarrels between neighbours, for instance, tend to suspect that there is some clever theatrical direction behind this violent sequence. Others take the scene at face value and have no doubts about its authenticity. The artist, in turn, pursues a strategy of renunciation. He does so by publishing a profoundly humiliating scene in his life: although he is years younger than his neighbour, he has to put up with physical violence from an old-age pensioner. His act of artistic creativity enables him to distance himself from the scene and thus to cope with it.

Seen against the background of notoriously propagandist war reporting, sensationalist live broadcasts and so-called docu-soaps, it is appropriate and indeed necessary both for the viewer and for the affected protagonists to reflect upon the scene. There is mutual interaction between the source of the scene (if there is a source), the motivation of the protagonists, the intention of the image-maker and the attitudes of the viewers. This interaction has its own effect on the "decoding" of the motion picture. With his video works, which now run to about 150 in all,[4] Banz submits an experimental set-up that occupies precisely this interface. All the sequences are everyday domestic family scenes. Some take no more than a few seconds, while others go on for several minutes. Yet all of them skilfully play off these paradoxical variables against each other, producing an equilibrium that is both enchanting and unsettling and which is threatening to collapse any moment. They are also expressions of a familiar environment: a petty bourgeois nuclear family, with a healthy façade that conceals something rather monstrous – a monstrosity which is in fact capable of causing this social narrowness and which very rarely appears in the videos themselves (except for "Door to Door") but is only conjured up through the images created in the viewer's head.

One element that characterises Banz's videos is their so-called documentary content, on the one hand, and their alienating, ambiguous effect causing associations to run through the viewer's mind, on the other. This effect develops its specific visual impact and independent-minded view of things. In "Scarborough Fair" (see page 162-163), for instance, we hear Banz's son Jonathan singing this well-known song (which, ironically, in its version by Simon & Garfunkel, is one of the most popular telephone tunes inflicted on people waiting for their calls to be answered). However, Banz does not show the lad directly but uses a translation technique which has quite a tradition in art history: he shows his mirror image, reflected by the smooth surface of some water. We can see straight away that this choice of imagery was influenced by the Narcissus myth. However, this only appears to be the case, like some virtual reality. What we see is not the silhouette of the boy, but of his sister Lena.[5] Yet, unless we actually know the two children, or unless we can tell them apart after watching Banz's other videos, we are unable to perceive this reality shift. This example is an excellent illustration of the complicated game that Banz plays with reality. Moreover, from time to time, we can see the artist's figure shining through the surface of the water, armed with a camera and evoking an entire new chain of further associations, ranging from Vermeer via Velazquez to Umbo and commenting on the subtle inclusion of the artist in the picture itself – somehow showing the author, yet shrouding him in mysterious semi-darkness.

In his work, Banz uses photography, video, installations, text and painting – techniques which, at first sight, display clear differences. While installations and painting are generally seen as genuine artistic statements, and photography suspends the space-time continuum for a fraction of a second, video prolongs the traditional illusion that it can record and depict reality. Banz's use of these media, however, is a plea for an interdisciplinary approach, emphasising the points they have in common, while at the same time pointing out differences. Despite the everyday character of his motifs, Banz is thus examining the very nature of the media in his œuvre. This was particularly noticeable in an installation set up by Banz at the Ars Futura Gallery in Zurich in summer 1999.[6] While presenting a series of small-format imitations of Francis Bacon paintings in acrylic ("Baby Bacons") in the main hall, he also confronted visitors with a provocative ensemble of paintings and videos in a small cabinet. He placed several small-format paintings on the wall, which he painted using motifs from his own photographic works. What was originally a rather mundane snapshot from a photograph album but had been absorbed by the art market, was now given an additional aura of art through this traditional artistic medium.

On the floor of the cabinet there were two television monitors showing short video loops entitled "Lick (Doggy)" (page 26-27) and "Jump (Doggy)" (page 18-25) – two sequences with special significance in the context of these art media reflections. They showed Banz's daughter Lena imitating a dog, crawling around grandma's house on all fours, barking and sitting up and begging in a doggy-like manner. Banz had started by capturing this juvenile activity with his camera. He then duplicated it, recorded one of the duplicates backwards and put together the forward and backward sequences in a loop. In this way he not only constructed a strange, persistent sequence but also reflected upon the role of the subject – a girl who, like the rest of the family, has long ceased to take any notice of the continuously present camera, thus showing a genuinely novel understanding of the media. This new understanding is directly opposed to

Roland Barthes' view, which used to be accepted as universal: "When I pose before the lens," he wrote, "(I mean, when I know that I am posing, be it only temporarily), I don't take much of a risk (at least not for the moment). [...] Yet no matter how imaginary this dependence may be (and it is pure imagination), I do experience it with the same apprehension with which one anticipates an uncertain childhood: a picture – my picture – is about to be created."[7]

[1] *Paul Watzlawick,* How Real is Real?: Confusion, Disinformation, Communication, New York 1977

[2] *On the occasion of the* NONCHALANCE *exhibition at the Centre Pasqu'art in Biel from August 31 to October 26, 1997.*

[3] *On the subject of cultural perception among the educated middle classes, see the study by the French sociologist Pierre Bourdieu,* Distinction: a Social Critique of the Judgement of Taste, Cambridge 1994. *Bourdieu recently also wrote a study on the role of television against the background of the reality shift between the world and images. Pierre Bourdieu,* On Television,*London 1998.*

[4] *Cf. pp. 164-165,* Video Works 1997-1999. *The only item that is missing from this list is Banz's first one of 1994: "Where Did You Sleep Last Night" – a video about the reality and the death of the teenage idol Kurt Cobain, who had just died at the time.*

[5] *"Scarborough Fair" was conceived as a further development of* "Where Did You Sleep Last Night" *– Cf. note 4.*

[6] *Stefan Banz,* Gods + Monsters, *Ars Futura Gallery, May 22 – July 10, 1997*

[7] *Roland Barthes,* Die helle Kammer, Bemerkung zur Photographie, *Frankfurt am Main, 1985, p. 19 (Roland Barthes,* Camera Lucida: Reflections on Photography, *New York 1981)*

STEFAN BANZ – WIRKLICHE WIRKLICHKEIT
Christoph Doswald

«Wie wirklich ist die Wirklichkeit?» fragte der Psychologe und Kommunikationsforscher Paul Watzlawick bereits 1976 in seinem gleichnamigen Buch und stellte damit die objektive Wahrnehmung der Realität zur Disposition.[1] Seither hat sich unser Bild von der Welt, die Wahrnehmung des Realen, nochmals radikalisiert. Denn aus unmittelbaren Lebenserfahrungen sind mediale Übersetzungen geworden. Werbung, Fernsehen, Illustrierte, Video und neuerdings das Internet definieren zunehmend den Ausschnitt und die Perspektive unseres Blicks. Welt wird heute grösstenteils als Bild erfahren. Wir wissen: unsere Eindrücke, unsere Perzeption der Wirklichkeit, ist niemals objektiv – genausowenig wie das Wirkliche objektiviert werden kann. Technische Hilfsmittel, wie etwa die Fotografie oder das Video, von denen wir uns Wahrheit versprochen hatten, sind in Verdacht geraten. Bilder, das scheint heute klar zu sein, sind oftmals Simulakren.

Trotz diesem Prozess, der Relativierung von medialer Wahrnehmung, tragen wir noch immer den sentimentalen Wunsch nach dem Authentischen im Herzen. Und wenn wir Bilder sehen, dann fragen wir uns immer, ob das Gezeigte so stattgefunden hat. Diesem Paradox sind auch die Betrachter der Fotografien und vor allem der Videos von Stefan Banz ausgesetzt. Deutlich konnte diese Verunsicherung der Wahrnehmung beobachtet werden, als Banz das Werk mit dem Titel «Door to Door» erstmals der Öffentlichkeit vorführte.[2] Das mehrminütige Videoband zeigt eine Auseinandersetzung des Künstlers mit seinem Nachbarn in einem Luzerner Reihenhausquartier. Obwohl der Disput über 'unartige' Kinder und 'asoziale' Künstler zur handfesten Schlägerei eskaliert, handelt es sich beim Gezeigten um keine exotische, abstruse Handlung, sondern um ein alltägliches Geschehen in der Enge der kleinbürgerlichen Existenz. Frustrationen und Vorurteile entladen sich nun einmal in einer 'zivilisierten Gesellschaft' als derartige verbale und manches Mal auch körperliche Gewalthandlungen, die allerdings den Rahmen des Domestizierten selten verlassen.

Wenn das Profane in den Rahmen des Museums gestellt wird, wenn es eine auratische Überhöhung durch künstlerische Diktion und kuratorische Inszenierung erfährt, dann stellt sich bei den Betrachtern die Entscheidungsfrage: artifiziell oder real? «Door to Door» steht als prototypisches Beispiel für diesen Diskurs des 'feinen Unterschieds'.[3] Betrachter, denen nachbarschaftliche Streitigkeiten fremd sind, neigen etwa dazu, hinter der gewalttätigen Sequenz eine raffinierte theatralische Inszenierung zu vermuten. Andere Betrachter nehmen die Handlung zum Nennwert und hegen keinerlei Zweifel an ihrer Authentizität. Der Künstler wiederum betreibt mit dem Veröffentlichen einer zutiefst erniedrigenden Begebenheit aus seinem Leben – obwohl um Jahre jünger als der Nachbar, muss er sich vom Rentner Schläge gefallen lassen – eine Strategie der Entäusserung. Seine künstlerische Setzung schafft Distanz zu seinem unmittelbaren Erleben, ja, sie dient der Vergangenheitsbewältigung.

Vor dem Hintergrund notorisch propagandistischer Kriegsberichterstattung, sensationslüsterner Reality-TV-Übertragungen und sogenannter Doku-Soaps sind solche Überlegungen der Betrachter und der beteiligten Akteure berechtigt und nötig. Die Quelle des Bildes (wenn es denn eine gibt), die Motive der Akteure, die Intention des Bildermachers und die Haltungen der Betrachter stehen in einer wechselseitigen Beziehung, welche die Decodierung des laufenden Bildes mitbestimmt. Banz legt in seinem videastischen Werk, das mittlerweile an die 150 Bänder umfasst[4], eine Versuchsanordnung vor, die exakt diese Schnittstelle besetzt. Die dem häuslichen Alltag mit seiner Familie entstammenden Sequenzen – manche sind nur einige Sekunden lang, andere dauern mehrere Minuten – spielen gekonnt und präzis diese paradoxalen Variablen gegeneinander aus und erzeugen ein zugleich bezauberndes wie beunruhigendes Gleichgewicht, das jeden Moment zu kippen droht. Hier artikuliert sich gleichzeitig das vertraute Dasein der kleinbürgerlichen Kernfamilie, hinter deren heiler Fassade das Monströse lauert, welche diese gesellschaftliche Enge hervorbringen kann – Monströses, das nur selten im Video selbst (mit Ausnahme von «Door to Door») zu sehen ist, sondern vielmehr erst durch die Bilder im Kopf der Betrachter evoziert wird.

Charakteristisch an den Videos von Banz ist einerseits ihr sogenannter dokumentarischer Gehalt und anderseits die verfremdende, vieldeutige und assoziationsreiche Wirkung, die seine spezifische Optik, sein eigenwilliger Blick auf die Dinge entwickelt. Im Video «Scarborough Fair» (Abb. S. 162-163) hören wir beispielsweise seinen Sohn Jonathan beim singenden Vortrag der bekannten gleichnamigen englischen Volksweise (in der Version von Simon & Garfunkel ironischerweise eine der beliebtesten Melodien, die dem in die Warteschlaufe delegierten Telefonierer zugemutet wird). Banz erfasst jedoch den Buben nicht direkt im Bild, sondern benutzt eine Übersetzung, die als Motiv in der Kunstgeschichte Tradition besitzt: er zeigt das Spiegelbild des Singenden, wie es von einer glatten Wasserfläche reflektiert wird – es ist auf den ersten

Blick leicht zu erkennen, dass bei dieser Bildfindung der Narziss-Mythos Pate gestanden hat. Diese Erkenntnis aber hat nur scheinbare oder virtuelle Gültigkeit, in Wirklichkeit nämlich sehen wir gar nicht die Silhouette des singenden Buben, sondern die seiner Schwester Lena.[5] Wer die beiden Kinder aber nicht wirklich kennt oder sie nicht aus der Kenntnis von anderen Banz'schen Videoarbeiten zu unterscheiden vermag, ist nicht in der Lage diese Realitätsverschiebung wirklich wahrzunehmen. Dieses Beispiel zeigt ausgezeichnet, welch vertracktes Spiel Banz mit der Wirklichkeit spielt. Wenn dazu noch die Figur des Künstlers, bewaffnet mit einer Kamera, immer mal wieder in der Wasserfläche aufscheint, dann evoziert das eine neue Kette von Assoziationen, die von Vermeer über Velazquez bis hin zu Umbo reicht und das subtile Ins-Bild-Setzen des Bildproduzenten thematisiert, den Urheber benennt und ihn dennoch im geheimnisvollen Halbdunkel belässt.

Banz arbeitet mit Fotografie, Video, Installation, Text und Malerei. Diese Techniken weisen auf den ersten Blick deutliche Differenzen auf. Während zum Beispiel die Installation und die Malerei gemeinhin als genuine künstlerische Setzungen gelten und die Fotografie das Raum-Zeit-Kontinuum für einen Sekundenbruchteil aufhebt, verlängert das Video die klassische Illusion, Wirklichkeit erfassen und abbilden zu können. Die Banz'sche Benutzung dieser Medien plädiert hingegen für Interdisziplinarität. Er betont in seinen Werken das Gemeinsame, weist auf Differenzen hin und führt somit, trotz der gängigen Motivik, einen regelrechten Mediendiskurs innerhalb seines Gesamtwerks. Besonders evident wurde dies in einer Installation, die Banz im Sommer 1999 in der Zürcher Galerie Ars Futura vorstellte.[6] Während er im Hauptraum der Galerie eine Serie von kleinformatigen, in Acryl gemalten Imitaten der Gemälde von Francis Bacon präsentierte («Baby Bacons»), setzte er den Ausstellungsbesuchern in einem kleinen Kabinett ein provozierendes Ensemble von Malerei und Video vor. An der Wand platzierte er kleinformatige Bilder, die er basierend auf den Motiven eigener Fotos angefertigt hatte. Der ursprünglich profane Schnappschuss aus dem Familienalbum, bereits vom Kunstmarkt absorbiert, wurde mit Hilfe der Malerei, des klassischen künstlerischen Mediums, zusätzlich auratisiert.

Am Boden des Kabinetts befanden sich zwei Fernsehmonitore, die – unter den Titeln «Lick (Doggy)» (Abb. S. 26-27) und «Jump (Doggy)» (Abb. S. 18-25) – kurze Video-Loops zeigten. Beide vorgestellten Sequenzen besitzen im Kontext dieser Kunst-Medien-Reflexion besondere Bedeutung. Sie zeigen seine Tochter Lena, wie sie einen

Hund imitiert, auf allen Vieren auf dem Boden von Grossmutters Wohnung herumkriecht, bellt und Männchen macht. Banz hat diese kindliche Handlung zuerst einmal mit der Kamera festgehalten. Dann hat er die Bildfolge dupliziert und eines der Duplikate mit rückwartslaufender Handlung aufgezeichnet. Indem er nun die chronologisch richtige und die falsche Sequenz in einem Loop zusammenbringt, konstruiert er nicht nur eine befremdliche, eindringliche Bildfolge, sondern reflektiert auch die Rolle des Bildobjekts – eine Tochter, die genauso wie die ganze Familie längst keine Notiz mehr von der permanent anwesenden Kamera nimmt und damit der einstmals gültigen Beobachtung von Roland Barthes ein genuin neues Medienverständnis entgegenhält. «Wenn ich mich vor dem Objektiv in Pose setze», schrieb Barthes, «(will sagen: wenn ich weiss, dass ich posiere, und sei es nur vorübergehend), so riskiere ich damit nicht viel (jedenfalls nicht für den Augenblick). [...] Diese Abhängigkeit mag aber noch so imaginär sein (und sie ist reinste Einbildung), so erlebe ich sie gleichwohl mit der Beklommenheit, mit der man einer ungewissen Kindschaft entgegensieht: ein Bild – mein Bild – wird entstehen.»[7]

[1] *Paul Watzlawick*, Wie wirklich ist die Wirklichkeit?; Wahn, Täuschung, Verstehen, München 1976

[2] *Anlässlich der Ausstellung* NONCHALANCE *im Centre Pasq'art, Biel, 31. August bis 26. Oktober 1997.*

[3] *Vgl. zur Thematik der bildungsbürgerlichen Kulturwahrnehmung die Untersuchung des französischen Soziologen Pierre Bourdieu,* Die feinen Unterschiede – Kritik der gesellschaftlichen Urteilskraft, *Frankfurt am Main 1987. Bourdieu hat vor kurzem auch eine Untersuchung über die Rolle des Fernsehens vor dem Hintergrund der Realitätsverschiebung zwischen Welt und Bild vorgelegt. Pierre Bourdieu,* Über das Fernsehen, *Frankfurt am Main 1998.*

[4] *Vgl. S. 164-165:* Video Works 1997 – 1999. *Auf dieser Liste fehlt nur die erste, bereits 1994 entstandene Arbeit «Where Did You Sleep Last Night», die sich mit Realität und Tod des damals gerade verstorbenen Teen-Idols Kurt Cobain beschäftigte.*

[5] *«Scarborough Fair» ist konzeptionell die Weiterentwicklung von «Where Did You Sleep Last Night», vgl. Anm. 4.*

[6] *Stefan Banz,* Gods + Monsters, *Ars Futura Galerie, 22. Mai bis 10. Juli 1999*

[7] *Roland Barthes,* Die helle Kammer, Bemerkung zur Photographie, *Frankfurt am Main, 1985, S. 19*

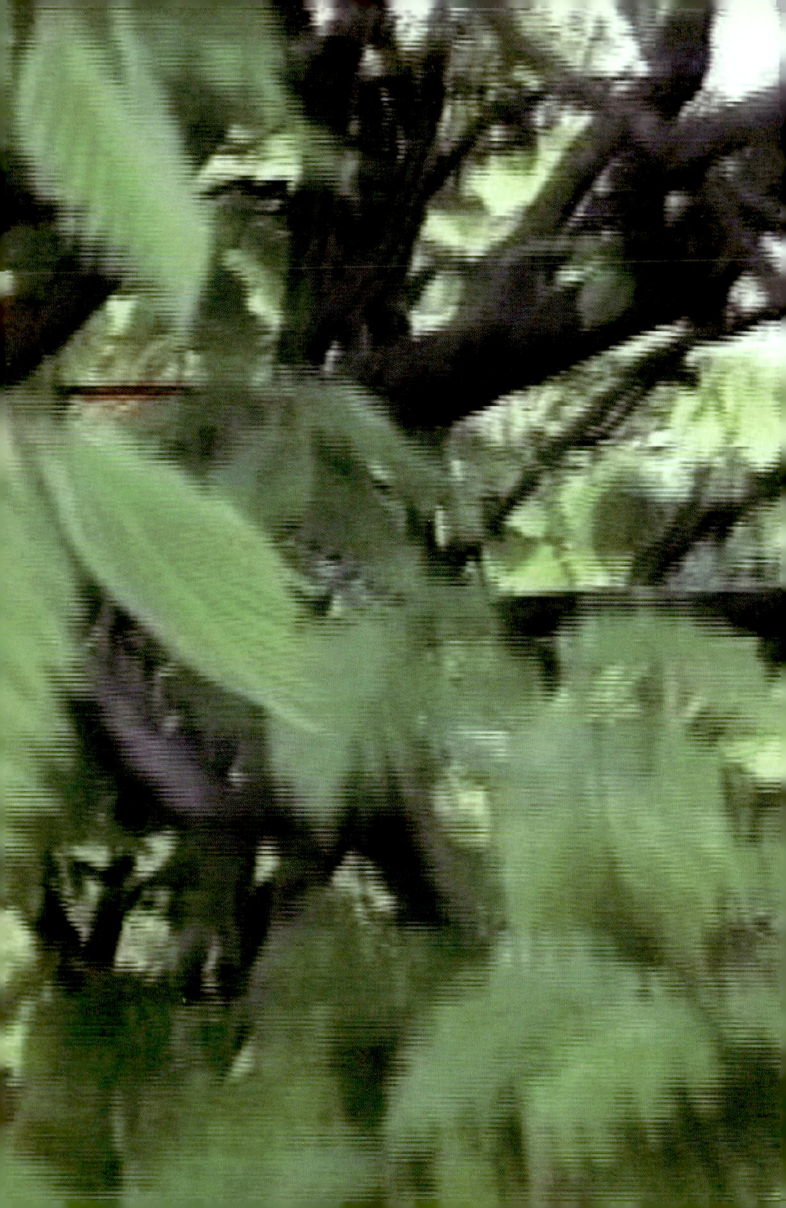

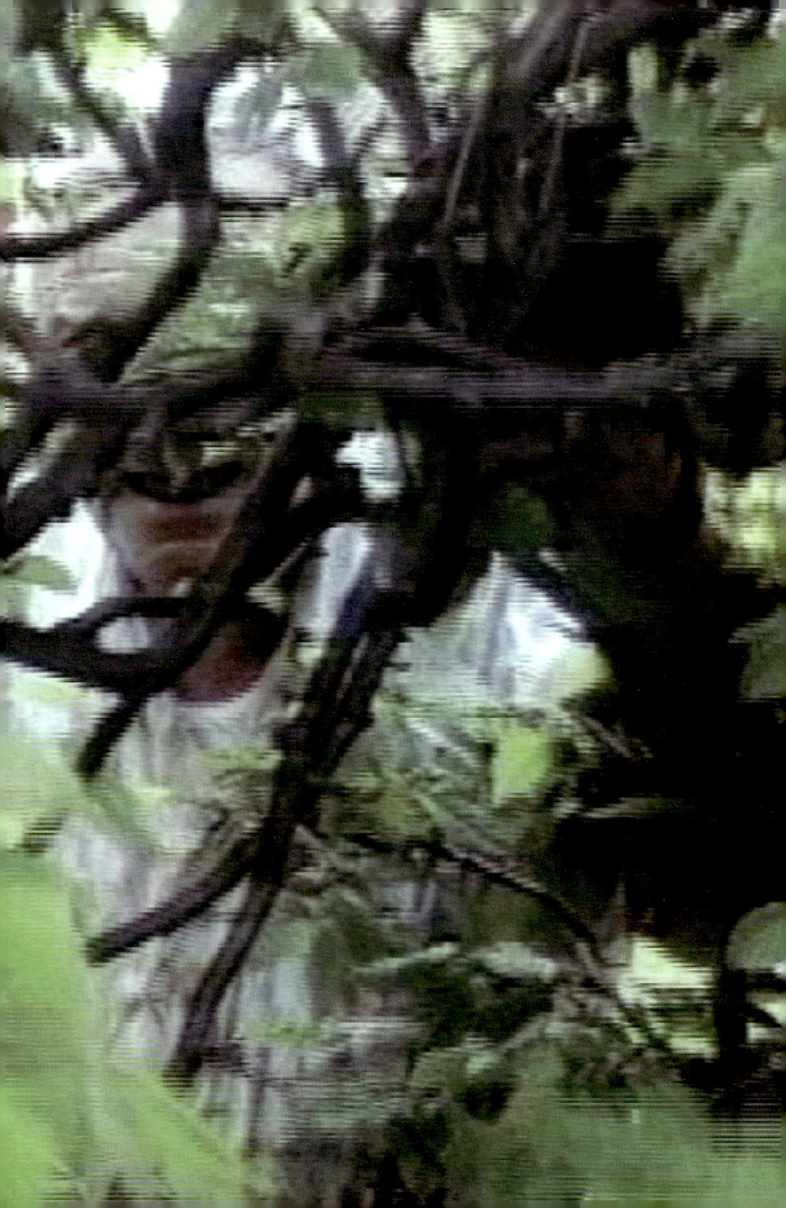

THE FIGURATION OF THE COMMONPLACE
Thomas Wulffen

What's Left?

Not much, we might say at the end of this decade and this century. All systems –
whether technical or ideological – are being integrated into a comprehensive whole.
Alternative options are only possible to the extent that they stabilise the overall system. Any antagonisms become a saleable perfume (*Contradiction* by Calvin Klein). Art
becomes an appendage of advertising in the tourist industry or dissolves in its own
Bermuda triangle of service, entertainment and the theory of knowledge. "What is more
fluid than water? Art – it's superfluous."[1] The familiar boundaries between genres have
cancelled each other out. A *white cube* becomes a *club event*. Art picks up where art
leaves off, because photography is of the same value as painting. The Internet is a way
of painting with different means, even though it pretends to be something quite different. But the present has always existed, although 'presence' is the motto of our time.
The public media are doing their utmost to demolish the borderline between privacy
and publicity. Yet all they do is move in such a way that the familiar dichotomy stops
being perceived altogether. Dissidence only occurs on the edges, so that it is almost
unnoticeable. It does not make itself known with any clarity, but mimics others to avoid
being absorbed and to remain effective.

Middle of the Road

They don't pretend to be different from the others. What Stefan Banz shows on his
videos are everyday stories which do not deny their private family background. The main
characters are called by name: they are his own children – the characters who figure
in his photographs. Whenever they stop short for a moment, an event is put at the centre of these videos. We only see an extract of the event, though it obviously has a beginning and an end. Yet the viewer knows that this beginning and this end are only part
of another beginning and another end. The diachronic aspect of the videos distin-
guishes them from the synchronicity of a photograph. Synchronous exposure and light-
ing give each photograph its own specific artificiality, which a video could not have
achieved without the artist's intervention. In 'The Transfiguration of the Commonplace'
Arthur C. Danto writes: "… the greater the degree of realism intended, the greater the
need for external indicators that it is art and not reality, these becoming decreasingly
necessary as the work itself becomes decreasingly realistic."[2] In a video, there are very

few "external indicators". The means used by the artist are repetition (loops), reversal, slow motion and the sound that goes with it and which is sometimes no more than a droning noise. The reverse conclusion is therefore quite rightly that realism was unintended. After all, realism is a 19th-century concept, and even 20th-century forms of realism refer back to it. We lead middle-of-the-road lives, surrounded by media images and sounds, which also means that we cannot perceive 'reality' without images (of images). Every single take of the videos is marked by the sort of images and sounds which we have experienced and stored before. Reality only comes about through an adjustment to these images, whether they are our own or whether they belong to others. As a concept it is no more than a form of shorthand for this procedure.

Right in Front
Stefan Banz's videos are marked by this difference between adjustment and concept. They play with the reality content which we can see but which we do not believe them to be capable of. The essential ingredient is indeed a familiar environment, which, in turn, points to its own environment. The apparent publicising of privacy, on the other hand, poses a question on a different level: What is the difference between public and private? In other words, where does ordinary life end and where does a family series begin? This issue remains ambivalent, and the decision is in the eye of the beholder. What we are faced with is some kind of mimicry which is effective and leads to the figuration of the commonplace.

[1] *Cf. the scene in Stefan Banz's* Video What Is ... *(No.11/1998) where his son Jonathan is sitting at the kitchen table, having a cup of coffee and a sandwich. The table is laden with coloured test tubes, and Jonathan asks cheekily: "What is more fluid than water?" – a question he answers himself straight away: "Art. Because it's superfluous." The sequence is repeated in an endless loop by the artist, so that the statement becomes something of a curiosity or indeed a ritual.*

[2] *Arthur C. Danto,* The Transfiguration of the Commonplace – A Philosophy of Art, *London 1981, p. 24.*

DIE KLÄRUNG DES GEWÖHNLICHEN

Thomas Wulffen

What's Left?

Nicht viel, könnte geantwortet werden am Ende dieses Jahrzehnts, dieses Jahrhunderts. Die Systeme, ob technisch oder ideologisch, werden zu einem großen Ganzen integriert. Alternativen sind nur insoweit vorgesehen, als sie das große System stabilisieren. Die Widersprüche werden zu einem Parfüm, das sich verkaufen lässt (*Contradiction* von Calvin Klein). Kunst wird zu einem Anhängsel der Tourismuswerbung oder löst sich auf im eigenen Bermudadreieck von Dienstleistung, Entertainment und Erkenntnistheorie. «Was ist flüssiger als Wasser? Kunst. Sie ist überflüssig.»[1] Die gewohnten Gattungsgrenzen heben sich auf. Der *white cube* wird zum *club event*. Wo die Kunst endet, beginnt die Kunst, weil das Foto gleichwertig neben der Malerei steht. Das Internet ist Malerei mit anderen Mitteln, obwohl es vorgibt, etwas ganz anderes zu sein. Aber Gegenwart ist immer schon gewesen, obwohl Gegenwärtigkeit die Parole der Zeit ist. Die öffentlichen Medien geben ihr Letztes, um die Grenze zwischen Privatem und Öffentlichem niederzureißen. Aber dabei vollziehen sie nur eine Bewegung, die die gewohnte Dichotomie gar nicht mehr wahrnimmt. Nur noch an den Rändern zeigt sich Dissidenz, kaum wahrnehmbar. Sie gibt sich nicht deutlich zu erkennen, treibt eine Mimikry, um nicht aufgesogen zu werden und um wirksam zu bleiben.

Middle of the Road

Sie geben nicht vor, anders zu sein als die anderen. Es sind alltägliche Geschichten, die Stefan Banz in seinen Videos zeigt. Die Herkunft aus einem privaten familiären Hintergrund wird nicht geleugnet. Die Hauptpersonen sind benannt, es sind die eigenen Kinder, die schon in seinen Fotos auftauchten. Wo diese einen Moment festhalten, gerät bei den Videos ein Geschehen ins Zentrum. Dieses Geschehen ist nur ausschnittsweise zu sehen, wobei es dennoch einen Beginn und ein Ende kennt. Aber der Betrachter weiß, dass dieser Beginn und dieses Ende nur Teil eines anderen Beginns und eines anderen Endes ist. In dieser Beschreibung unterscheiden sich die Videos in ihrer Diachronie vom Foto in der Synchronie. Synchrone Belichtung und Beleuchtung geben den Fotos eine spezifische Künstlichkeit, die den Videos ohne den Eingriff des Künstlers nicht zukommen würden. Arthur C.Danto schreibt in 'Die Verklärung des Gewöhnlichen': «Je größer der Grad des beabsichtigten Realismus, desto größer auch die Notwendigkeit äußerlicher Hinweise, dass es sich um Kunst und nicht um Realität handelt.»[2] Für die Videos gilt, dass der 'äußerliche Hinweis' gering ist. Eingesetzt werden Repetition (Loop), Umkehrung, Zeitlupe und der damit verbundene Klang, der zum Teil nur eine Art Brummen ist. Der Umkehrschluss heißt dann auch zu Recht: Realismus ist nicht beabsichtigt. Denn Realismus ist ein Konzept des 19. Jahrhunderts und selbst die Realismusformen des 20. Jahrhunderts beziehen sich noch darauf. Wir leben *Middle of the Road,* umgeben von medialen Bildern und Klängen, und das heißt auch, dass wir ohne Bilder (von Bildern) 'Realität' nicht wahrnehmen können. Jeder einzelne Take der Videos ist geprägt von diesen Bildern und Klängen, die wir schon vorher erfahren und gespeichert haben. Realität kommt nur im Abgleich mit diesen Bildern, eigenen und fremden, zustande und ist als Konzept nur eine verkürzte Redeweise für diesen Vorgang.

Right in Front
Die Videoarbeiten von Stefan Banz zeichnen sich durch diese Differenz zwischen Abgleich und Konzept aus. Sie spielen mit dem Realitätsgehalt, den wir sehen und den wir ihnen nicht zutrauen. Wesentliches Ingredienz dafür ist da tatsächlich das familiäre Umfeld, das wiederum verweist auf das eigene Umfeld. Die scheinbare Veröffentlichung des Privaten stellt dagegen auf einer anderen Ebene die Frage nach dem Unterschied von Öffentlichem und Privatem. Wo beginnt das gewöhnliche Leben und wo endet die Familienserie? Das bleibt ambivalent und die Entscheidung liegt im Auge des Betrachters. Was wir vor uns haben ist eine Art Mimikry, die wirksam ist und zur Klärung des Gewöhnlichen führt.

[1] *Vgl. Stefan Banz' Video «What is ...» (Nr. 11/1998), in welchem sein Sohn Jonathan am Küchentisch bei Kaffee und Butterbrot und vor farbigen Reagenzgläsern keck die Quizfrage «Was ist flüssiger als Wasser?» stellt, um sie sogleich selbst mit den Worten «Kunst. Sie ist überflüssig.» zu beantworten. Die Sequenz wird schliesslich vom Künstler endlos geloopt, was dem Statement sowohl etwas Kurioses als auch Rituelles verleiht.*

[2] *Arthur C. Danto,* Die Verklärung des Gewöhnlichen – Eine Philosophie der Kunst, *Frankfurt am Main 1984, S. 49*

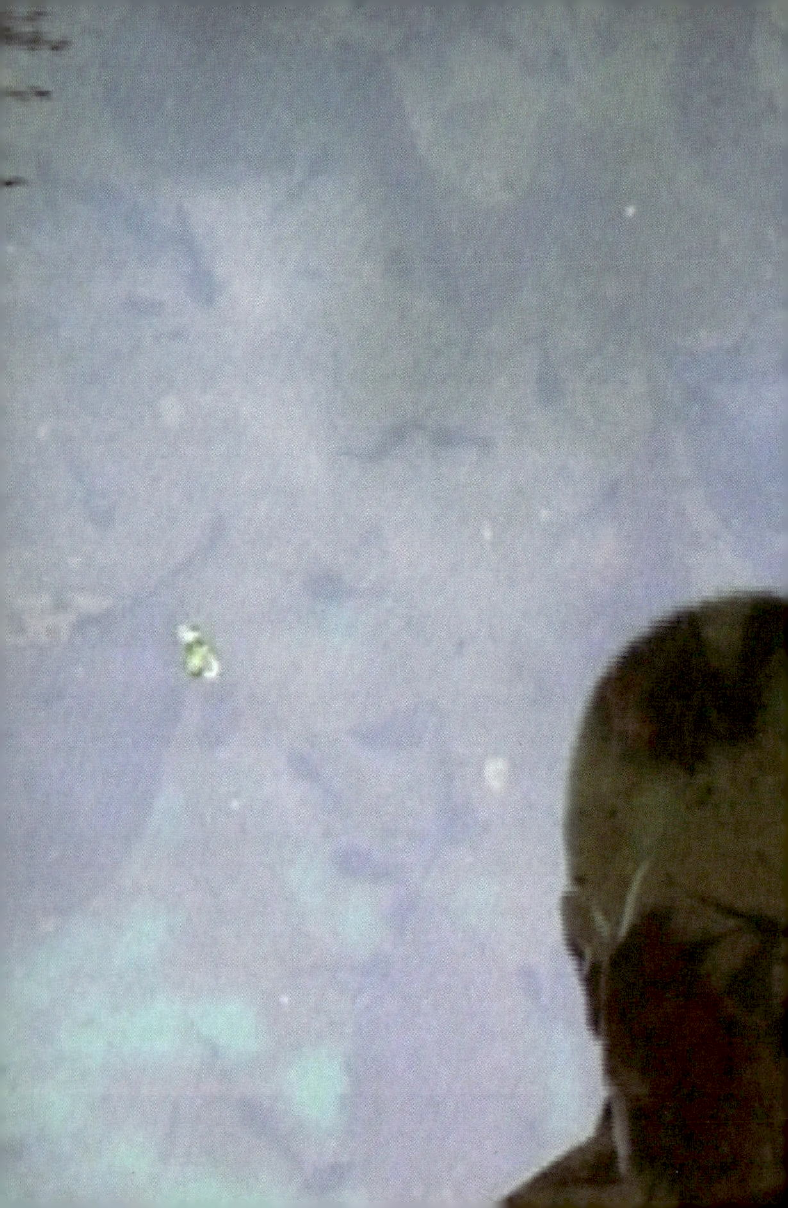

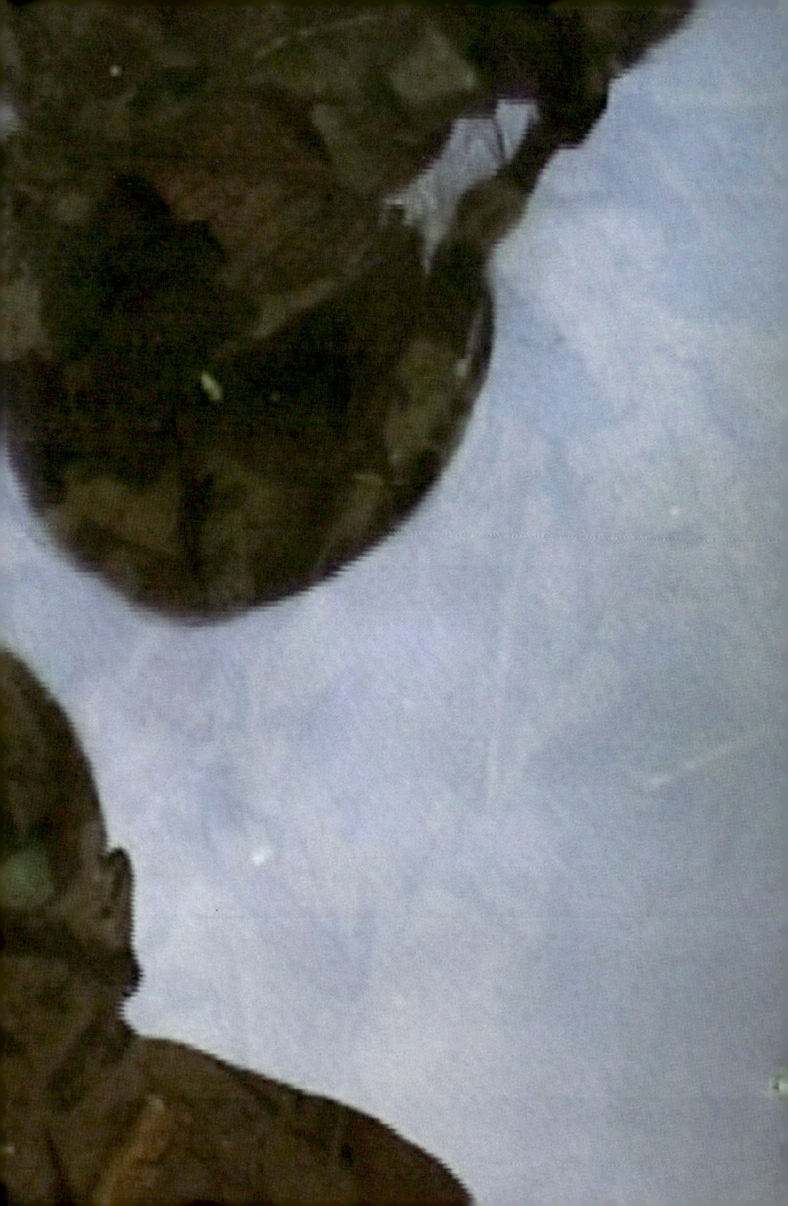

VIDEO WORKS 1997 – 1999

1997
1   Door to Door; 132-147, 156-157
2   Bip Bip Bip; 28-35
3   Hitzfeld
4   Dresses

1998
1   Blow
2   Labyrinth; 126-131, 166-167
3   Labyrinth (Slow Motion)
4a   Park (Left)
4b   Park (Right)
5   Everybody Loves You When
        You're Dead
6   Eating Vampire (1)
7   Eating Vampire (2); Cover
8   Eating Vampire (3)
9   Shot (Short Version)
10   Shot (Long Version)
11   What Is ...
12a   Nintendo 64 (1)
12b   Nintendo 64 (2)
13   Ants
14   Bush (1); 44-53
15   Bush (2)
16a   Boot
16b   Away
17a   Amazing Grace (1a)
17b   Amazing Grace (1b)
17c   Amazing Grace (1c)
18   Amazing Grace (2)
19   Amazing H
20   Night
20b   Ventilator
21a   Promenade (1); 118-125
21b   Promenade (2)
22   Mask; 86-87

23   Back (1)
24a   Back (2a); 76-77
24b   Back (2b)
24c   Back (2c)
24d   Back (2d)
24e   Back (2e)
25a   Scarborough Fair (1)
25b   Scarborough Fair (2)
26   Scarborough Fair (Water); 162-163
27   Mach ...
28   Mach ... (Slow Motion)
29   Flute (1)
30   Flute (2) (Promenade)
31   Scream and Water (D)
32   Scream and Water (E); 92-99
33   Glow; 68-69
34   Cannes, August 1998
35   Guinea Pig; 84-85
36   Duel; Inner Sleeves
37   Nod; 36-43
38   Flying Dragon
39   Stone's Throw
40   Stone's Throw (Slow Motion)
41   Walking the Circle
42   Playing the Dog
43   View
44   In the Car; 4-11
45   Face; 82-83
46   Light
47   Ray of Light
48   Atlanta
49   Lena
50   I Want to Meet My Mother Going to
        Live With God
51   Be Our Guest
52   Lena's Experiment
53   Breaking the Test Tube (1)
54   Breaking the Test Tube (2); 90-91
55   In the Car (Night)

STEFAN BANZ

1961　　　　　Born in Sursee, grew up in Menznau, Switzerland
1975-1981　　Collects the music of Frank Zappa
1977-1984　　Poems, texts & Super 8 films
1979-1980　　Singer with the rock band «Food for Fools»
1982-1991　　Studies art history, German language and literature, and literary
　　　　　　　criticism at the University of Zurich
1987　　　　　Birth of son, Jonathan
1987-1992　　Strong interest in the philosophy of Jacques Derrida
1988　　　　　Marriage with Sabine Mey
1989　　　　　Birth of daughter, Lena
1989-1993　　Co-founder and director of the Kunsthalle Luzern

Selected Solo Exhibitions Since 1995
1995　　　　　*Give me a Leonard Cohen Afterworld*, Kunstmuseum Luzern
1996　　　　　*Dive, OK*, Centrum für Gegenwartskunst, Linz
　　　　　　　You Can Spend Your Time Alone, Ars Futura Galerie, Zurich
1997　　　　　*Switzerland*, Westwerk, Hamburg
　　　　　　　Door to Door, Espai Lucas, Valencia
　　　　　　　Hitzfeld, Galerie Urs Meile, Lucerne
1998　　　　　*Ein gewisser Hang*, Kleines Helmhaus, Zurich
　　　　　　　Eating Vampire, Kunstverein Schichtwechsel, Vaduz
1999　　　　　*Black Cat's*, Kiosk, Berne (with Daughter Lena Banz)
　　　　　　　Gods + Monsters, Ars Futura Galerie, Zurich
　　　　　　　A Shot Away Some Flowers, MAMCO, Geneva
2000　　　　　*Gulliver*, Migros Museum für Gegenwartskunst, Zurich

Selected Group Exhibitions Since 1997
1997　　　　　*Someone Else with My Fingerprints*, Galerie Hauser & Wirth, Zurich,
　　　　　　　curated by Wilhelm Schürmann
　　　　　　　Disaster and Recovery, Swiss Institute, New York
　　　　　　　Nonchalance, Centre Pasquart, Biel, curated by Christoph Doswald
1998　　　　　*C'est la vie*, Centre d'Art Contemporain, Brussels, Centro de Fotografia
　　　　　　　de la Universidad de Salamanca, La Biennale de Montréal, Centre In-
　　　　　　　ternational d'Art Contemporain de Montréal, curated by Hilde Teerlinck
　　　　　　　Freie Sicht aufs Mittelmeer, Kunsthaus Zurich, Schirn Kunsthalle
　　　　　　　Frankfurt am Main, curated by Bice Curiger & Juri Steiner

Stefan Banz, Cosima von Bonin, Matti Braun, Kunstraum Kreuzlingen, curated by Dorothea Strauss
Diana 98, Migros Museum für Gegenwartskunst, Palais X-tra, Zurich, curated by Jean-Noël Jetzer
Nonchalance Revisited, Akademie der Künste, Berlin, curated by Christoph Doswald
Mütter, ihr habt's ja so gewollt, ACC Galerie, Weimar, curated by Frank Motz

1999   *Videothek «Ideal»* – Kunstschiff auf dem Vierwaldstättersee, Lucerne, curated by Karin Frei
Level Zero Cinema, W139, Amsterdam, curated by Hilde Teerlinck
Images, Independent Video-Festival, Toronto, curated by Deirdre Logue
Faiseurs d'histoires, Casino Luxembourg, invited by Marc-Olivier Wahler
D.A.CH., Benger Park, Bregenz, curated by Ursula Krinzinger
Videos aus der Sammlung, Kunsthaus Zürich, curated by Tobia Bezzola
Missing Link. Menschen-Bilder in der Fotografie, Kunstmuseum Berne, curated by Christoph Doswald
On Paper 1999, Stalke Galleri, Kopenhagen, curated by Sam Jedig

Public Works
1998   *Echos*, Haft- und Untersuchungs-Gefängnis Grosshof, Lucerne-Kriens

Selected Publications
1991   *Serendipity*, Helmhaus Zürich
1993   *Kunsthalle Lucerne*, Kunsthalle Luzern
1994   *Das Dilemma der Kriterien*, in: Artis, 5/94, Bern, p. 52-55
1995   *Give me a Leonard Cohen Afterworld*, Ostfildern/Stuttgart
1996   *Dive*, OK, Centrum für Gegenwartskunst, Linz
        Platz der Luftbrücke, with Friedrich Kittler, edited by Iwan Wirth, Cologne
1997   *Delta X*, Interview mit Hans Ulrich Obrist, in: Artis 2/97, Bern, p. 34-39
        Logik der Sammlung und Wahrheit in der Fotografie, Interview mit Boris Groys, in: Artis 3/97, Berne, p.54 - 61
1998   *Echos*, 01/3, edited by Manuel Bonik, Berlin
1999   *Komplexes System Kunst*, in: Kunstklasse, HGK, Zurich, p. 43-49
        Dieses Echt, es ist ein ganz seltsames Wort, Ein Gespräch von Thomas Wulffen, in: Kunstforum International, No. 145, p. 266-277
        I built this garden for us, edited by Christoph Doswald, Edition Patrick Frey, Scalo Verlag, Zurich

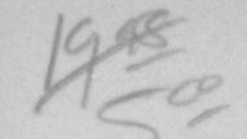

THANKS

The artist wants to thank Sabine, Jonathan and Lena Banz for acting and helping in almost all the videos; Christoph Doswald and Thomas Wulffen for their texts; and Patrick Frey for his dedication in publishing the video stills. He also wants to thank Walter Keller, Pia Rohr, Anna Helwing, Erich Keiser and Simon Lenz, who all had a strong helping hand in making this second edition possible. And not least to Christian Bernard, who invited Stefan Banz to make the show *a shot away some flowers* at Musée d'art moderne et contemporain (MAMCO), Geneva, from October 19 to December 22, 1999.

This book is the twin of *i built this garden for us,* which is also edited by Christoph Doswald and published by Patrick Frey: ISBN 3-905509- 23-7

Editor:
Christoph Doswald, Berlin and Zurich

Publisher:
Edition Patrick Frey
c/o Scalo Zurich-Berlin-New York
Head Office: Weinbergstrasse 22a
CH-8001 Zurich / Switzerland
Tel. +41 1 261 09 10 ; Fax 261 92 62
E-mail publishers@scalo.com
Website www.scalo.com

Distributed in North America by D.A.P., New York City; in Europe, Africa and Asia by Thames and Hudson, London; in Germany, Austria and Switzerland by Scalo.

Translation:
Hugh Beyer, Leverkusen

Art Work:
Stefan Banz

Printing:
Druckerei Odermatt, Dallenwil

Binding:
Schumacher AG, Schmitten

Video Stills:
© 1999 by Stefan Banz

Texts:
© 1999 by Christoph Doswald
and Thomas Wulffen

First Edition:
© 1999 by Edition Patrick Frey

Second Edition:
© 2000 by Edition Patrick Frey

Copies printed of this 2nd edition:
1500

ISBN 3-905509-28-8

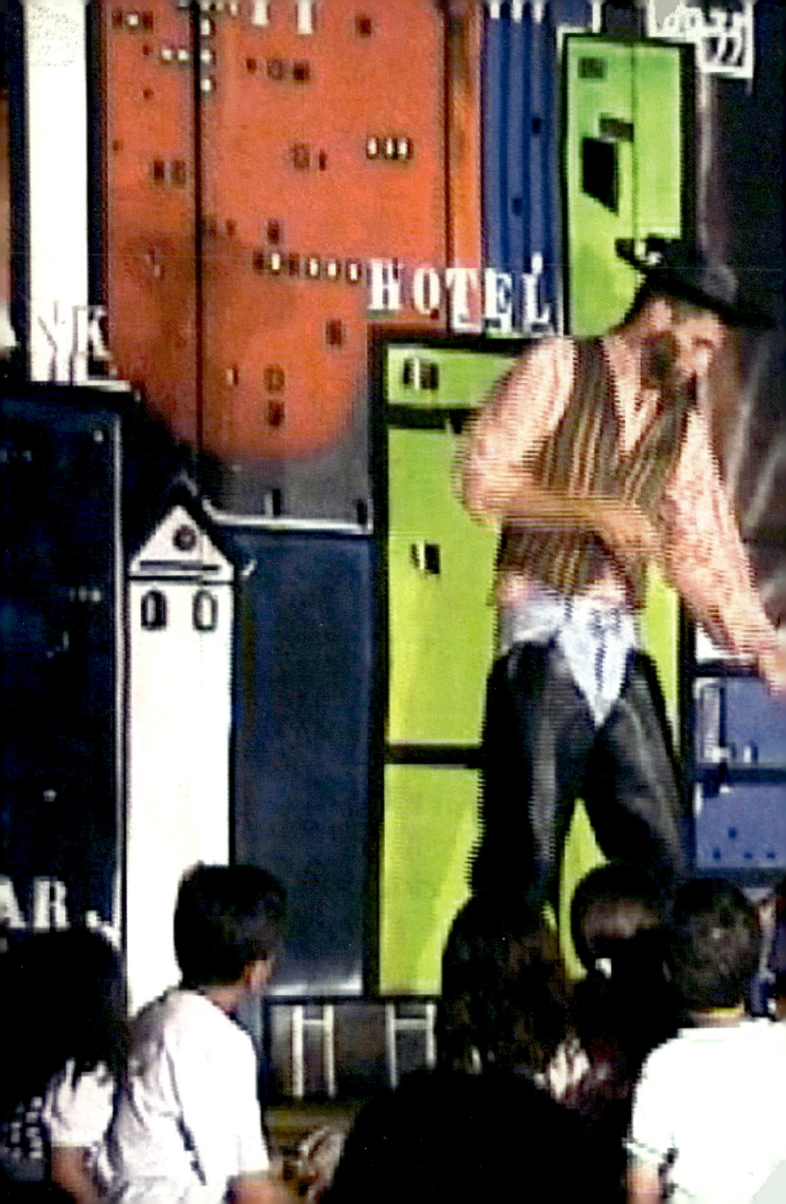

HOTEL
AR